Imagineering an American Dreamscape

Imagineering an American Dreamscape

Genesis, Evolution, and Redemption of the Regional Theme Park

Barry R. Hill

Foreword by Rob Decker

Rivershore Press

Published by Rivershore Press. Visit us at www.rivershorecreative.com.

ISBN: 978-1-7321210-7-2 (Paperback)

ISBN: 978-1-7321210-6-5 (Hardcover)

Cover design by Churchill Strategies

CONTENTS

FOREWORD

Rob Decker, former Senior Vice President of Planning & Design for the Cedar Fair Entertainment Company

Let's face it—the context for regional theme parks will always be in the shadows of Disney parks (and others) in terms of storytelling, wayfinding, immersion, and so on. But they also come up second-fiddle for how well people know where they came from. Bits and pieces have been scattered about for those willing to dig deep, but at long last someone took on the task of filling the void, to compile and unravel the stories behind how these parks were developed and where the creators found their inspirations.

So how do I fit into all this? I am an architect, urban designer, and themed entertainment developer who recently retired from a fantastic industry after working with over thirty theme parks for over 35 years. What kept me focused on the entertainment sector is curiosity. What is it about the attraction to a theme park? Is it the emotional connection, visceral engagement, or immersive departure from reality that attracts people and keeps them coming back? Duh, it is all of that, and twelve-plus breathtaking rides on the roller coasters! But behind the scenes, there is a considerable amount of research, strategy, planning, and ultimately shifting philosophies for the evolutionary course in the theme park industry that occurs. I never imagined that I would be one of the folks who dream up the parks and attractions, or that these fascinations would continue to be explored so intently and wonderfully brought to life by my colleagues throughout their lifetimes.

My first read through an early draft of this book was a drive down memory lane with a lot of familiarities and also new discoveries. The more exciting content for me underscores the evolution of the parks from inception to survival—fascinating to me since I lived a part of that. So here is how I relate my experiences in the theme park industry to this book. As a young but experienced architect, I took part in the design of a few start-up parks out of the gate. The first was a small bit part of preparing detailed drawings for the storied main entrance and set street design of Universal Studios Florida. Then came an expanded role in the design and development of Fiesta Texas. However, construction on new theme park development slowed to a halt in the '90s when the master planning of the Indianapolis-based Garfield Park got no further than my drawing board. Seeking opportunity and recognizing the growing popularity for broader entertainment options, my new focus became developing entertainment zones in sports arenas and ballparks for NFL, MLB, and NBA teams. It was an awkward period in time when nearly every entity in the entertainment sector was trying to broaden their appeal to families, as were a few unfortunate clients with failed intent in Las Vegas. But I never gave up on regional theme parks and am fortunate that I could consult with Six Flags on strategic and capital planning before joining the Cedar Fair Entertainment Company in 2000.

But alongside creating experiences for casinos, professional sports teams, and even grocery stores, regional theme park growth came marginally slower, forcing focus toward highly competitive tactics to find space in the out-of-home entertainment realm. As you will see in this book, control of regional theme park destiny began to change hands from the creators and custodians to the media marketers. This shift brought with it a calling for what we now know as an overlay of intellectual property with fashionable flair—some of which are perhaps enduring, but none of which can compete with the mega-media park entities with the resources to create or acquire new media and take concepts to scale. As for the regional parks, a paradigm reversal became inevitable by either retaining and reinforcing or rebuilding the park's identity. But for me personally, I was fortunate because the timing was right. Within this context, my focus on providing a "stronger sense of place" found its voice within the Cedar Fair organization, which at the time was led by President and CEO Matt Ouimet, a former Disney executive. It was from his point of reference that as regional park operators, we own who we are and who we are is our story, our brand.

My most recent position as Senior Vice President at the Cedar Fair Entertainment Company gave me the responsibility of executing strategic direction in the lead role for all planning and design of capital improvement projects. This period crossed over three eras of CEO's strategies and investment platforms. Each had been successful in their own right. However, in my later years my objectives included taking a pause with my colleagues and reversing the course of the capital investment program, which, by my own admission, had begun to erode the core identity and heritage for some of the regional parks in which I served. But just as important, I was not only focused on restoring the heritage and soul of the parks, but fascinated to materialize this movement as a reflection for ever-changing guest needs. Although we all took part in these transitions, the theme park continued to be my perfect laboratory for endless curiosities. I will miss that opportunity. Over time, my passion for creating and executing the strategic objectives will be evaluated through the lens of the guests' perspectives. Ultimately, contemporizing experiences to enthrall new audiences formulated how we all should shape and grow the business of theme parks and entertainment. The betterment of the guest experience remains my passion.

Today, I can attest that I have an advantage that comes along with retirement by always looking back, and this book certainly takes me there to another place in time. From the first draft to this final version, I remain enthralled with this book. Barry Hill's in-depth perspectives take us back through the evolution of regional park development to the good, the bad, and the opportunistic. I was humbled and honored when Barry asked me to write the Foreword for this book; it is through its content that I remain connected to the world of theme park design and development, and I hope it does the same for you.

Isn't it great that the excitement of entering a theme park has been passed along for so many generations? On the surface, the line between the real world and the gated fantasy world of theme parks appears to be physically abrupt and sometimes commercially over-leveraged. Still, the redemption for all who enter is the ultimate social experience, and the memories that are created from within these kingdoms have no boundaries in our minds—and hopefully never will.

Rob Decker
Sandusky, Ohio
April 2020

The above painting shows the area of Magic Mountain wh

ted, as visualized by the amusement area's art directors.

INTRODUCTION

There was something magical about walking through the majestic columns of the grand mansion to buy your ticket, then strolling through the breezeway to search for your county inscribed on the plaza bricks. Head on over the bridge as the narrow gauge passenger train hissed and clacked underneath on its journey around the park. The themed lands represented local culture, past and present, such as Pirate Island, Contemporary Carolina, Plantation Square, Country Crossroads, and more. Though obviously inspired by its famous predecessor, the park had a local identity that made it, well, different from Disneyland. It was *our* park. It was personal, even. Oh sure, some things had nothing at all to do with the Carolinas, like the majestic sternwheeler that plied the small waterway around the tiny central island. But what an icon! And the sleek monorail that provided such a grand tour of the park before winding its way over long rows of parked cars, past the empty site where a once-planned resort hotel would have accommodated eager park guests, then silently gliding across the entryway pond back toward the station. Disneyland–lite? You bet, but it was our brand of magic—local, accessible, and a part of us.

The 1960s and 70s were the golden age of the regional theme park.

Once Disneyland opened in 1955, forever changing the landscape of outdoor amusements, everybody wanted one in their own yard. A few ambitious entrepreneurs rose up to lead the evolution of taking Walt's grand ideas, scaling them down to a more budget-friendly level, and making them relevant for their particular location. After a few false starts, designers quickly gained their footing and built scores of parks around the country over the next twenty or so years. Many of these were steeped in local culture, creating a unique bond and identity with guests who grew up with each particular park—*their* park.

As time passed, however, changes of ownership brought in people who weren't versed, or even interested, in the ways of themed design. Few of these parks had the heritage and a built-in fairy-dust factory like Disney Imagineering to keep the magic alive. Original designs, backstories, and theming guidelines were tossed aside and forgotten as random layers of paint and corporate intellectual property took over. Many, but not all, of these parks have lost their identity, most likely forever. Of course, millions of guests visit them each year, largely oblivious to the changes, happy to buy their tickets for the latest rides, slides, and shows. What you don't know can't hurt you, I suppose, so no harm, no foul. We're certainly not going to set up a picket line out front with signs warning folks "Story is King!" "Bring Back the Theme!" or the ever-effective "Beware of the Evil Corporate IP!"

There must be something, however, that even the most casual visitor can sense when experiencing a park rich in theme, culture, and story. After all, the concept of theme has begun permeating all aspects of society in recent years. Restaurants, shops, museums, and even airports are getting into the act. This is what experts call the experience economy, where we don't merely want good food. We want to enjoy the entire dining experience from the moment we walk up to the building until the check is paid. Immersive activities, including interactive entertainment, cosplay, and virtual reality are all the rage. People don't want to sit back and watch—they want to be part of the action. Surely the idea of a physical, themed, immersive environment where people can live inside the story would fly these days, right?

Well of course—just look at Disneyland, which is more popular (and crowded) than ever. Harry Potter at Universal Studios re-energized the whole notion of living the movies, with Star Wars: Galaxy's Edge taking it to the next frontier. So what about those regional parks who lost their soul so many years ago? Hope springs eternal...there are glimmers here and there of bringing back the concept of story, place-making, and local history. It'll take time and the right type of management to make this stick. We can hope the trend is true. And in the meantime, maybe you should polish your picket signs just in case.

This is the story of the genesis, evolution, and yes, even redemption of the American regional theme park. Its roots extend further back than you might think. And telling the complete story requires getting to know some of the larger-than-life personalities who made it happen, individuals who have remained largely obscure through the years and deserve to have their day in the spotlight. Their vision and plain hard work brought a new brand of creativity and ingenuity to the task of building the modern theme park—the Imagineering of American Dreamscapes.

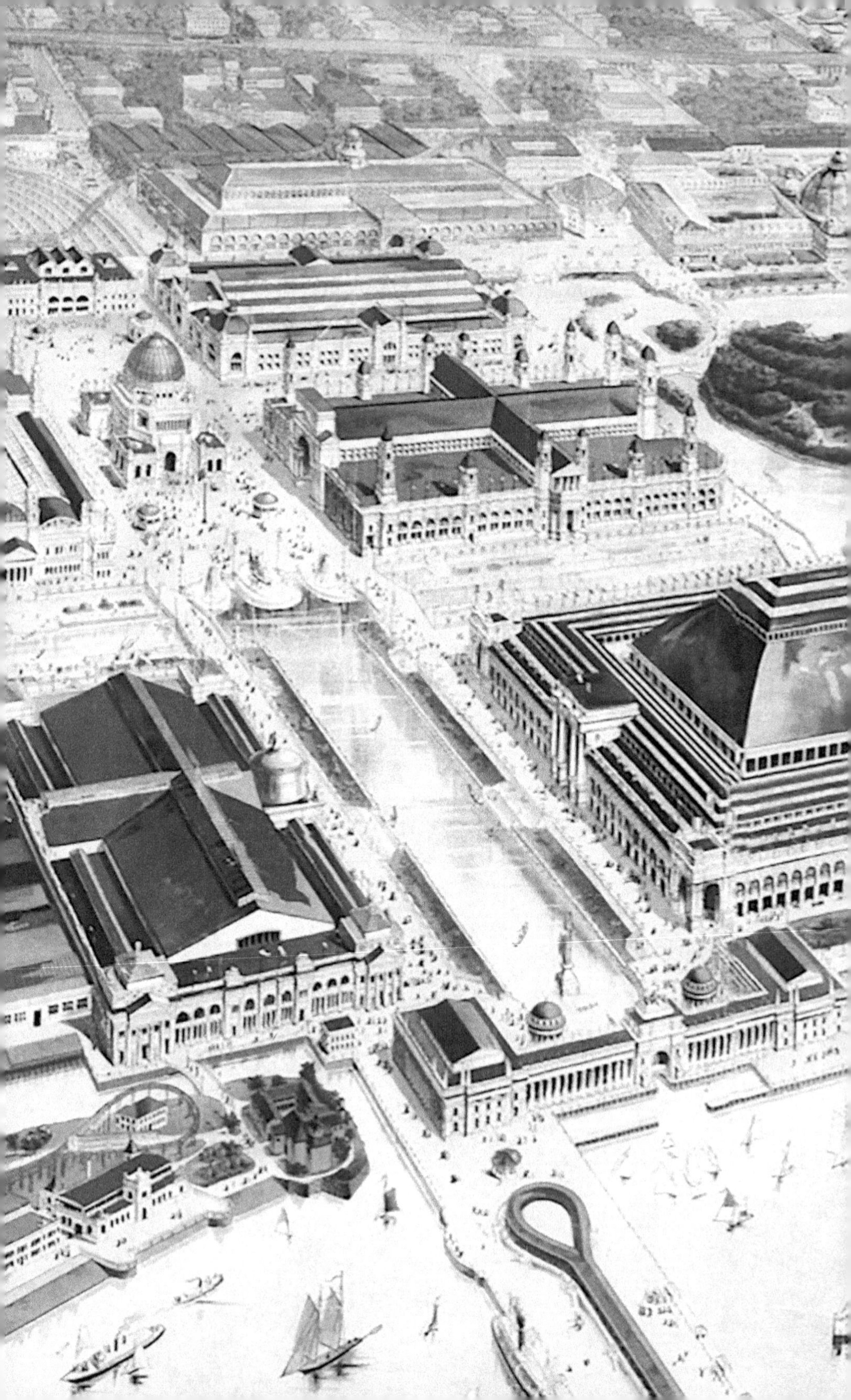

Chapter One

BEFORE DISNEYLAND

A park bench. A merry-go-round. A bag of peanuts. From such simple, unlikely circumstances comes inspiration that can change the world. Disneyland certainly did that, altering the landscape of entertainment for generations to come. Walt himself shared the story of sitting on that bench in Griffith Park, watching his daughters ride the merry-go-round while he did what he was exceedingly good at—watching people, seeing how they do things, what they seemed to want.[1] Walt was an astute observer and infinitely curious. Whereas most of us assume life is what it is, he was always wondering what it might be.

The issue with amusement parks of the time, fun as they might be, was that they generally featured a haphazard collection of rides, food, games, and seedy characters. Most were dirty, not well maintained, and the employees were unfriendly. Many were not really fit for taking your family.[2] Even the better ones, such as Griffith and Beverly, didn't really offer that much for families to do together, and so he couldn't help but think there must be something more, something different that could be done.[3]

Beautiful gardens. Twinkling lights. Inspirational architecture. Immaculately maintained. Walt paused frequently, to the bewilderment of his friend Art Linkletter and others traveling with him, jotting notes in his little book. This visit to Tivoli Gardens in 1951 was surely one of the key moments when things began to click in Walt's mind.[4]

What made Tivoli different was the *intentional* design behind the landscaping and layout, bringing a beautiful, reassuring order and peace notoriously absent in typical parks of the day. It demonstrated that you could craft an ordered, controlled environment that not only was nice to look at and walk through, but that affected one's psyche in a profound way. You let your guard down in such a place. You talk to strangers. It's inspirational and uplifting.[5]

Beautiful gardens. Twinkling lights. Inspirational architecture. Immaculately maintained. No, not Tivoli. Living on a farm in Missouri opened up all kinds of adventures for a little ten year old tike. He had room to roam and explore, to build forts, to just be a boy. And in the evenings, he and his sister Ruth would walk the fifteen blocks to Electric Park, the second so-named park in Kansas City inspired from both Coney Island and the "White City" architecture of Chicago's 1893 World's Columbian Exposition. Originating as a trolley park and built during the heyday of grand amusement extravaganzas, Electric Park was a beautifully designed, carefully laid out, peaceful retreat for recreation. Sure, there was a roller coaster and a few other thrill rides, but it presented a sense of order and sophistication with its carefully manicured green areas, intricate architectural detail, and inspiring structures lined with thousands of popcorn lights. At night the place simply radiated, sending thousands of guests home with a magnificent fireworks display.[6]

And so the seeds were planted for something different, something that would go far beyond the barkers, ugly rides, and freak shows. Both seem fitting as the genesis for the vision of Disneyland...and yet, as with anything in life, it's not so simple. As satisfying as it is to confidently proclaim this to be *the moment, the thing that started it all,* there's much more to the story.

DEVELOPMENT OF AMUSEMENTS AND THEMATIC SPACE

The genesis of the theme park concept can mark a significant transformation and turning point at the opening of Disneyland, but pieces of it actually go back centuries. The creation of public spaces for various purposes, including fun and entertainment, education and exposition, food and games, and just plain getting together with friends are a common thread. Although the 17th and 18th century pleasure gardens of Europe, such as London's Vauxhall Gardens,[7] had early traces of park-like features, we'll trace our *thematic* amusement park roots to the large expositions and world fairs of the late 19th and early 20th centuries. At various times a celebration of the past, others looking toward the future, these events featured increasingly symbolic architecture and thematic experiences in the pavilions and attractions. They featured built-for-purpose space, meaning the layout, structures, and activities were intended to support the specific motives of the fair. The grounds were enclosed from the surrounding environment, requiring ticketed entry at the front gate. Each event followed an overall theme, such as energy or the future. Originally intended to be primarily educational, expositions helped usher in an age of intellectualism beyond the elite social class. Middle-class citizens thronged to these expos and enjoyed fine art, music, history, and science exhibitions, often for the first time. Our nation's art, history, and science museums can be traced largely to these events, providing lasting opportunities to enjoy and learn long after the fairs closed.[8]

But, people being people, the balance between educating and entertaining was unsurprisingly lopsided as we morphed from informational world fairs to amusement parks. People generally want to have fun, after all, and the operators of these fairs and expos learned early on to include food, games, entertainment, and even rides in order to financially support these extravagantly expensive endeavors.[9] It was for this purpose we got the word *midway* from the 1893 Chicago World's Columbian Exposition, when planners insisted on establishing an amusement area separate from the more serious, educational offerings.[10] And so the concept of *attractions* took form. Innovative rides such as roller coasters, Steeplechase, and Ferris wheels were developed, providing repeatable thrills—something the lofty educational exhibits somehow didn't quite command. The idea of a ride was nothing new—existing amusement parks featured all sorts of rides and thrills. But scale and imagination took on new directions and heights, literally. The Philadelphia Centennial of 1876 showcased a 300-ft tall iron tower, the Sawyer Observatory.[11] One could grab a bird's-eye view of the 1934 Chicago World's Fair from an aerial tram ride,[12] or an even loftier perspective on the 1915 San Francisco Pan-Pacific International Exposition *Aeroscope*. It leveraged over one hundred people up to 330 feet at the end of a 285 foot long, pivoting steel arm.[13] For the 1893 Chicago World's Fair, George Washington Gale Ferris, a young engineer from Pittsburg, envisioned a 250 foot diameter revolving steel wheel with seats that rotated up and around.[14] And forget such sedate, charming affairs...the *Parachute Jump* for the 1939 New York World's Fair hauled what looks like a flat board with canvas straps across the back some 20 stories up before letting go and bouncing to an uneasy landing near the ground.[15]

In an age before film and television, people's exposure to past civilizations and far-away lands was restricted to photos in a book. The notion of relaxing on a gondola as it floated past recreations of Venice, or riding a miniature railway through Switzerland, or even being "submerged" in a submarine was novel, exciting, and growing increasingly sophisticated. One could relive the 1913 Dayton Flood, complete with gushing waters and burning buildings, or marvel at a five-acre reproduction of the Panama Canal.[16] *A Trip to the Moon* was a staggeringly ambitious dark ride first presented at the 1901

Buffalo Pan-American Expo where guests boarded an airship and "sailed" upward to the moon. Large, mechanically driven wings flapped away as fans simulated wind and the "engines" roared and vibrated the ship. Passengers followed their journey's progress as canvas prints rolled by the portals with images of an increasingly distant planet Earth. Lighting and sound completed the experience, all housed in a gargantuan eighty-foot high, 40,000 square foot show building.[17]

It wasn't only the rides and simulations themselves, but the facades of the buildings often reflected the theme of what was to be discovered inside. Some of these were quite elegant, others garishly overstated. The *Zone*, a seven block long midway at the 1915 Pan-Pacific International Exhibition, was a notable example of wildly symbolic architecture—the four-story tall Uncle Sam leaning over the Souvenir Watch Palace, the dominating winged angel inviting you to witness Creation from Genesis, the hand-held cone hovering over the ice cream window, and of course, *Toyland Grown Up*, featuring 14 acres of oversized toys, figures, and alphabet blocks.[18] The result was a visual cacophony that surely generated sensory overload. But it was all new and exciting for a growing, increasingly mobile population looking for places to go and things to do.

THE MIDWAY COMES TO TOWN

The problem with all of this was that world's fairs and expos were temporary. They only lasted a couple of years or so, and once people got accustomed to all these thrills and experiences, well, they didn't want to stop. It's one thing to part ways with the St. Louis Louisiana Purchase Exposition, but to not be able to ride the Ferris Wheel again? When the World's Columbian Exposition wrapped up in 1893, people rioted when the Wheel shut down.[19] The Buffalo extravaganza, focused on a university-style curriculum in object lessons, was a certified flop—except for the amusement Midway.[20] When it came down to it, people were far more interested in the rides and attractions than the lofty exposition halls, and so amusement parks flourished across the country, benefiting from the advances and experiences realized by the expos.

Many of these were the so-called trolley parks, conveniently and inexpensively connected to nearby towns via the electric streetcar. They were largely simple affairs at first, essentially space for people to enjoy entertainment, leisure, and sports. Names familiar to park enthusiasts today got their start at the turn of the century, such as Kennywood, Lake Compounce, Quassy, Dorney Park, and Canobie Lake Park. Along with swimming pools and dance pavilions, amusements such as carousels, chute-the-chutes, and roller coasters were added, turning many of these recreational areas into full-fledged amusement parks.[21] Trolley parks flourished through the 1920s, a time of prosperity and enthusiasm, but then saw a decline toward the end of the decade. The automobile allowed greater opportunity to explore beyond the tracks, urban parks suffered from limited parking, and the Depression was beginning to dampen everything in American society. A number of the original trolley parks survives today, but most have been gone for decades.[22]

None of these would come close to qualifying as a theme park. The extravagant attractions from the world expos were simply too expensive, too grand, and, well, not really suited to a local recreational area. But there were others, direct descendants of the grand fairs, that carried forward concepts that would be key for the future of theme parks. The Big Three made their home at Coney Island, New York: Steeplechase, Luna, and Dreamland.

CONEY ISLAND

Honeymooning George Tilyou wandered the grounds of the 1893 World's Columbian Expo in Chicago with his new bride, seeking ideas for the land he owned on Coney Island in New York.[23] When his eyes fell upon Ferris' wheel, he knew he had found it. An attraction that could hold up to 2160 people at 50 cents each was a business bonanza,[24] and so after discovering it had already been sold for relocation after the fair, he decided to have his own built. The new wheel, half the size of Ferris', joined other attractions scattered about his property, including double dip chutes, an aerial slide, and an imported bicycle railroad.[25] What he didn't understand at first, though, was the concept of grouping everything together and charging general admission. This was pioneered by Captain Paul Boyton with Sea Lion Park, the first gated amusement park in the country, also located at Coney Island.[26] Searching for a headlining attraction for a newly reimagined park, Tilyou discovered a mechanical horse-themed racing ride by English inventor J.W. Cawdry. He bought the rights, improved the concept, and opened Steeplechase Park in 1897.

Steeplechase featured a combination of traditional amusements along with attractions originating from the world's fairs. Some of these were relocated to the park pretty much as-is, similar to how Walt Disney brought attractions developed for the 1964 World's Fair back to Disneyland. *A Trip to the Moon* was one of these, from the 1901 Buffalo expo. Many were new inventions, such as an early roller coaster from LaMarcus Thompson, the Steeplechase race, and a series of wild rides that certainly pushed the envelope of current social etiquette.[27] Still, most of these were amusement attractions, and aside from the moon experience, not anything necessarily thematic or immersive. And the park was certainly not intended to convey any particular theme or placemaking; Tilyou was merely looking for the biggest return on his investment no matter what the attraction happened to be.

Luna Park and Dreamland opened in 1903 and 1904 respectively. Both were responses to the wildly successful Steeplechase, and each tried to outdo the other. After making a fortune with his moon excursion after only one season at Steeplechase, 28 year old Fred Thompson, the consummate showman, teamed up with Elmer "Skip" Dundy to build their own money-making enterprise. They leased the failed Sea Lion Park property, transforming its 22 acres into Luna Park. Widely considered the first sort-of-a-theme-park, Luna brought key components from the expos, primarily the concept of an enclosed, built-for-purpose space separate from the rest of the surrounding environment. The park had its own version of *Sleeping Beauty Castle* for an icon—a two hundred foot tall tower covered in bright, multi-colored lights that were quite the sight as night fell on Coney. Symbolic, thematic architecture that was fun and entertaining was in, traditional straight lines and pure form was out. Overall, however, what made it different from Steeplechase's emphasis on rides and amusements was its sense of another place—of fantasy and illusion. Architecture and attractions were elevated to new heights and offered visitors simulated, immersive experiences of historic events, world cultures, and future dreams.[28]

Dreamland was intended to be a bigger and better version of Luna. And it was, but with a different approach. Architecture was more refined, buildings were painted white for a majestic, traditional feel similar to the 1893 Chicago World's Fair. It also boasted its own magnificent tower, and the park absolutely radiated from the glow of a million lights. William Reynolds, the park's founder, copied liberally from attractions found at other parks, but of course making them bigger and more sensational. Themes were more educational and with a moralistic twist—major attractions sought to teach Biblical principles, even demonstrating what was in store for unbelievers at *End of the World* and *Hell Gate*. And none of this really worked; the park never reached the popularity of Steeplechase and Luna, and in a spectacular twist of judgmental irony, burned to the ground from an accident that set *Hell* on fire.[29]

From a sheer scale and financial investment standpoint, these parks were easily the equal of a Disney park. Luna brought in over four million guests per year at one point;[30] Dreamland cost three and a half million dollars to build more than half a century before Disneyland.[31] Though certainly very different constructs, with little cohesive sense of storytelling, placemaking, and with primitive thematic immersion, they were the pinnacle of spectacular entertainment and social gathering in their day. Key ideas were in place that would later find fruition in the modern theme park. All of these early parks were proof of concept that people wanted to gather and engage in social discourse, experience immersive environments and simulation, have fun, and perhaps learn something along the way. And they didn't mind paying for the privilege. The millions of dollars spent pushing the envelope of rides, shows, and theme-based attractions was a precursor to the current day theme park arms race between Disney and Universal. It just took several intervening decades before an ambitious cartoonist jumpstarted and transformed the entire industry.

WALT'S LITTLE PARK

It was no secret around the studio that Walt was thinking of building a park. He'd been talking about it for years, first looking at storage space on his backlot, then across the road from the studio.[32] Of course, in those days everybody's idea of a park was something on the order of a carnival or seaside amusement area. California had become quite the entertainment and architectural scene. The state was full of parks, drive-in movies, and roadside restaurants and concessions themed like you'd find in Roller Coaster Tycoon. It was a mecca of recreation, catering to a wave of post-World War II blue and white collar families who were first-time home buyers, relatively prosperous, and eager to jump in the family car and explore. This mobility and range of options presented challenges to parks, who suffered with increased competition for the family dollar and attention.[33]

Along with a desire for some sort of family-friendly attraction, one of Walt's early reasons for a park was in response to all the letters he'd get asking for a behind-the-scenes tour of the studio. Universal Studios Hollywood had been doing this quite successfully for years, but it's one thing to let people gape at their favorite movie stars on a live-action set. Walking around seeing animation come together was on the order of watching the grass grow through the window. So maybe a small park with things for families to do with their kids. They could meet Mickey Mouse, and of course take a miniature train ride. It certainly had to be more interesting than the local amusement areas he'd been taking his daughters to.[34]

It was Walt's love of trains that led him to grab Ward Kimball, one of the studio artists who actually ran a full-size railroad in his not-so-full-size backyard, to attend the 1948 Chicago Railroad Fair.[35] Along with scores of trains on display, each company set up a scenic representation of their home territory: the French Quarter of New Orleans, the Wild West with trading posts and teepees, a generic national park complete with a mechanical geyser that shot up every fifteen minutes. Authentically costumed employees completed the illusion of being in a different place at a different time. The most poignant moment for Walt was a depiction of Lincoln's funeral train, including an original railcar and the singing of "The Battle Hymn of the Republic." But it wasn't just the individual scenes that captivated Walt; there was an overall cohesiveness and unity with all these aspects pointing toward a common goal, a common good. Disneyland would later take this idea and elevate it to a whole new level.[36]

Afterward Walt and Ward stopped off at Henry Ford's Greenfield Village, featuring recreations and relocated structures of historic places in America. One could meander through Thomas Edison's laboratory, explore the Wright Brothers' home and bicycle shop, and practice spelling at Noah Webster's house. There were traces of Ford's own childhood and past as well, such as the farmhouse in which he grew up, staged with various items that reinforced fond memories. Patriotism and personal nostalgia would surface time and again as one of Walt's inner themes, and such experiences surely left indelible impressions on him as he sifted through various ideas for his park.[37]

Up until this point Walt had been pursuing the small Mickey Mouse park along with an idea for his deep interest in miniatures: a traveling railcar exhibit filled with tiny, authentically detailed scenes of Americana. Animator Ken Anderson had been hired from the studio to help him develop what became known as *Disneylandia* or *Walt Disney's America*. One set included Walt's own handmade replica of Granny Kincaid's cabin from the movie *So Dear to My Heart*. But other than a recorded narration and lights that turned on, it just sat there. A trip to New Orleans netted him a mechanical bird that flapped its wings while it sang, so he had Wathel Rogers, the studio's quiet genius, tear it apart to see how it worked.[38] From this came Project Little Man, a dancing miniature set on an opera stage. The goal was to make it as real as possible, so actor Buddy Ebsen was filmed against a grid so his dance movements could be translated to the mechanical figure. Over time, though, as various scenes developed, the logistics of how to display it all began to reveal a dead end. The railroad industry was changing significantly, reducing opportunities for excursion trains to easily move about from city to city. The costs for right-of-way also began to skyrocket as industry officials learned about the plan and tried to cash in. And capacity would be severely limited as people casually wandered through and watched each tiny scene's action.[39]

Meanwhile Walt had been researching amusement parks, fairs, carnivals, zoos, and anything else that seemed remotely related. Along with the big ideas that were forming from his experiences with miniatures, Tivoli, the railroad fair, and so on, he spent a great deal of time sitting on park benches observing how things worked—how people moved around, what they seemed to enjoy and what frustrated them, the role of landscape and architecture. After a few frustrating attempts with traditional architects, it became clear a different approach was required. Walt began pilfering a small team of artists from the studio to work at WED, his personal design company, and they alternately sweated and froze in a rundown shack that was a holdover from the original studio on Hyperion Avenue. They visited parks on the weekends, including Knott's Berry Farm, whose owners were initially quite eager to answer an avalanche of questions about the park's design and operation. Bud Hurlbut, owner of a small park in Los Angeles, would notice Walt spending hours looking at his rides. He eventually became a good resource for Walt (and ultimately industry fame as the designer of the *Calico Mountain Mine Ride* and *Timber Mountain Log Ride* at Knott's).[40]

On a visit to London in 1951, Walt by chance met an artist and fellow rail buff by the name of Harper Goff. They hit it off, and Harper eventually came to work for Walt. His first mission? Start work on the Disneylandia project, but then almost immediately he got assigned to the *20,000 Leagues Under the Sea* movie while Walt was in England.[41] The third assignment, though, was to lay out a site map for a sixteen acre park across the street from the studio.[42] In a detailed 1948 memo, Walt had described what Mickey Mouse Park would entail, and it was vastly different from typical parks of the day.[43] Guests would spend a relaxing day in a miniature town complete with fire and police stations, a town hall, drugstore, opera house, various shops, and of course a train station. A horse-drawn streetcar would transport you to Western Village, an old west inspired section. But after his recent experiences and further thinking, he was already plussing the ideas. Harper's instructions were to add some Tivoli, Greenfield Village, and Colonial Williamsburg to the original concepts of family amusements. "I don't want to just entertain kids with pony rides and swings. I want them to learn something about their heritage."[44]

Goff's concept art from this project is an early glimpse of Disneyland architecture and placemaking with scenes straight out of yesterland. The initial plan included an old west area, riverboat, stagecoach ride, small boat ride, a farm, a tiny lake in the middle, and of course a miniature train circling the park. Considering the obvious pressure for maximizing limited acreage, the layout is quite spacious, scenic, and fairly immersive. The influence of Tivoli and Greenfield is obvious, but even these don't quite feature the same level of placemaking, meaning immersing guests into a different time or place. Walking through Goff's layout would take you back to another period in American history, albeit on a small scale.[45] Early signs from Burbank officials had been positive, and the final presentation to the city council was delivered in typical Walt style—dynamic, animated storytelling, describing the beautiful scenes and activities for families to enjoy, the educational opportunities, pointing to the detailed artwork arranged around the room.[46]

This was the first time all of these various concepts began to tangibly meld together into what would evolve into Disneyland: the beauty and intentionality of Tivoli, the American heritage and thematic symbolism of the fairs, the recreations and history in Greenfield Village, the Disneylandia miniatures, mechanical recreations of historic figures, childhood memories, and of course model trains all grown up. But the presentation did not go well—Burbank killed the proposal for that little park across from the studio, lacking the vision to understand the difference between Disney's dreams and carny fairs. And we'll forever be in their debt...because we got something far grander instead.

Chapter Two

WALT SETS A NEW STANDARD

What made Disneyland so ground-breaking? So transformative? So amazing? What made the park an indispensable catalyst for the regionals that were to follow? The story of how Disneyland came about is well-documented, so we're not going to rehash it all here. But we must examine some key principles that laid the foundation for how the later parks came to be. We've followed the trajectory from the earliest pleasure gardens in Europe, the grand world expositions, Coney Island, and changes in society, seeing how the process of getting to Walt's magical little park wasn't completely revolutionary. We often read about how Walt transformed the cheap local carnival and simple roadside park into the modern theme park. There's much truth to this, but there was a long string of influences, not only on his personal experiences that shaped his thinking, but also on the very enterprises he was being exposed to. History is always more complex than we prefer, but in the end it really doesn't make that much of a difference. Disneyland, no matter the myriad ways in which it became what it was, indeed altered the landscape of outdoor entertainment forever. Let's take a look at some of the ways in which the park's design and impact on society affected the regional parks soon to come.

Taking cues from the world's fairs and the Big Three at Coney Island, Disneyland provided a built-for-purpose space that controlled the environment, provided a safe haven for people to socialize, and immersed you in a story. Unlike the typical carnival of the day, which was chaotic, random, and usually unfit for families, these places were encouraging and reassuring. All is well within our walls; you can let your guard down and just have fun—together.

Part of what created this atmosphere was the intentional design of everything, from the overall organization of buildings and attractions, layout of pathways, beautiful landscaping, and even the architecture itself. You could just *feel* something different about the place, even if you weren't quite aware of it and had no idea why. It wasn't just the fact that everything was so much grander than in one's own neighborhood; careful design lowered anxiety by reducing visual and mental chaos. Everything seemed to belong together, more or less.[1]

Disneyland took this into the next dimension, and not only with intentional design of its layout, landscaping, and architecture. The park was a *show*, and for the first time one could pass through the tunnels, leave the messy world behind, and step directly into the story.[2] All the good stuff from the expositions and Coney were there, but much better. This is because the park was dreamed up and executed by *storytellers*. Walt gave up on traditional architects because they couldn't quite conceive of what he had in mind. His artists, long experienced with producing stories on film, knew exactly how to do this. They brought along their storyboards and sketch pencils and approached the park from a completely different angle.[3] Walt set the tone and scope: history, patriotism, nostalgia, and his rich library of animated films would serve as guideposts for what the park would look and feel like. His people knew how to set a scene, even in three dimensional form due to their work in live action movies. Concepts from backlot building sets, impact of scale, and use of forced perspective directed the physical design of the park.[4]

Disneyland is a narrative adventure.[5] Main Street immediately takes you back in time, and for many in the park's early days it was a time they actually remembered at the turn of the century. Everybody seems to remember the good ole days. No matter that often they weren't all what they're cracked up to be, but that's how memory and nostalgia works.[6] Take your time ambling up the street, window shopping and enjoying the sounds and scents of a better-than-real town. Main Street opens gently out into the Hub, a circular open area designed as a gathering space, a place to get one's bearings and figure out what's next. Decision making is enabled through visual cues at Disneyland, with clearly indicated pathways off the Hub leading to the various lands.[7] Wienies beckon from beyond; enticing structures such as the fairytale castle and majestic sternwheeler lure one to go find out what's so interesting back there.[8] Transitions to these various destinations are cross-dissolves straight from film production, gradually switching over to a different place in time.[9] The Hub is an ingenious concept that allows you to change the channel and pick which scene you want to explore.[10]

Placemaking is the key to all of this. Once designers determine a backstory for a park, land, or attraction, everything points toward making that feel real, to suspend one's disbelief and really buy into the thing. Attention to detail is crucial and is what sets Disneyland apart from previous affairs (and, frankly, most everything after it).[11] Everything guests see, hear, and touch is carefully specified: building architecture, signage, color, textures, materials, costuming, equipment, vehicles, and on and on. The book for each land sets the rules for designers (and generations of maintenance) to follow to the letter. Visual intrusions, whether from neighboring lands or outside the park, are to be avoided at all costs. Thus sight lines are pre-determined through extensive use of physical models (and virtual environments today). A landscaped berm surrounds the park to keep the outside out. Breaking any one of these components potentially destroys the show and shatters the suspension of disbelief.[12] Walt famously went off on an early photographer who left his 20th century car parked within sight of guests in 19th century Frontierland.[13] The harmonious nature of a carefully-conceived and implemented thematic environment is soothing, reassuring, and quite different from real-world places around us. John Hench, Disney Legend and the philosophical voice of Imagineering, put it this way:

> "Most urban environments are basically chaotic places, as architectural and graphic information scream at the citizen for attention. This competition results in disharmonies and contradictions that…cancel each other. A journey down almost any urban street will quickly place the visitor into visual overload as all of the competing messages merge into a kind of information gridlock."[14]

Inspired and encouraged by Walt, Disneyland took customer service and care to new heights. Employee training became much more than how to operate the cash register and push the go button; Van Arsdale France was hired not long before the park opened and tasked with developing a training program. As he walked about and talked with people he got a sense there was something different about this place. Taking cues from Walt, he realized they weren't merely servicing customers and collecting cash to haul away to the bank at the end of the day. With Van's "We Make Happiness" approach, new nomenclature entered industry lexicon for the first time such as "guests," "host & hostess," "cast members," and "on-stage." Attitudes were different than ever seen before, and this approach has been adopted far and wide across not only the entertainment industry but in business, hospitality, and so on (admittedly with much variability of success).[15]

The park paid close attention to their guests, observing how they moved, how they made decisions, what they liked, what they didn't. Walt instructed his designers to spend time in the park, eat lunch there, to listen to what people were saying.[16] The practice of guest surveys to measure all this, compile demographic data, and get feedback on future ideas has been standard procedure in the industry ever since.[17] Attraction queues progressed from long, tiresome lines to *pre-shows,* immersing guests into the attraction's story as they wound their way toward the entrance.[18] Even the food got better, in some cases serving as an attraction in its own right.

One of the reasons Walt wanted his park was so he could continue playing with it, trying new ideas, re-thinking old ones.

> "Disneyland is something that will never be finished. Something that I can keep developing, keep plussing and adding to. It's alive. It will be a live, breathing thing that will need change. A picture is a thing, once you wrap it up and turn it over to Technicolor you're through...Not only can I add things, but even the trees will keep growing...And as I find out what the public likes...I can change the park, because it's alive. That is why I wanted that park."[19]

To this end he poured tons of money back into the place, plussing in grand fashion to the everlasting dismay of his accountants.[20] It worked, however, proving that reinvestment in an enterprise is essential for repeat business. Most—but not all—regional parks would follow this rule, though in wildly varying ways and usually contrary to the original design. But as we shall see throughout the book, sufficient start-up capitalization and continual reinvestment are crucial for the success of the business.

In an era after World War II, while the Cold War raged on in the backdrop of daily life, Americans sought new ways for escape. Many of them found it every week on their black and white television sets, eagerly taking in every word as Uncle Walt showed them around his magical playland. With the development of a national road network, families looking for things to do, and disposal income with which to do it, Disneyland came along at just the right time. The park provided hope, inspiration, and encouragement. It invited you in as a participant to live out the stories you grew up with. It was refreshingly new, and it caught the entire nation by storm. Evolutionary though it may have been, it was revolutionary enough to have completely transformed an entire industry. As stated by James Rouse, respected master planner and builder, before a distinguished gathering at the 1963 Harvard University Urban Design Conference:

> "I hold a view that might be somewhat shocking to an audience as sophisticated as this—that the greatest piece of urban design in the United States today is Disneyland. If you think about Disneyland and think about its performance in relation to its purpose; its meaning to people—more than that, its meaning to the process of development—you will find it the outstanding piece of urban design in the United States. It took an area of activity—the amusement park—and lifted it to a standard so high in its performance, in its respect for people, that it really has become a brand-new thing. It fulfills all the functions it set out to accomplish unself-consciously, usefully, and profitably to its owners and developers. I find more to learn in the standards that have been set and in the goals that have been achieved in the development of Disneyland than in any other single piece of physical development in the country."[21]

All of these principles would be the basis for the upcoming regional parks. Their designers, some of whom earned their wings from Disneyland, tried their best to incorporate all of this within severely constrained budgets. Turns out, though, this wasn't to be so easy after all.

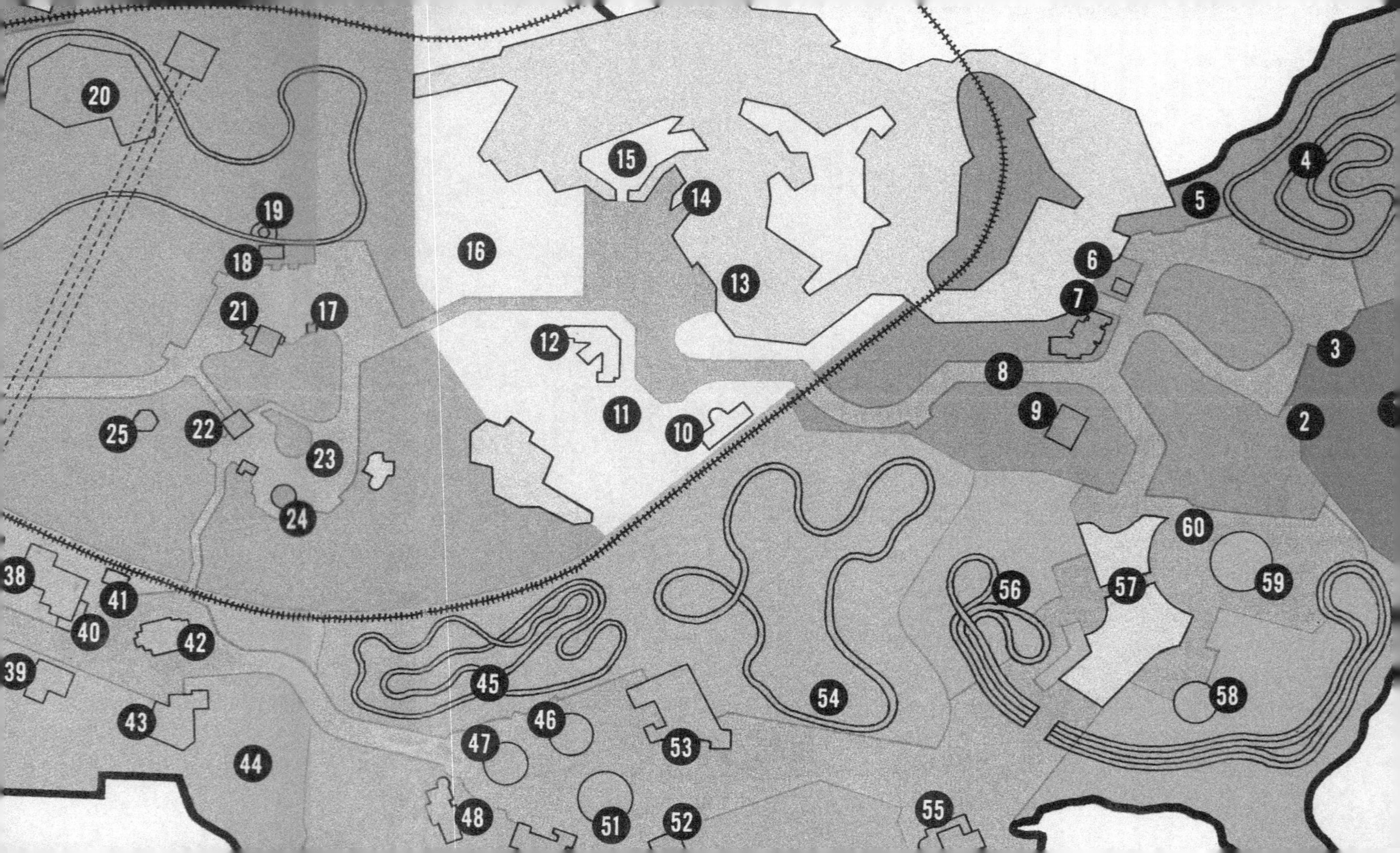
20
15
14
19
16
13
18
6
5
4
21
17
7
3
12
8
11
9
2
25
22
10
23
24
60
38
41
56
57
59
40
42
39
45
54
58
46
43
47
53
44
48
51
52
55

Chapter Three

DUPLICATING DISNEYLAND IS HARDER THAN YOU THINK

Cornelius Vanderbilt Wood Jr. is the singular definition of an enigma. Few Disney fans have ever heard the name. The ones who have, have read anything from *genius, showman, shuckster,* to *con man.*[1] The self-confident kid who got into college on a rope twirling scholarship was pure Texas and a born leader.[2] His friends were known as the Bombers, and they remained loyal to the very end.[3] Woody, as he was called, could talk anybody into anything. Could sell anything. Had the chutzpah to will anything into existence if he wanted it. And his Texan drawl was so charming you'd never know what hit you.[4] First meeting the Disney brothers as one of the team at Stanford Research Institute, his no-nonsense, easy-going, confident manner was so impressive he was quickly hired to oversee completion of Disneyland on a tight budget.[5]

That he did, against all odds. There was no way that park was going to make it on time with the cash they had available. Previous attempts to lease space in the park to large companies had been unsuccessful, so they let Woody take a stab at it. Sponsorships are an iffy thing. How do you set a value on something that's so intangible? For example, say a company would operate a shop or restaurant on Main Street. They paid for all internal construction, equipment, and operations, on top of a sponsorship fee, in hopes that it would pay off with future sales.[6] Yet Woody talked a long list of companies into jumping on board.

Swift's Packing Company was the first to sign on, but it seemed hopeless for a long while. Nobody could see far enough down the road to imagine how this might be different from their normal advertising experience. Swift's was the last gasp at making this whole thing work, and after the initial pitch Woody and his sidekick were thrown out of the president's office. He sat in the lobby for several minutes before heading back up, striding into the office to retrieve his "forgotten" briefcase. Turns out the guy had a few minutes to think about the concept and decided to sign on. Swift paid a lease of $110,000 per year to run their restaurant in the park, and this opened the gates for others to join in, including Upjohn Pharmacy, Richfield Oil, and the Santa Fe Railroad. Could anybody else have pulled this off? Maybe P.T. Barnum, but at any rate C.V. was instrumental in getting Disneyland opened, on time, and (sort of) on budget.[7]

Seven months later he was gone. Two egos don't easily co-exist, and Walt couldn't take it anymore. And there had been plenty of talk about some of Woody's deals, things that might not show too well on the company's accounting statements.[8] Roy Disney let him go in 1956, and C.V. promptly set up his own company, Marco Engineering. His objective? As "master planner and builder of Disneyland" he could bring the magic to anybody's home turf.[9] He began hiring designers and engineers, including a few key individuals from Disney such as Wade Rubottom. But his most significant hire was straight from the movie industry, the highly successful art director Randall Duell.[10] More on him later, as his story eventually overshadows that of Woody in the realm of regional theme parks.

MAGIC MOUNTAIN

C.V. started out strong, beginning work on four parks in the late 1950s. First up was Magic Mountain, outside Golden, Colorado. Originally envisioned as a Mother Goose Storyland themed park,[11] art directors Wade Rubottom and Dick Kelsey, another Disney studio artist,[12] worked to reimagine some of the early ideas from the park's owners. In a pattern that would be revisited time and again, many attraction ideas were adapted from Disneyland, though scaled down in detail and cost.

Visitors would enter under the railroad bridge, with steam trains leaving the station elevated majestically just off to the right. The period is the mid-to-late 18th century, and the guest has just entered a cavalry fort, complete with blockhouses, medicine shows, and *Hobo Jungle*, where one could eat beef stew served in tinware such as what hobos would presumably have used. This area paid homage to how the cavalry made expansion possible into the west, providing safe zones for settlers to build villages. And so on the other side of the fort lay Magic Mountain's version of Disneyland's Main Street. Magic Mountain Village (renamed Centennial City in 1959) was laid out with the same clever use of four large industrial structures hidden by period-authentic facades. Designed to resemble city blocks from Colorado in the 1880s, each housed multiple shops and attractions.

Beyond that lay...well, not much of anything. The plans called for six themed lands: Cavalry Post and Stockade, Magic Mountain Village, Fairgrounds, River Ride, Magic of Industry, and Storybook Lane. Beyond Cavalry Post and the Village, here is how the park described upcoming attractions:

> "At the edge of Magic Mountain Village, it is planned to have a Fairgrounds, much the same as every Western Town had its own fairgrounds area, where families met for picnics and entertainment. In the Magic Mountain Fairgrounds, plans call for various types of amusement facilities, such as a "Mine Ride" and "The Creation of the Earth Ride." All such rides will have authenticity and educational concepts as their underlying theme.
>
> Included in the plans for Magic Mountain are areas for such things as: a river ride, that will tell the story of early-day fur trappers and the experiences they had on the Colorado River; a Magic of Industry exposition, telling the story of a century of progress in the West; a

> "Storybook lane" for the younger set; a full scale narrow gauge railroad circling the entire park; and an authentic reproduction of the Cherrylyne horse-drawn streetcar that used to operate between Denver and Englewood."[13]

Surrounding everything was the *Magic Mountain Railroad,* an authentic, narrow gauge steam train. Conestoga wagons explored undeveloped lands. The *River Ride* was to be the first knock-off of Disney's *Jungle Cruise,* with guided boat tours of the backwaters. Of course you'd encounter all sorts of animated wildlife, get caught in the crossfire of battles between cowboys and Native Americans, and narrowly avert sinking when an old bridge collapses just shy of the boat. The *Outer Space Land* ride concept was a simulated flying saucer experience, blasting off from Earth and making guests feel as though they've journeyed far beyond the atmosphere. *Creation of the Earth* would tell the pre-historic story of the Rocky Mountain regions.[14]

Most of this never came to pass. The park struggled continuously to finance construction, and a senior executive skipped the state with the remaining company funds.[15] It was so iffy the park actually opened its gates in 1958 for visitors while construction was still ongoing. The train began operation in 1959 on weekends, essentially sightseeing a vast construction site, and the first full season of "regular" operation was 1960. This would also be the last. They managed to complete the stage coaches, which were used for tours of the property, the train, an *Indian Village, Market Street* (Village/Centennial City), and *Road Racer* (a standard Arrow auto ride). Much of the *River Ride* was excavated with concrete rocks, structures, and gags built on site and in the show building of the *Creation* ride, which was used as a workshop similar to how Disney used the *Opera House* in the early days.[16]

The park, what there was of it, sat idle for eleven years, when in 1971 it was reopened as Heritage Square amusement park.[17] Other than the existing structures of Centennial City, this park had nothing to do with the original vision of a Disney-type experience. As of this writing, that park has also closed and the land is planned to be redeveloped.[18] The very first theme park to be designed and built after Disneyland was finally gone. Lost history? Or getting rid of a bunch of cheap industrial structures with fancy facades? It's all in the eye—and heart—of the beholder.

PLEASURE ISLAND

Pleasure Island was announced at a Boston press conference on October 28, 1958.[19] Marco's second theme park was underway at the same time the first one was struggling to find its footing. The original concept came from the publisher of Child Life magazine, Bill Hawkes. Child Life World, full of storybook and fantasy, was transformed into the country's second theme park to be patterned after Disneyland, using the same design team of artists Woody had brought over from Disney and elsewhere.[20] Many of the same themes and design ideas would be employed here as at Magic Mountain.

168 acres in Wakefield, MA, much of it swampland, was dredged, filled, and reshaped to feature Main Street, Clipper Cove, Western City, and Hood's Farm. Main Street was angled a bit toward the right just beyond the hub, with the farm located to the far right. As you turned and walked toward the end of Main Street, the waterfront and the park's iconic *Hawkes Point Lighthouse* would come into view in a Disney-like cinematic reveal. Clipper Cove resembled a New England fishing village, with various boats, docks, and *Cap'n Snow's Chowder House* (a corporate sponsor). Back to the left of the front hub were the *Jenney Cars* (an Arrow auto ride sponsored by the Jenney Oil company) and the Western City section.

Shoving off from the waterfront were two destinations for danger. The *Moby Dick Hunt* was a play off the *Jungle Cruise,* this time with a narrated hunt for the great white whale that has terrorized the area. If the menacing cannibals didn't get you on the way past their island, the sound of the whale's blow hole surely signaled all was over. Soon the whale itself was in sight, rising out of the water, blowing to beat the band, then submerging again (to reset for the next boat). If you survived, you could regain your land legs for a moment and then head over to the other dock. "Bamboo-thatched pirate boats embark from Clipper Cove for the perilous safari to *Pirate Cove,* just beyond the Western section." This popular attraction was in the outer harbor, beyond the causeway and railroad trestle. The island featured a tree house, fort, shipwreck, and other fun, piratey kinds of things.

The park featured two dark rides. *Wreck of the Hesperus* was located near the waterfront, clearly visible with the remains of a great sailing ship dominating the entrance. Or at least that was what the original concept art depicted. Reality being what it is, the actual entrance featured two tall masts planted at angles in the cement with various ropes and torn flags. Ride vehicles shaped like small sailing vessels set off across the sea, only to be sunk by a hurricane. Drifting along the undersea realms, you finally escape after a warning by King Neptune himself. The *Old Chisholm Trail* ride, located in Western City, was a horseless carriage vehicle that took you into a Western town where you witness a live hanging and a gunfight while the piano player blissfully plays away in the corner.

The narrow gauge *Pleasure Island & Western Railroad* (later renamed *Old Smokey RR*) departed from Western City on a roundabout tour of the back country and outer harbor, crossing over a trestle that separated it from the inner harbor (where Clipper Cove was located). The railroad locomotive and passenger coaches were leased from Edaville Railroad in Massachusetts. Edaville had a popular Christmas season that used a lot of equipment, but the slower summer seasons left some of this sitting idle. So it was trucked back and forth to Pleasure Island each year.

Live entertainment was a major draw for the park, with much of it consisting of "streetmosphere" actors roaming about the grounds. The *Diamond Lil Saloon* show was the big deal, and later the *Show Bowl* hosted a variety of big name entertainers.[21]

Along with his designers who were working on Magic Mountain, Woody called in an old friend from Texas who had developed Disneyland's new employee training program. Van Arsdale France's "A Guide for Pleasure Islanders" was in the same vein as Disneyland's "We'll Create Happiness" and Freedomland's "Be a Friendly Freedomlander."

His approach, focusing on treating park customers as *guests,* was a major departure from typical amusement park operations and helped define the modern theme park experience.[22]

Unlike the Colorado park, Pleasure Island would be completed and survive–more or less–for eleven seasons. Corporate sponsors, like C.V. had arranged for Disneyland, made a big difference in funding initial construction. Sponsors paid for a five-year lease along with interior construction costs, taxes, and fire insurance.[23] Keeping the doors open, though, wasn't easy, and the park went through multiple changes of ownership along the way. Initial construction costs ran higher than planned, and the park reportedly took in only $700,000 during the 1959 season (gross, not profit).[24] That first year was also the rainiest in the area since 1927, hindering construction as well as dampening outdoor activities, and with the short New England operating calendar they barely saw half of the expected 750,000 guests.[25] By the time the last owner gave up in 1969, total attendance had clocked in at a mere three million. All of this combined with a lack of sustained capital investment led to the park's decline with little in the way of new attractions and lots in the way of deferred maintenance. Once the downhill spiral begins it's increasingly difficult to dig out.[26]

While much of the original park is long gone, the site itself isn't entirely transformed into modern development.[27] Memories live on through the efforts of Friends of Pleasure Island,[28] an enthusiastic bunch who meets to reminisce, take tours of the grounds, and compile memorabilia.

FREEDOMLAND

On May 25, 1959 in the Empire State Building, C.V. Wood and partners held a press conference to announce the largest Disneyland-type park to be built east of Anaheim.[29] Freedomland was to be 85 acres of American history, billed as "The World's Largest Entertainment Center." From the opening season guidebook:

> "...You see, hear, feel, and *live* the true history of our land, as it actually happened. In Old New York, at the Chicago Fire, in the Indian-fighting West, in the Civil War, *you are there*, playing a real part in the great moments that shaped our country's destiny. *You* help fight the Chicago Fire, *you* are "attacked" by hostile Indians, *you* participate in the dramatic action stories that highlight our American heritage. Freedomland is *your* adventure in living history."[30]

Well, who could pass that up? Indeed, in a region full of amusements of all types, including the original Coney Island, Freedomland was an entirely new thing, and enough people had watched Walt show off his park for so long they were hungry to try a taste of it for themselves.

Getting the park ready for them, however, was a complicated affair. Freedomland was Woody's idea and Marco Engineering handled all design aspects. The land was owned by Webb & Knapp, Inc, which was a major shareholder in National Development Corporation. International Recreation Corporation, including investors in Pleasure Island, was the parent company to Freedomland, Inc. They leased the land from National Development for a reported $767,400 per year. Stock purchases as part of the deal cost $7 million. Construction overruns added another $4 million beyond the estimated $16 million for the park. The actual inner workings of who was in control of what are far more complex and resulted in a structure where no single individual or entity was actually in total charge of everything. It would have to perform exceedingly well to recoup this and sustain operations over the years.[31]

The site was on 205 acres in the Bronx, mostly marshland and a former landfill.[32] In a unique design twist, the park was laid out in the shape of the United States. Visitors entered along the mid-Atlantic seaboard and found themselves in Little Old New York. The time period is 1850-1900; you might witness a holdup at the bank, cruise the lake in the *Harbor Tug Boats*, drive a *Horseless Carriage* through New England (standard Arrow auto ride), or take the *Horse-Drawn Streetcar* or *Surreys* over to Chicago. Set in 1871, Chicago featured the

Santa Fe Railroad, bound for San Francisco on the other side of the park, the two majestic *Sternwheelers* (*American* and *Canadian*), and the *Stockyards Restaurant.* Youngsters were encouraged to chip in and help fight *The Great Chicago Fire* (catastrophe breaks out every fifteen minutes as posted on the attraction sign). Burned timbers outside the attraction building were remnants of an actual fire during park construction.

Venturing westward we found ourselves in The Great Plains (1803-1900). *Fort Cavalry* provided a safe haven from the various hostiles to be found beyond its gates, but the brave could hop on the *Fort Cavalry Stage Line* and ride the stage coaches over Lewis and Clark's route. Post a letter at the *Pony Express* station and watch the rider tear off at full speed for delivery at Old Southwest. *Borden's Farm* was here on the Great Plains, complete with a real-life Elsie the Cow and other various farm animals. Elsie, who was always well-coiffed and ready for a night on the town, lived in supreme comfort with a lavish stall designed by a New York interior design firm.

San Francisco covered the west coast of the U.S. map. Step off the train in 1906 and take in the shops of *Chinatown,* entertainment of the *Barbary Coast,* and hear grizzled fishermen tell tall fish tales at *Fisherman's Wharf.* Two major attractions were located in this section of the park, the first described as follows:

> "On April 18, 1906, the ground fell from under San Francisco's feet. You will safely see the San Francisco earthquake and fire re-created in harrowing detail. You will ride past buckling sidewalks, open fissures and collapsing buildings. You will see houses slide sideways and crack in two, then burst into flames. These thrills are yours in Freedomland's *San Francisco Earthquake* ride."[33]

This was a classic dark ride designed by Marco and engineered by Arrow Development consisting of antique autos that wound through the town streets, first enjoying the peaceful atmosphere of townspeople enjoying everyday life, then frantically careening through complete disaster as the world crumbled around you.

Northwest Fur Trapper was yet another adaptation of the *Jungle Cruise,* set in 1820s Oregon. Boarding a fur trapper's bullboat, you set sail up the Snake and Columbia Rivers, your armed guide desperately trying to ward off danger from wild animals and Totempole Indians. Since Marco was simultaneously working on design concepts for all three parks there was much overlap and common experiences, in this case narrowly avoiding a falling tree and collapsing bridge, as was originally intended for Magic Mountain.

Walk through the tunnel toward The Old Southwest and notice the *Tuscon Mining Company Ore Buckets* gliding overhead. This was a standard Von Roll sky ride, though it had two complete circuits side-by-side for double the capacity. Additional attractions that you could also find in the other Marco parks were the *Burrow Trail* (slow saunter on a small donkey), live entertainment at the *Opera House and Saloon,* gunfights in the streets, and a tilt house where nothing was straight and objects appeared to roll uphill. Board an Arrow mine train car and descend deep into the *Mine Caverns,* encountering all sorts of creatures, exploding TNT, and narrowly avoiding a head-on crash with another out-of-control mine car.

New Orleans was next, featuring the gaiety of Mardi Gras. Take a spin on the *King Rex Carrousel,* lose yourself in the *Crystal Maze* glass-walled house of mirrors, and watch your kids hop on the back of *Danny the Dragon,* an Arrow-developed multi-vehicle train designed to resemble a long, twisting dragon. *Danny* (mostly) followed a wire buried in the pavement, an adaptation of guided vehicle technology from factories. A similar approach would be employed much later at Epcot for *Universe of Energy* and *The Great Movie Ride* at Disney's Hollywood Studios. The last veterans from the Civil War were just about gone, and the park paid homage to that terrible period with an "intensely realistic recreation of the Great War Between the States." A war correspondents' wagon took you through encampments, burning houses, and a derailed train, suddenly finding yourself trapped by cannon cross-fire. Escaping over a pontoon bridge, the wagon drove past *Appomattox Court House* where Lee surrendered his Army of Northern Virginia to Grant. Transfer over to a Model T in *Tornado* where large fans blew every which way, cows and chickens went flying through the air, residents held on for dear life, and you got swept up in the rotating eye of the monster storm.

Of course pirates are a major aspect of history in this region of the country, so the tall mast planted in the concrete with flags, crow's nest, and a dead pirate hanging from the yardarm was an inevitable draw to ride *Buccaneer*. Arrow was certainly busy for Freedomland, and for this attraction they provided eleven cars designed like pirate ships, winding their way along a track past scenes of merriment, hidden treasure, a sea serpent, and…blundering right into the midst of a battle between two pirate ships firing cannon in all directions. And you thought Disney was first.

The last land of the park focused on the future. Satellite City offered a glimpse toward where the country was headed with *Science and Industry Exhibits*, the futuristic sports cars of the *Satellite City Turnpike*, and the moving sidewalk that took you over the lake to *Space Rover*. Similar to what had been planned for Magic Mountain, this attraction simulated space travel with a bone-shaking launch and high-altitude views of America's great cities. The park's second season featured the *Moon Bowl*, an expansive outdoor dance floor built over the former lake. This was a highly successful addition with concerts by major stars of the day.[34]

Freedomland opened June 19, 1960. Five seasons later it was all over. There has been great speculation and mystery surrounding its demise, with most accounts echoing the long-held belief that the 1964 World's Fair in New York did it in. But as in most cases, the story is far more complex than this. First was the overly complicated ownership and management structure. Disneyland survived because one man was in total charge of everything and was passionate about making the whole thing work. Factor in an expensive annual land lease and the math quickly becomes unsustainable, especially with attendance falling far short of Wood's predicted five million per season.[35] The land itself was terrible, consisting of marsh and landfill; stories abound of mattress springs sticking up through the asphalt, tripping staff and guests alike.[36] Short operating seasons, about four months, did not offset the significant amount of year-round financial commitments. After pouring the foundation for the announced Freedomland Inn, all construction on the hotel was abandoned and the land put up for auction as early as 1963.[37] Lack of capital resulted in the decline of show over time, such as selling *Tornado* to Kennywood Park[38] and replacing the horse-drawn Civil War correspondents' wagons with regular farm tractors.[39] For the 1964 season San Francisco was closed off completely, with a sticker in the park's guide book claiming "We're fixin' it for you! Closed in order to build...a bigger and better Freedomland."[40] The park struggled to find new attractions that were necessary to maintain attendance, but these often ran contrary to the original historic intent and story.[41] Management claimed at the end of the 1964 season that the park would reopen the following year with only Little Old New York, Old Chicago, and Satellite City.[42]

It never did. The cash drain for building and operating the park, along with the highly complex financial dealings for the involved companies, caused serious fiscal issues before the park even opened for its inaugural season in 1960.[43] The park filed bankruptcy in September 1964, presenting a plan to maintain a small portion of the park while building a housing development on property.[44] This wasn't accepted, and so developers moved in with the blessing of state and local government and began building Co-op City, a series of high-rise apartments.[45] It has been claimed this was the actual intent from the very beginning, but that the land needed to be "proven" acceptable for such development. Building the park, with its multi-story structures, and running it for five years supposedly satisfied the condition for allowing construction of much larger buildings.[46] More likely it was simple economics—the land became much more valuable for anything except a park in decline, especially in New York City.[47] At any rate, the park was done, and with it the last of C.V. Wood's dream of building his own Disneylands around the country. Of the four major parks he was directly involved in realizing, only one has survived. That's our next tale to weave.

Marco Engineering was hired for a variety of other park and entertainment projects, most never realized. The company provided a range of services, from feasibility studies to design and engineering. All of them were billed with headlines such as "The designers and builders of Disneyland, California, may very well lend the magic of their fairy wand to New York's Aquarium next year."[48] And you wonder why Disney set his legal beagles loose on them. There was a proposed Circusland in Orlando;[49] Discoveryland in Miami; Magic Harbor in Houston;[50] Jungleland in Thousand Oaks, CA;[51] a "Disneyland type gold rush center" in Rocklin, CA;[52] San Antonio's River Walk;[53] a Boston Exposition Center revamp;[54] and a major makeover for Cedar Point.[55] The "man who built Disneyland" confidently informed the city of San Antonio in 1958 that a park in that region was feasible and would attract over a million visitors each year.[56] And on it went, but the main ones that will forever be associated with his (in)famous name started in the mountains of Colorado and wound up as concrete foundations for housing outside the Big Apple.

Woody went on to develop Lake Havasu, a planned community in Arizona, featuring the actual London Bridge he bought and shipped from England. Stone by stone. Every single one. Or so it was claimed.[57] For all his supposed faults, lack of self-assurance was not one of them.

FRANCE
Bon Apetit
Trading Post
The Flying Jenny
Rabun Gap Depot
Jean Ribaut's Adventure
Lafayette's Shooting Gallery
Rest Rooms
Gaslight On The Green
Baskin Robbins
The Sweet Tooth
The Animal Fair
Refreshment Stand
Clem Greene School House (Lost Parents)
Ralston-Purina Petsville
Tales of the
TALES OF OKEFENOKEE
First Aid
Treasure Chest
Happy Motoring Freeway
The Emporium
Rest Rooms
THE CRYSTAL PISTOL
GEORGIA
Log Jamboree #1 and #2
Refreshment Stand
Souvenirs

Chapter Four

ANGUS WYNNE GETS IT DONE

The young mayor had only been in office for four years, but clearly the town was headed in a new direction. First elected at the age of 25, the broadcast journalist had just successfully bagged a new General Motors assembly plant, gotten approval to build a lake to serve as a regional water supply, and was working on plans for a turnpike, a hospital, and other major industrial development. Sandwiched between Dallas and Fort Worth, Arlington at the time featured a population of around 8,000, and Tommy J. Vandergriff wasn't finished. He was transforming the town from a largely agrarian region into a transportation-centered suburb, focused on new industry. And then he took a trip to visit some new place called Disneyland.[1]

Angus Wynne, president of the Great Southwest Corporation and quite the dominant force in the region, was buying extensive tracts of land around Arlington with the intent to develop one of the nation's largest industrial centers featuring a railway, warehouses, and a new freeway. He, too, visited Disneyland shortly after it opened and came away impressed. This was the ticket, both of these gentlemen knew, to not only spur growth, but to generate maximum publicity for the region. A park would also provide a much quicker turnaround in recouping the costs of Wynne's massive development plans, which had stalled out for the moment. Few people in the country had ever experienced anything like Disneyland, and most could not make the cross-country trip. How fabulous it would be, both men agreed, to convince Walt to build a similar park here in Texas.[2]

It wasn't for lack of trying. Vandergriff appealed directly to Walt... along with scores of other civic leaders across the country. Everybody wanted one, and of course, no one would get it. Wynne pushed ahead, determined to build a similar amusement enterprise which initially included a major sports and recreation complex along with the theme park. The two men, one a mayor, the other a business developer, realized they needed help from folks who actually knew how to design and build a park. But at this point in time there were only two individuals who fit this description: Walt Disney and C.V. Wood. Walt was out, but Woody, the fellow Texan building parks around the country with his new company Marco Engineering, was eager to jump in.[3]

One of Woody's well-known hires from the movie industry had been adapting to designing for spatial environments for a few years now. The former art director for *Singing in the Rain* had become Marco's principal designer,[4] working closely with Woody and participating in high level meetings with Wynne and other park officials between Arlington and Marco's offices in Los Angeles. Whether or not he had any notions of going solo in the business was made irrelevant when one day the news came down—Marco Engineering and Woody were out. Wynne was asking Randall to continue work on the park under his own name.[5] And thus was founded one of the most influential and successful park design firms outside of Disney. When Six Flags Over Texas opened in 1961, it was but the first in a long series of successful projects over the next forty-two years, from 1959 until 2001. R. Duell and Associates would ultimately design—and actually build—over forty parks in the United States and abroad. No other company has come close. They led the way throughout the golden age of regional parks in the 1960s and 70s, ultimately touching the lives of millions of guests over the decades.[6]

SIX FLAGS OVER TEXAS

Originally conceived as *Great Southwestland,* during the planning stage the park was briefly thought of as *Texas Under Six Flags,* referring to the six nations that have ruled the territory at various periods in history. *You can't call it that—Texas is never under anything!* And so with that indisputable bit of logic the name was cleverly reimagined into *Six Flags Over Texas,* which apparently made all the difference.[7]

Few states possess a history and culture as rich as Texas, and so thematic ideas for lands and attractions in the park weren't exactly hard to come by. Six Flags was a heavily themed park, divided into six lands representing the ruling countries: Spain, France, Mexico, the Republic of Texas, the Confederate States of America, and the United States of America. Each section was essentially a self-contained mini-park complete with a mixture of attractions, shows, food, merchandise, and restrooms. This concept became the model for future parks as designers worked to ensure that all guests' needs and interests were taken care of.

Not surprisingly, C.V. Wood and Marco Engineering's experience building Walt's park is clearly evident as Disneyland influences can be seen in many of the attractions and other elements. The single front gate was the only way in and out, a concept Walt got from Bill Pereira, one of the architects he consulted early in his park dreaming.[8] In fact Six Flags Over Texas was the first to implement a single admission charge that covered nearly everything in the park.[9] Disneyland was still using their A–E ticket books, charging a nominal fee to get in, then letting guests choose which rides to spend their tickets on. A fence around the park served a dual purpose: preventing people from sneaking into the park, but also as a berm to block out the real world.

The park's overall shape was an inverse of the Disneyland triangle, with the larger base at the front instead. The park was encircled by a narrow gauge railroad, though with only a single station it didn't serve as transportation to the far reaches. For that matter, neither did Disneyland's at first—guests would embark at either the Main Street or Frontierland stations, then complete an entire loop around the park to return where they started. For the foot-weary both parks had overhead sky rides; at Six Flags it provided a scenic hop from United States all the way across to the western frontier of Texas.

Rather than a Disneyland-style hub and spoke layout, or the completely random pathways found in most amusement parks, the primary guest path followed a meandering circle. It's nearly impossible to get lost, and you're guaranteed to see most everything. That was intentional, as park officials didn't want to waste anything they spent money on.[10] But the meandering serves more than this, such as hiding what's around the next corner. This cinematic concept of the *reveal* is far more adventurous and exciting than just laying everything out where you can see it. In order to transition from one land or themed area to the next along the loop, designers can alter the environment in various ways. Landscaping changes from the desolate pines and scrubs of the wild frontier to manicured flowerbeds of modern America. Signage, lighting, and architecture take on the styles, colors, and materials of that place. Even the sounds around you, such as background music and environmental noises (animals, townspeople, transportation) contribute to the feeling that you've traveled to a different land and time.[11] This approach to a circular pathway around the park would come to be known as the *Duell loop*, from Randall Duell's company who conceived and refined it over time. It would be the standard approach for a great many parks they designed for years to come.[12]

A visitor to Six Flags would enter over the railroad into the *Star Plaza*, which featured a large floral Lone Star of Texas, synchronized water fountains, and the six flags flying over everything. If you decided to head toward the right, a habit engrained from weekly grocery shopping, you'd next enter the United States period, representing Texas after it became the 28th state in 1845. Instead of the old west and frontier history, this section focused on modern times with a rocket-themed scrambler, *Humble's Happy Motoring Freeway* (named after the

Humble Oil Company), and *Sidewinder,* a Herschell-designed wild mouse roller coaster (this would be moved to the Mexican section for the park's second season and renamed *La Cucaracha*). For over twenty years the *Animal Kingdom* petting zoo featured your standard fare of goats, cows, and donkeys, but also more interesting monkeys, seals, and baby elephants.

Moving along we would find ourselves back in the late 1800s. France's stake in Texas territory consisted of a single tiny colony, Fort St. Louis, established as a base of operations for further exploration. Lasting all but four years, this small foothold was apparently enough to qualify as one of the six flags. Park designers worked to instill the concept of theme as much as possible, so this section featured a very rustic, log-construction fort and a gift shop designed to mimic the original Fort St. Louis style. Merchandise focused on relevant items such as rocks and jewelry. You could play in the fort, shop in the shop, but like the historical colony before it, the heart of this land was quite small. The major attraction, though, was *La Salle's River Adventure,* the latest descendant of Disneyland's *Jungle Cruise.* The historically-based story focused on the colony's leader, La Salle, and his quest to find the Mississippi River. Your boat captain wove a tale of Texas history while watching ahead for signs of trouble. And trouble was everywhere, in the form of an attacking Spanish fort, alligators, falling trees from beavers, and Native Americans unhappy about their homeland being overrun. As at Disneyland, physical animation brought the attraction to life, meaning crude animatronic figures, cannon shots that splashed around the boat, cave doors that opened and closed around you, and a falling tree that nearly smashes the boat as it passes. This was authentic theming at its finest for regional parks; most people had never been to Anaheim, so this was a completely new experience.

Stepping a bit further back in time we found ourselves in the early 1860s when Texas had joined the Confederacy. Styled to a Southern town during the war, it featured a Confederate recruitment station comprised of tents and cannon. Reenactments were performed by actors in authentic uniforms, and kids could "sign up" for service as soldiers or nurses. Themed shops sold flags, history books, maps, and other typical souvenir items. The obligatory fried chicken dinner could be had in a Southern plantation home. Obliquely related to the Confederacy was the stagecoach ride; its backstory recreated the original *Butterfield Overland Stagecoach* company that ferried mail and passengers between Texas and California (predecessor to Wells Fargo; Knott's Berry Farm used the same name for their version of the ride). A more dubious placement in the Confederacy was *Skull Island*, where the famous French pirate Jean LaFitte would presumably hide his ill-gotten gain. This was essentially Disneyland's *Tom Sawyer Island*, featuring a playground for kids accessible by river raft. It was lushly landscaped, and the river journey surrounding it was quite scenic. Theming broke down somewhat with a fiberglass slide running awkwardly out of the imposing *Skull Rock's* left ear. But the island was fun for kids with room to run and play, suspension bridges to bounce on, and even a pier for fishing.

On the other side of authentic plantation columns was the Republic of Texas, formed after independence was achieved from Mexico. Due to the popularity of western movies and culture, it seems nearly every park in the 1950s and 60s featured a Wild West frontier section. But it was especially appropriate to include a western-themed Texas in this park. The largest of the lands, you could walk through a western town complete with jail, bank (an actual historic bank moved from the town of Tom Bean), general store, and so on. Gunfights broke out regularly, of course, and the town saloon featured live shows and authentic period furnishings. One of the few breaks from the land's backstory and theme was the inclusion of Judge Roy Bean, a famous justice of the peace in that area of Texas...but in the 1880s, long after Texas had juggled its membership between a couple of flags. Across the creek, the *Six Flags Railroad* departed for a relaxing trip around the park, while the not-quite-so-authentic *Astrolift* ride station tried its best to fit into its surroundings.

Somewhat sandwiched between Texas, Spain, and Mexico was the *Indian Village*. Not being credited with a flag of its own, this almost-a-land consisted of a large *Trading Post* souvenir store, stocked with authentic relics, and a small teepee area for live performances of Native American dances.

Although historically first, Spain was next in the park's layout. The difference in architecture was immediately apparent with structures built from stone instead of wood, the idea being to recreate the ruins of Spain's first mission built in Texas in 1690. Hop aboard a mule (if you were small enough) as the pack followed a conquistador through what was originally intended to be a majestic canyon. That major thematic feature never quite made it to construction, somewhat diminishing its historical significance and scenic enjoyment.

Last stop on the tour was Mexico, located directly to the left of the entrance plaza. Mexico, which included the region that would ultimately become known as Texas, was formed after breaking away from Spanish rule. The year is 1821, and this section of the park featured bright colors everywhere as is typical of Mexican culture. The bazaar sold authentic Mexican items that you'd find in-country, instead of typical park merchandise, and a Mexican restaurant offered appropriate cuisine. One of the more interesting attractions was the *Ferrocarril Fiesta Train,* distinctive with oversized sombreros that topped each car. The winding narrow gauge track passed by beautiful gardens and colorful, comical animatronic figures such as mariachi bands, dancing tamales, and a bullfighter scene. The *Fiesta Train* hardly represented authentic, historical vistas, but instead captured the flavor of a festive, joyful society.[13]

Similarities to Disneyland abound, from overall park layout, attractions and themes, to how they actually pulled it off. Attractions are near-duplicates of those found at Marco's earlier three parks, many of which, of course, were first pioneered in Anaheim. The commonality is not merely design influence, but practical. It's much cheaper and more efficient to copy existing successful ideas and buy off-the-shelf rides and components from third party companies, dressing them up as need be to fit local themes.[14] One of these outfits was a fledgling two-man operation from Mountain View, California, who started out in the machining and metalwork business, then transitioned into building small rides such as miniature freeways and boats for amusement parks. Walt's team discovered them, commissioning development and manufacture of the ride vehicles for *Mr. Toad's Wild Ride, Alice in Wonderland, Dumbo* flying spinner, and later the water-flume systems for *Pirates* and *Small World*. Their invention of the tubular steel track for Disneyland's *Matterhorn* in 1959 upended the coaster world, and each of these early theme parks would add a family-friendly runaway mine train based on this approach. Arrow would go on to dominate the roller coaster industry for many years, but in 1961 they were just gaining a foothold in the business.[15]

Corporate sponsors, crucial for getting Disneyland to the starting line, also played a major role for Six Flags Over Texas. Companies such as Westinghouse and Eastman Kodak signed up, paying a fee to showcase their products and services. In those days these were fairly significant displays, much grander than merely having your logo on a "picture spot" plaque.[16] Most of the shops in Walt's park were originally operated by outsiders, including the film concession awarded to his friend Art Linkletter in exchange for hosting Disneyland's opening TV special. This approach meant you had experienced industry professionals who could come in and just do their thing, freeing the park from having to figure it all out. It takes time to learn the restaurant or retail business, train employees, and finesse operational patterns, but over time parks realized the profit they were losing and gradually took over all merchandise and food operations.

Though some aspects were more authentic than others, Six Flags designers should be credited with establishing solid themes that were relevant to this particular park, in this particular location. Texans are rightfully a proud lot, and this park was *theirs*. It represented their state's rich, diverse heritage. The flags flew proud over the entrance plaza. Merchandise in the shops wasn't generic, touristy dribble; you could take a piece of Texas history home with you. Kids probably learned more about their state's history here than they had in school.

C.V. may not have made it to the finish line, but at least there's one park he had a hand in that has survived to this day.

SIX FLAGS OVER GEORGIA

The success of Six Flags Over Texas inspired Angus Wynne to explore opportunities for a second park. In 1964 he had negotiated a sale of 49% of Great Southwest Corporation to the Pennsylvania Railroad, maintaining his role as president and CEO and accessing a bigger checkbook for expansion.[17] Similar to his original Texas concept, the announcement boldly predicted a $400 million industrial and recreational development plan. A 3,000 acre site just west of Atlanta was secured in 1965 for $3 million,[18] and two years later the company became the first chain park operator in the United States.

Opening June 16, 1967 for a total cost of $12 million,[19] Six Flags Over Georgia followed the same principles as its predecessor, tuned to its specific region. An early conundrum involved the fact that Georgia has actually never been ruled by six different countries, and so the original title was *Georgia Flags*. Reason won out, and the growing brand of Six Flags was used after all, the sixth flag filled in by using Georgia's own state flag.[20] The five countries announced for representation included the United States, the United Kingdom, France, Spain, and the Confederate States of America. This then set off a second controversy among local historians who were puzzled at the inclusion of France. Apparently the only claim the French could make was from sailing along the rather modest coastline in the 17th century for a few weeks charting and temporarily slapping names on places.[21] Oh well, the show goes on.

As with the Texas park, the opening day admission price of $3.95 provided access to all the rides and attractions. R. Duell and Associates were back to help develop the Georgia property;[22] joining them was art director Hans Peters, another veteran from the film industry with credits such as *The Red Badge of Courage.*[23] Similarities were everywhere, such as the Duell loop pathway layout, local interest theming, and many of the attractions. It was a somewhat ragged loop, though, in order to provide interest, suspense, and allow for wandering through the various architecture and scenery.

The ornate entrance plaza, more extensive than in Texas, was clearly designed to evoke images of a Southern plantation. Brilliant white classical statuary, planters, and fountains were arranged in a symmetrical box layout typical of well-manicured plantation gardens. Towering over everything from the back of the plaza, grand Corinthian-style columns, presumably inspired by the ruins of Windsor Plantation house in Mississippi, beckoned the visitor toward the park proper. Such an elaborate welcoming area immediately established the unique theme and regional place setting for the entire park; this was no mere copy of its older Texan sibling—you were now in the heart of Dixie. As you wound around toward the right, though, each section featured similar attractions and concepts found in Texas. The British area featured the obligatory miniature antique car ride with Colonial British-themed shops. A replica of the Liberty Pole installed in Savannah during the Revolutionary War connected the United Kingdom with Georgia history. The early-to-mid 1860s was next with the Confederacy, again with the Southern fried chicken restaurant and one of the park's two train stations. *Marthasville* depot comes from one of the original town names for Atlanta, and the two locomotives, the *Texas* and the *General,* were named after the famous great locomotive chase in the Civil War. As at Disneyland and Six Flags Over Texas, the train looped the park providing a relaxing journey back in time, but in Georgia also served as transportation between two stations.

A gorgeous music hall, the *Crystal Pistol,* was reminiscent of the 1855 Athenaeum theater on Decatur Street, near the old railroad square in Atlanta;[24] it featured architecture straight out of the Old South with its tall, circular, columned portico. Tubular steel roller coasters were ushering in a new era of thrill rides, and Arrow Development, manufacturer of many of the park's original rides, wowed visitors with the *Dahlonega Mine Train.* Close by was the *Yahoola Hooler,* a kid-friendly mine train coaster named after the Yahoola Creek in Dahlonega. Simple attempts at attraction theming throughout the park included static and animated figures that represented each scene, such as loggers, soldiers, Native Americans, and so on. The *Mine Train* featured moonshiners and gold prospectors; Dahlonega is a small Georgian town that enjoyed a very brief gold rush in 1828…long before the war. Close enough.

The park's major dark ride was *Tales of the Okefenokee.* The experience for opening day was rather underwhelming, and so it was reimagined for the park's second season by Sid and Marty Krofft (well known at the time for their children's television programming). This was a classic Disney-style boat ride through a show building, filled with animated scenes from the Uncle Remus stories adapted by an Atlanta journalist, Joel Chandler Harris.

Directly across the main pathway from *Okefenokee,* Spain was represented almost exclusively by a single structure designed like a fort that housed shops and a Mexican restaurant. Spanish conquistadors stood watch at *Castillo DeSoto,* the actual name of a castle in Spain, the structure of which appears to have been modeled after the Castillo de San Marcos in Florida. Just beyond Spain, typical rustic New France architecture signaled the era of frontier exploration by France between the 16th and 18th centuries. That is, except for the *Dolphin Show,* situated next to the *Watermelon Waterloo* watermelon seed spitting area. Ah, history. The main attraction for France, though, was a near copy of Six Flags Over Texas' river adventure, which in itself was a near-copy of Disneyland's *Jungle Cruise.* But instead of the explorer LaSalle, it's the legend of French explorer Jean Ribault we're interested in. The adventures were nearly identical to those found in Texas, with gun fights, threats from Native Americans, cannon fire from an opposing fort, and even the same gag where the tree nearly falls onto the boat as it passes. The skipper, costumed in a rather questionable brightly festive striped shirt and hat, drove the boat while spieling corny jokes and incessantly warning of danger and disaster ahead.

After leaving France, there was a bit of the American frontier with old west structures providing an appropriate setting for the *Rabun Gap* railroad station, an actual town located in the extreme northeastern tip of Georgia. This transitioned into a more modern United States section that would have never been mistaken for an immersive, themed environment. For the most part it was a small collection of off-the-shelf amusement rides with current American touches, such as a "modern" miniature car ride sponsored by a Texas oil company, complete with scaled down billboards. A puppet theater featured shows by the famous Krofft brothers, the same team who would redesign the dark ride for the park's second season. As in Texas, there was a petting zoo that must have been quite the thing those days. Soon to come, other thoroughly American things to do included the *Chevy Show* (a point-of-view wide screen theater which took guests on a roller coaster ride and wild car journey), and an indication of where these parks were headed over time—a towering Y-shaped *Sky Hook* ride that hauled a couple baskets of guests way up and back again. The ride wars had started.

And lastly, in the minuscule land of Georgia, the *Log Jamboree* opened with one flume, with a second to be added the following year. Maybe it goes without saying, but the thematic idea of using a fiberglass log flowing down a waterway comes from the logging industry where they'd float their cut trees down rivers. Occasionally an ambitious lumberman would hop on for quite the thrill ride. For the Georgia attraction, oversize, animated logging figures encountered along the journey were more spectacle (and freaky) than immersive characters, but they provided interest and motion along the ride.[25]

Like in Texas, Six Flags Over Georgia was an immediate success that has continued to this day. Duell's group took a formula that worked quite well in the first park and continued improving and adapting it for a new audience. It's clear to see their experience from Texas in the more elaborate designs for Georgia. The park brought a piece of Disney magic to the local region, thrilling guests with adventures steeped in Georgia history. It became *their* park, like so many regional parks yet to appear across the country. And Angus wasn't yet finished...his company was to attempt striking gold for the third time —just west of the mighty Mississippi River.

SIX FLAGS OVER MID-AMERICA

The third site was located near Eureka, Missouri, about thirty miles southwest of St. Louis. 502 acres were optioned at a cost of $1,500,000 for development just off Allenton Road, which runs north from nearby I-44. Over a dozen other locations had been rejected, most due to lack of room and the desired "pastoral" setting. They found it here for sure, with the unincorporated town of Allenton just south of the property with its 500 residents, Eureka just east with around 2400 folks, and equally tiny Pacific to the west. It was small-town quiet at its best, and local reaction to the proposed entertainment center was typically mixed. Naysayers claimed the usual, worried about water, sewage, traffic, noise, and an irreparable hit to their low-key way of life.[26] Sensing the inevitable, though, home builder Kenneth Edwards pretty much summed it up at a local proposal hearing: "It's not hard, after seeing all these big guns arrayed here tonight, to see how the Texans held the Alamo against the Mexicans for 13 days."[27]

Most, though, including area businesses, were highly enthusiastic, thinking it was high time *something* happened in their sleepy corner of the world. Even more giddy were officials from the three local municipalities, which soon initiated competing annexation plans (and counter-lawsuit threats) for the park property. Helpless to intervene, Six Flags wanted no part of it, but it was St. Louis County itself that pointed out the obvious—none of these places had the resources to provide adequate government services for such a large facility.[28]

And so the $22 million project commenced on what was then called Six Flags Over Mid-America. This was a turbulent time for Penn Central, Six Flags' parent company, and an ongoing struggle with financing, corporate debt, and changeover in management was the backdrop for getting this project to the finish line. The park division, however, had been going strong in Texas and Atlanta, so progress rolled forward to complete the park by mid-1971.

There were challenges, of course. As project director John Everett Smith knocked the mud off his boots climbing out of the jeep, he kept looking around wondering how they were fairing after one of the rainiest seasons in recent memory. Entering his rather plush office in what might have passed for a small barn, he sank into his chair to examine the plotting maps on the walls: one was a color-coded map of the park, indicating each section and progress updates, the other tracked construction costs.[29] Smith was no stranger to this sort of thing, being one of the very few in the country who could say they'd built a park before. After supervising construction of the Texas pavilion at the World's Fair for Angus, he moved to Georgia and got the company's second park up and running. "I don't know the (opening) day, but it'll be at 10 o'clock in the morning, and at 9:59 we'll be cleaning out the back door." Recalling similar pressure getting Six Flags open in Atlanta, "They were coming in the front door as we were hosing out the back."[30]

Early construction ground to a temporary halt when a local farmer showed up with a small problem—he still had Angus cattle and unharvested wheat on a portion of the park's property, something completely overlooked in all the complicated business dealings. But he was optimistic about the whole thing. "Those people mean to do right," and the giant earth movers cranked back up soon thereafter.[31] Smith recalled several problems that you just have to expect during such large-scale construction, especially for something as atypical as an amusement park. The railroad tracks had to be rerouted five times as they figured where to put everything. The park's sky ride, imported from Switzerland, had to be ordered early in the process if it were to be completed on time; the manufacturer needed exact land details for engineering the large support columns, and so Smith just drew a line and fit other stuff around it. Then what do you do when you finish a building and it looks taller than what you had in mind? No problem. Just lift it with a crane, dig a deeper hole, and drop it back in.[32]

Opening June 5, 1971, it is clearly evident that the park's layout was a departure from the earlier Duell designs. Randall's company had been developing plans for Astroworld in Houston, and apparently Six Flags considered this too close for comfort to their Dallas park. Duell argued that the locations were far enough away in terms of their respective demographics, but to no avail. Six Flags apparently launched their newest project without them, although they'd be back at some point to help out.[33]

When that might have occurred, though, is difficult to determine. The park seemed to have a bit of the Duell touch with thematic elements, architecture, and attractions, but these could have been adapted by local designers. The layout was radically different, with little hint of the Duell loop that had proven so effective. By contrast, all of Randall's parks, before and after Mid-America, exhibited a very similar implementation. The pathway design here could be characterized more as a hub-and-spoke design pioneered at Disneyland. Walt's thinking was that there should be a central location that served as a meeting place and jump-off point to each of the different lands. At Disneyland it's the plaza in front of the castle. At Mid-America, once you entered the front gate, the building complex in front of you became the hub. The front mall consisted of shops and such, but walking around toward the back you'd find the main entertainment theater, *The Palace,* facing toward the rear of the park. The spacious courtyard located here made a perfect meeting location. All around this central complex were access paths that branched out to each area of the park. Pathways within and connecting each of the lands were numerous and meandering, often requiring a visitor to get their bearings when seeking the next destination. But *The Palace,* majestically facing out toward the park, provided a homing beacon that didn't take too long to locate.

Interestingly, the visual effect of this hub and spoke layout when looking at a park map or aerial photograph is that of an arch... perhaps inspired by the great St. Louis arch? The railroad, instead of passing along the front of the park, takes a horseshoe shaped turn inward and around this central hub layout, crystalizing the visual of an arch. Other entrance architectural details coincide with this idea, such as the guest services buildings on either side of the ticket gates and the turnstile gateway structure. Arched, Neo-classical peristyle columns adorn these structures, strongly suggesting a link to the famous landmark.

The first flag represented was Missouri, encompassing the central hub area. The front mall, directly in front as you passed through the turnstiles, was straight out of the 1904 St. Louis World's Fair (officially dubbed the Louisiana Purchase Exposition). Architectural design recalled such regional touches as the well-known LaFayette Square terraced townhomes and historic neighborhood of Soulard. In back of this, the grand *Palace* theater, featuring the *Stars and Stripes Salute,* faced across the courtyard toward the *St. Louis* train station, which provided transportation service around the park to a stop in Illinois. Six pathways led across (or under) the railroad tracks into the rest of the park, but to the lower-left sat the entrance to *The Moon Antique Car* ride, named after the Moon Motor Car Company that was based in St. Louis from 1905–1930.

On the other side of the hub, off to the lower-right corner of the park, the modern USA section featured the ubiquitous sports car ride (creatively named *Super Sports*), a down-to-earth American fare *Good 'N Plenty* restaurant, ultra-rad glass-walled *Mod Mod Whirl* shop with posters and black light, and of course the *Chevy Show* that had made an appearance in the other parks. The Krofft brothers had been revitalizing entertainment for the Six Flags chain, and so the *Krofft Theater* sat nestled in the sports car figure eight track.

France was next as we continued counter-clockwise around the park; there are deep French roots in Missouri, the most obvious being the founding of St. Louis in 1764 by Pierre Laclède, a fur trader from France, who named the city after a revered king. The main attraction filling the upper-right corner of the park was the *River King Mine Train*. This was another Arrow tubular steel family roller coaster that had become so popular in the other parks, but the unique twist here was that it featured *two* coasters running non-identical layouts. To tie in the old mining theme, as in the previous Six Flags parks, rustic frontier structures set the scene. *Marquette's Market* honored Jacques Marquette, who sailed the Mississippi in 1673 and recorded the first use of the name "Missouri" on his map of the journey.

A smooth transition into 1800s Illinois continued the log and clapboard look with *Trapper's Tradin'* and *Honest Abe's Hats*. At the very far tip of the park sat the *Dolphin Show*, which presumably had little to do with Illinois or history, but served to draw guests into that corner of the park. *Allenton RR Station* was named after the tiny hamlet across the highway from the park that popped up during the Civil War. A most curious inclusion here was *Jesse James Hideout*, appearing as a rock formation of sorts on the map. This comes from Meramec Caverns, known as a hideout for James, but actually located in Missouri. And the notorious outlaw was a Missourian, but apparently either they wanted no part of him, even in 1971, or more likely it fit the surroundings better in the land of Lincoln.

French and Spanish interests dominated early America, but England attempted to stake their claim as well, and so there was a barely noticeable section in the park under the English flag. It was essentially the same as the frontier surroundings above it in Illinois and to the right in France, but it served the purpose in recognizing England's participation in American history.

Moving toward the left side of the park, past the now-obligatory *Pet-A-Pet* petting zoo, were two major attractions that paid tribute to the mighty Mississippi and early American literature. *Adventures on the Mississippi* was the latest incarnation of the *Jungle Cruise* knockoffs, featuring a river boat ride past animatronic wildlife, charging alligators, furious Native Americans, waterfalls, caverns, cannon fire from an enemy fort, and the arm of a poor soul drowning in a whirlpool of raging waters. Across the pathway was the park's dark ride, *Injun Joe's Cave*. Like *Tales of the Okefenokee* in Georgia, this was a boat flume ride that cruised the bayou and introduced guests to awkwardly crude figures such as Tom Sawyer and Becky.

Spain was last, located in the lower-left corner of the park. Along with typical mission-style architectural touches to the shops, restrooms, and *Casa Meramec Seafood* restaurant, the main attraction was a log flume ride from Arrow. *Hoo Hoo Log Flume* got its unusual name from the lumber industry, where "hoo hoo" became a popular term for lumberman. No connection to Spain can be found in the world of logging, however; perhaps the intention was to continue honoring trades that used rivers for transportation. Life being ever practical, it could also simply have been a matter of finding enough acreage left in the park for it to fit.

A celebration of history and life in the middle America region of the country, the park made its distinctive mark the same as the parks in Texas and Georgia had. However, Six Flags Over Mid-America would be the last park the company designed and built from the ground up. From then on the company would buy existing parks and rebrand them with the Six Flags name, and so fundamental design similarities among them end after 1971. As we shall see, however, although you cannot rebuild a park's fundamental layout and infrastructure, retheming and rebranding by the company would eventually remove many distinctions from these early parks, bringing a franchise-type commonality to them all. But for the time being, residents in the greater St. Louis area had their own taste of Disneyland magic.[34]

There's a clear progression in design development from Texas to Mid-America, each successive park becoming more refined in its layout and functionality. They learned as they went, figuring how to provide necessary components such as attractions, shows, food, shops, and restrooms in ways that maximized guests' time and enjoyment. The entrance plaza and hub at Mid-America was far more extensive with support services, shops, and so on than at Texas. The

Duell loop was clearly more defined in Georgia, though Mid-America was a completely different animal, presumably due to the change in designers along the way. Large attractions such as the mine train and river ride were pushed farther back in Georgia than in Texas, reclaiming more precious central real estate for other uses.

They planned for future expansion, anticipating the parks' growth over time, and so chunks of land were reserved in the far edges and corners in which to build larger attractions and additional themed lands.[35] There was also much compromise along the way, usually due to budget constraints. Comparisons between concept art and final build are always interesting to study to see what got chopped. At the Georgia park, for example, the queue for *Tales of the Okefenokee* looks to have included an Uncle Remus cabin and plantation in front of the show building. England was quite impressive with an array of Tudor structures that never materialized. Disney fans have drooled over such never-realized plans for decades.

Although theming choices might not have been their first priority, careful research for regional, historical stories and influences is evident. Many attraction names reference local towns, historical figures, trades, rivers, companies, and so on. Architecture was often fairly generic, such as the typical rustic wooden shacks of the old west and mission style from Spanish colonists, but then there are the entrance columns at Georgia, modeled after an actual Southern estate, or the more subtle details at Mid-America that perhaps draw from the famous gateway. Graphic design of the 1960s prevailed all too often, with rather bland signage for attractions that are reminiscent of the generic "Family Restaurant." The local references, however, along with creative design touches brought a sense of regional identity to the park. This made it personal and not merely something from a universally famous movie or fairy tale.

But it wasn't just the logistics of putting together a park that functioned well and looked nice. Learning from the earlier mistakes of Magic Mountain, Pleasure Island, and Freedomland, Duell's team, working with park management, figured how to scale a Disneyland concept down to a local level. For Disneyland, Walt had the advantage of television, where he could advertise and tease his park directly into the homes of millions of viewers each week. Disneyland was a national attraction; Six Flags wasn't intended to compete with that. Instead of attempting to build completely immersive environments and recreating film stories for guests to "step into," the designers settled for a sense of place and time that was enough to make a guest know they were somewhere special and fun. Being former film art directors, and not merely run of the mill architects, they knew a thing or two about how to creatively dress a set within budget. And so for about $10 million dollars they got the ball rolling in the right direction.

It's difficult for us to relate at this point in time, but water splashes from imaginary cannon balls, boats on rails, and simplistic animated figures were exciting and new for the time, there being few people who had experienced Disneyland. So early thematic elements were relatively crude, low budget, and yet utterly thrilling for park guests. The core concepts that made Disneyland successful—social interaction, fun, education, history, nostalgia, and leaving the real world for just a bit—were all there. After the early failed attempts to copy Disneyland's magic around the country, Angus Wynne's vision and Randall Duell's growing understanding of park design had found the right recipe for making it work for the regional market. And in so doing, ushered in the golden era of the modern American, *regional* theme park.

END OF THE RIDE FOR ANGUS

Not long after opening the Arlington park, Angus Wynne tried exporting the same brand of Texas-sized magic to the 1964 New York World's Fair. By personal request of the governor, John Connally, and with the promise to reimburse him once the state legislature reconvened the following year, Wynne spent $9 million dollars building attractions and running the operation. The massive Texas pavilion complex was positioned in an area away from the main fair and therefore suffered from low attendance. Walt Disney had tried to convince

Robert Moses, organizer of the fair, that this arrangement wouldn't work and to build a monorail to entice people to make the effort. It was a money pit from the very beginning and never improved. When it was all over Wynne got the next bit of bad news: Texas refused to make good on the governor's promise to pay up. He was wiped out, losing the Great Southwest Corporation and the Six Flags parks as a result of bankruptcy proceedings. At least he still had a management role in the company, for now, although tumultuous times were brewing for the new owner.[36]

SEVEN SEAS

While all of this was going on Tommy Vandergriff hadn't let off the gas, still looking for ways to boost the local economy. While nailing down a major league baseball franchise, it occurred to him that since Six Flags was doing so well, why not a second park? His first thought was a Western-themed park, so he contacted a few famous movie stars to gauge interest. Finding none, he reached out to Walter Knott in California about bringing his brand of boysenberry and cowboy goodness to Texas. Mr. Knott begged off, claiming he was too old at that point. But he suggested Vandergriff take a look at George Millay's SeaWorld, which the mayor did. That was the ticket, and after George ignored his phone calls, he decided that Texas could certainly do a sea life park on their own.

He found a willing partner much closer to home; Angus Wynne was enthusiastic about the idea and suggested it be built on land adjacent to Six Flags. They could even have a riverboat ride connecting the two properties with a two-park single ticket admission, which would have been revolutionary for the time. Although none of these ideas transpired, the project accelerated forward. Six Flags entered into an agreement to design, build, and operate Seven Seas while the city of Arlington financed the whole thing. The concept was bulletproof, and so they commenced designing a park with beautiful landscaping, various animal shows, an Arctic-themed dark ride, and lots of waterfalls, bridges, and so on. Construction started in late 1970, animals were purchased...and then Six Flags' parent company, Penn Central, imploded. One of the casualties was Angus, who was sent packing for good. The company pulled out of the deal, and so the city was left with an incomplete park, a bunch of creatures that required expensive care and upkeep, and no current income until they could get things opened. They trudged ahead on their own, convinced by the earlier financial predictions that it would be a bonanza for them.

It would not be. Attendance declined year-over-year and the park lost money each season. For the third season, 1974, they were looking for help. Six Flags signed on to operate the park that year, but that didn't go so well. Then George Millay finally showed up, interested in doing something in the area. He struck a deal, a pretty good one, and really made a go of it for 1975. But it was clear that nothing was going to turn it around at that point. His attention turned to obtaining the property for a new idea he was chewing on—a gated water-activity park called Wet 'n Wild. The city wouldn't play ball, so he found a site elsewhere; it worked out quite well for him. Seven Seas floundered and drowned completely, a financial boondoggle on the city's books.[37]

So what happened? Management was inexperienced in running a park. Exotic animals are extremely expensive, and off-season costs were $250,000 with no offsetting income. The financial outlook was overly optimistic and disregarded operational issues unique to the project that nobody considered (such as having no local source of salt water). There are small bits of the place still there, with the Arlington Sheraton Hotel as the current occupant. Although most people have never heard of the park, it's always sad to see the rusting bones of yet another special place that's no longer making memories.

Lost Parents
REST ROOMS
Rub-A-Dub
The Barnyard
Carrosel
CHILDREN'S WORLD
Boot Slide
Crystal Palace
Fred's General Store
Clown Show
Maypole
Post Office
Blacksmith Shop
WESTERN
REST ROOMS
The Mill Pond
Arcade
Mini Restaurant
PLAZA DE FIESTA
Wagonwheel
Skyrama
Emporium
Drug Store
Circus Shop
Arcade
Print Shop
Magic Shop
Toy Shop
AMERICANA SQUARE
Information
Sandwich Shoppe

Chapter Five

ENTREPRENEURS, VISIONARIES, & MAVERICKS

The really big ideas almost always come from a larger-than-life individual who has the vision, connections, resources, or at least the sheer guts to go out on a limb and do something everybody believes is foolish. Walt had a dream he believed in and a brother who stuck with him along the way. Angus Wynne had a vision and resources from his development company. Houston in the 1960s had such a fellow, someone who lived such a colorful, P.T. Barnumesque life that his influence would transform an industry and add to the American cultural lexicon.

ASTROWORLD

A graduate of law school at the age of 19, elected member of the Texas legislature at 22, (the) Harris County judge at 24, owner of radio and television stations, and then, why not, go on to become mayor of Houston at 40. He suffered no fools under his watch, whether they deserved it or not, and his mayoral tenure was littered with such juicy confrontations as having four of his city council members arrested (they were planning to boycott a meeting and he simply wanted them there), blithely ignoring his own impeachment from office, and taking his arguments directly to the people through his own television programming. In a bid to clean the slate, he successfully got a charter amendment passed that cancelled the remainder of his and the council's terms, forcing a new election. Unfortunately for him, it backfired with the good folks fed up with all the shenanigans and voting him out with everyone else.[1]

No matter, Judge Roy Hofheinz pushed forward into the most influential stage of his life, convincing the county to finance a fully-enclosed athletic arena, something unheard of in its day. Apparently hearing that the Roman Colosseum had a cover of some sort, and convinced by Buckminster Fuller (of geodesic dome fame…think Epcot) that it was feasible, he brought the Astrodome to life in 1965—saving generations of Houston sports fans the misery of melting in a mosquito-infested ball park. His self-proclaimed "Eighth Wonder of the World" was only the first step in his planned Astrodomain, which at first included the arena, the Astroworld Hotel, and Astrohall convention center. Next up was to be a world class theme park across the highway from the arena, taking a cue from Disney who had developed the concept of a complete destination resort in Anaheim. He wanted people to come stay for a week without needing to leave. His family certainly had little reason to get out much, having moved into their own lavish, garishly decorated thematic suite on the top floor of the hotel.[2]

Financial challenges in the early 1970s prevented full development of his plans, and so additional motels, theaters, museum, race track, an inland "Sea-Arama," and a monorail between everything never materialized.[3] Nonetheless, the Astrodome significantly impacted modern culture through its concept of a large-scale indoor recreation facility, the development of Astroturf (grass couldn't grow inside the dome), and of course, the name itself, which is as fundamental to American lingo as Chevy, the Alamo, and the Yankees…er…Astros.

In September 1967 plans for the theme park were announced to the public. Ever the showman, Hofheinz confidently declared it would become "the world's greatest tourist attraction, bringing untold millions of dollars into the Houston area economy."[4] Overseeing the park's design was R. Duell & Associates,[5] who had just completed Six Flags Over Georgia, and Harper Goff, the former Disney artist and Imagineer who had been responsible for early Disneyland concept renderings and the *Jungle Cruise* attraction. Arrow would furnish many of the park's ride systems, as they had become the go-to for park developers. Additional operational expertise came from Stan McIlvaine, from Great Southwest and Six Flags, as well as officials at Disneyland who were consulted in the hopes of reducing potential problems during construction.[6]

The 56 acres allocated for the park were located directly across Interstate Loop 610 from the Astrodome and the parking lot, necessitating a bridge for park guests to get to the entrance. The plan for the monorail beam had been to serve as transportation between the arena, hotels, parking lots, and the park; ultimately trams and foot power would have to suffice. Crossing the bridge, guests would also pass over the *610 Limited* steam train as it circled the park, making stops at two stations in Oriental Corner and Western Junction.

The entrance plaza led through the turnstiles and into Americana Square, a turn-of-the-century, smaller version of Disneyland's Main Street. Various shops lined the way with *The Emporium* dominating straight ahead. Off to either side were pathways to the rest of the park, so the next themed area in the lower-right corner of the property was Mod Ville, styled to the then-current hippie 60s. Along with an outdoor music amphitheater, the standard sports car ride, *Spin Out*, filled the lower corner while the *Astrowheel*, a giant double ferris wheel from Intamin, dominated the skyline.

Continuing along the pathway up the right side of the park would find us in the neighboring Alpine Valley and European Village sections. Appropriately enough was the *Astroway* sky ride station that was certainly at home in the Alpine surroundings, providing an aerial view of the park while gliding over to the other side in Oriental

Corner. Trying a bit harder to fit into Europe was a standard-fare, very American-sounding *Chicken Restaurant.* Along with a classic antique auto ride, *Le Taxi,* the major scenic backdrop towering over everything in this far-right corner of the park was *Der Hofheinzberg* mountain, clearly a Matterhorn-wanna-be featuring a custom-designed Arrow ride system. Presented in Arrow's sales catalogs as an Aero Glide, this one-of-a-kind tracked system with single, sleigh-themed cars was part scenic dark ride, part thrill ride. *Alpine Sleighs* wound through a forest, past a waterfall, into the mountain, and even past an abominable snowman. Snow machines were installed in one area of the ride, but that didn't work out so well. But the air conditioned mountain certainly cooled guests off from the Houston summer heat.

Western Junction was next at the very top of the park. One of the two train stations was here, *Western Junction Depot,* along with *Fred's General Store, Shooting Gallery,* and *Mini Restaurant* (several of these around the park), all themed with rustic, pioneer facades. You could pan for gold inside the *Hard Luck Mine* or take in a live show at the *Crystal Palace.* The pathway between European Village and Western Junction provided access to the towering *Astroneedle,* a two-layered rotating cabin that would be renamed to *Skyrama* the following season. Based along the edge of the central lagoon, it provided a beautiful panorama of the entire park and Astrodomain complex across the highway.

Next up was Children's World, with the *Rub-A-Dub* boat ride through brightly colored, oversized storybook pages, a big Texas boot with a slide inside, small carousel, and, of course, a petting zoo—*The Barnyard.* After the *Clown Show* concluded, the path led you through a giant carved pumpkin and straight down the left side of the park into Plaza De Fiesta. Of course you'd expect a Mexican restaurant, but a candle shop? The *Lost World Adventure* boat ride, yet another *Jungle Cruise* progeny, sailed down the Rio Misterio while viewing various ancient sites...in air conditioned comfort. Astroworld went to great lengths to keep their patrons from suffering in the Texas heat and was famous for providing air conditioning *everywhere,* even outside areas such as attraction queues, the boat ride, and notably at the outside tables of an ice cream stand, where cool air blew out of small vents in the umbrella posts.

Oriental Corner was the last themed area, located in the lower-left corner of the park. The second train station was here along with another *Astroway* station; year two would bring the Arrow flume *Bamboo Shute* and a mini coaster. Everything was designed with typical oriental architecture. Rounding the bend and heading back up toward the center of the park was the transition back to Americana Square.[7]

Disneyland influence continued with the single entrance, clearly defined layout and pathways, beautiful landscaping, thematic sections, and similar attractions such as the river boat ride, miniature Matterhorn with Alpine themed area, and of course the railroad encircling it all. The resort concept of a connected hotel was proven at Disneyland and would return time and again with other parks. The overall design and layout of Astroworld was more tightly compacted, controlled, and visually efficient than that of the first two Six Flags parks. The Duell loop was clearly evident, even more so than at Georgia, largely due to the symmetrical, nearly square shape of the park.

Water was a major feature, presumably not too difficult to achieve as the entire plot of land was previously subject to flooding and required much filling before construction began.[8] A lagoon with several small islands graced the center of the park, a design feature that would be slowly abandoned over time by Duell's team due to its inefficiencies with utilities maintenance and relatively poor use of prime real estate.[9] Over time, the river boat ride channel in the upper-left corner would be filled in and used for a coaster. This trend as parks develop and grow is not unusual, as the land becomes more valuable and necessary for attraction development.

Unlike the Six Flags parks, which were generally themed for each park's region of the country, the lands and attractions at Astroworld did not seem particularly tuned to Texas. The most obvious connection, of course, was the use of "Astro" for nearly everything at the complex, named after the newly established space program in Houston. But very little at the park had any thematic or physical resemblance to space exploration. Proximity to Mexico made sense for the Plaza de Fiesta area, though many parks would include such a theme no matter where they were located. Children's World was presumably because Judge Roy simply wanted an area for kids. The concept of a Matterhorn-type mountain ride automatically demanded a Swiss Alpine setting, even though it's a direct lift from Disneyland. Mod Ville came with the times. Overall, understanding Hofheinz's personality makes it certain that all design aspects conformed to his interests and wishes; this was certainly not a case where an owner hires a designer and then waits for the final result to arrive in the mail. Curiously enough, other than *Der Hofheinzberg* mountain, there wasn't apparently anything else named directly for the Judge or his family. One would expect him, of all people, to insist on more personal tributes of some sort. Then again, the entire park and complex was his stamp on humanity.

In the end none of the theming issues mattered a bit; opening weekend saw 50,000 guests and it never really let up. Houston loved this park. Six Flags would eventually take over the place, branding and changing as they always have. But this was the locals' home park, full of nostalgia, and then in 2005 came the announcement that ripped the community asunder—the company was in financial trouble, needed to reduce debt, and management believed the land was worth more as a real estate deal. So they bulldozed the park. Six Flags has done pretty well since, but that doesn't help loyal Houstonians who had a piece of their heart ripped out.[10]

Duell's artists, mostly coming from the film industry, were highly skilled and did beautiful work, but Disney-quality art and design was also represented at Astroworld with Harper Goff's contributions. Concept art and advertising posters clearly evidence his style and are beautiful works in and of themselves. It's reasonable to assume Goff's early work on Disneyland's Main Street had influence on the similar

Americana Square section. Most interesting, however, is Harper's work done personally for Hofheinz. The top floor of the Astroworld Hotel featured the Celestial Suites, thirteen highly thematic rooms such as the P.T. Barnum suite, complete with a three-ring tent-ceilinged room and a bed made out of an authentic Ringling Brothers band calliope (Hofheinz was part owner of the circus at the time). When available for rent, it was the most expensive hotel suite in the world, running between $2500–$5500 per night. But most of the time this was the family's home, and so everything was done to Judge Roy's taste. Goff also designed a personal railcar for the Judge that was intended to run on the park's railroad. True to Hofheinz's larger-than-life personality, everything had to be the best there was; it was an extraordinary, exquisitely designed affair intended to woo sales clients at the Astrodomain complex (and also surely for personal enjoyment). "When he inspected samples of things for trains, the judge would look at me real hard and say, 'It is the best of the lot, isn't it? I want the best,'" Goff said.[11]

However, not long after opening Astroworld, Hofheinz's empire started falling apart. Way over-extended in debt and with rising interest rates, and having been confined to a wheelchair after a stroke, he finally sold off his interests in the Astrodomain complex in 1975.[12] Part of this included figuring out what to do with his cherished play-toy, the *Astrodoma*. His people called a commercial developer searching for somewhere to store it, finally selecting a South Houston warehouse in 1976. Well, actually the warehouse didn't exist yet. The thing wouldn't fit through anybody's doorway, so they set it up on a lot and built the building around it. There it sat, behind a wall, for the next 42 years, along with the locomotive that pulled it around the park. In 2018, then-current owner Robert Harper finally decided to put it up for sale.[13]

OPRYLAND USA

Irving Waugh was president of WSM Inc., a Nashville radio station best known for the *Grand Ole Opry*. The iconic country music radio show had called Ryman Auditorium its home since 1943. But the Ryman, built in 1892, had been through the ringer and needed either a complete renovation or a match. And that was exactly what they were terrified about, what with the condition of the building and the fact that for years the old dirt floor had been saturated with oil to keep the dust down. "For years we used firemen for ushers and ticket takers so they'd be ready when we needed them. No one was ever more than 25 feet away from a fire extinguisher."[14]

What to do? As with Disneyland, the area immediately surrounding the building had fallen prey to the worst of American enterprise. This was not where you'd feel comfortable taking your grandmother or kids to see their favorite country music stars. Maybe we should build a new Opry elsewhere; it's not like the show hasn't changed venues before. A new building, though, would set us back at least five million dollars, so how do we pay for it?

In 1968 Elmer Alley, the program director at WSM, wrote out a memo to his boss sketching out the concept of a new Opry auditorium, complete with a state-of-the-art television studio and recording facilities. Adjacent to this magnificent facility would be an amusement area "situated in a setting which typifies the beauty of the Tennessee countryside, preferably a relatively flat area containing a stream and backed by the river bluffs or hills." The park would be "keyed to the broad theme of 'Music of America.'"[15]

Waugh was enthusiastic. Tossing ideas back and forth, they determined that this park would focus on authentic, live entertainment. "Other parks had cute robot bears popping up out of the woods. We wanted real performers singing and dancing their hearts out on a stage. That had always been the image of Nashville."[16]

The idea of a complete destination resort with a hotel, sports venue, and theme park that drove repeat business seemed brilliant and could be just the ticket to solve their problem. With the blessing of WSM's parent company, National Life and Accident Insurance Company, Irving flew down to see Roy Hofheinz at the Astrodomain to get an idea of how to go about their wild dream. The Judge's recommendation was to get a feasibility study, even though "you'll wind up throwing it away."[17]

Waugh did just that. The resulting Economics Research Associates report wasn't overly enthusiastic, recommending a 5,000 seat theater for the Opry, a mere $2.2 million in rides and amusements, a complex of exhibit centers and specialty shops, and a 150-room motor lodge. Attendance was predicted primarily for the Opry at 872,000 by 1976, with only around 71,000 for "the center."[18] Irving ignored it and pressed on, convinced that a full-fledged theme park, a new Opry auditorium, and a motel couldn't fail. The area was a hot tourist destination. The show itself had been extremely successful in attracting visitors; a theme park would be an additional draw, giving reason to visit multiple days and therefore requiring overnight stays in an on-site motel. Moreover, the park could help generate needed funds to build a new home for the Opry.[19]

He threw the dice and convinced the NLT board to push ahead, acquiring 369 acres along the Cumberland River just outside Nashville. 110 acres were set aside for the park, the remainder earmarked for the new Opry, hotel, parking, and a planned shopping district. Groundbreaking was on June 30, 1970 and, $28 million later, Opryland opened May 27, 1972.[20] Two years later the new auditorium was complete, and in 1977 the Opryland Hotel was in business. The resort was off and running, wildly successful and hosting two and a half million visitors a year over time.[21]

Few cities in the country could have been more tailor-made for theming a park. Nashville was known almost exclusively for country music, but the idea of expanding this and celebrating American music of all types was a no-brainer. It must have been pure joy for Randall Duell[22] and his team to craft a park with such rich design elements to draw from. The land was largely undeveloped and quite beautiful, a portion of it heavily wooded, so the approach was to preserve this as much as possible. "Bulldozing natural beauty is criminal" was one of Randall's oft-repeated principles.[23] Over four thousand trees were transplanted as needed,[24] and landscaping was carefully designed to fit into the natural surroundings. A wildlife area for mountain lions, bears, and other animals was established with carefully concealed fencing built into the landscape. True to Irving and Elmer's early thoughts, park developers proudly proclaimed that everything in this park was live—real musicians, artisans, and animals, but no mechanical animation like that found in the other parks.[25]

Opryland's shape was somewhat rectangular, with the entry plaza located at one end, the river running directly alongside the long left boundary, and the right edge paralleling the then-new Briley Parkway where the upcoming Opry house and hotel would be built. The park's grand sign as you took the exit into the parking lot was beautiful, built from stone with—what else—a floral mandolin. Once through the ticket booths you'd find yourself in Opry Plaza, intended to serve not only the park but the upcoming Opry hall complex. Architecture was Southern antebellum, welcoming visitors to the South and immediately setting the scene for the park. There was plenty to do here, including the twenty-minute *Great Moments from the Opry Show* at the information center, the *Roy Acuff Music Hall* museum, *Dee Jay USA Radio Show*, and various food and merchandise to hold you over for awhile. When you were ready, just head over one of the three short bridges spanning the Plaza River Walk stream and tackle the standard Duell loop.

Most likely the inclination would be to head left, with the Hill Country area in sight, but instead take a right and walk under the railroad overpass into Music of Today. As was the case with Astroworld and Six Flags Over Mid-America, the idea of a "mod" section was to recognize the changing music scene of the 60s and 70s. Radical architecture and paint colors made it clear this was a more modern time far removed from dulcimers and Dixieland bands. Shows were staged on the rooftops, presumably as a nod to the Beatle's final public concert atop their Apple Records building. One of the most interesting items at the park was a 1920 Belgian calliope that played arrangements of various music styles. The mod look would soon be out of vogue, and so the area would later be renamed Do Wah Ditty City and take on a 50s overlay.

Curiously, the sole coaster at park's opening was located in the Music of Today area, though it probably would have best fit in the American West a bit farther around the bend. *Timber Topper* was another mine train type ride from Arrow Development.

Along the path toward American West was one of the sky ride stations along with *Animal Opry*, showcasing animals performing various tricks and instruments. Who could pass up watching a dancing goat, a pig on the piano, and Burt Bachaquack the duck? Moving along, the *El Paso* train station provided transportation to the Hill Country, but you could take a right under the trestle and enjoy some peaceful moments at Eagle Lake. This was a beautiful three acre water feature located at what was then the far end of the park. Guests could ride *Ryman's Ferry*, small battery-powered rafts that cruised the lake, though there wasn't really anything else to see other than the beautiful wooded surroundings. Later this relaxing, rather tame experience would be replaced with *The Old Mill Scream*, a fairly elaborately themed Intamin "spillwater" type Shoot the Chute boat ride. Along with a deer petting farm, the short-lived *American Horse Pageant* was close by; the horses would be sent out to pasture for good for the second season.

El Paso, TX was the setting for the American West area, a theme that nearly every park in the country seemed to have at the time. Though by now losing ground to the space race, westerns were at the heart of American culture in the 50s and 60s. It was easy to build and theme such structures, and they all seemed to feature a general store and live gunfights in the street. But appropriately enough, at Opryland shootouts were replaced with sing-offs. Not quite fitting in were the *Tin Lizzies*, the ubiquitous Arrow antique car ride. These were great fun, but a fair stretch to place them in 1880s El Paso. (*Tin Lizzie* was the nickname for Henry Ford's Model-T, first introduced in 1908...close enough?)

Since the property edged the Cumberland River, some sort of tie-in seemed appropriate, and so the next section was known as Riverside. A grand performance theater, the *American Music Hall,* was home to an elaborate musical review that ran, off and on, throughout the history of the park. Facing the music hall was one of the park's signature attractions and photo spots. The carousel was originally built in Germany in the early 1900s and was actually a circular switchback type of ride. Carriages would slowly go around over a series of small hills, providing an undulating, wave-like motion for the riders.[26] It was a beautiful work of art and was uniquely placed out over a body of water, providing a centerpiece for park publicity and zillions of guest photos.

Riverside led directly into New Orleans, complete with intricate iron railing balconies straight from the French Quarter. Along with the usual assortment of shops and food, jazz filled the air every which way you turned. The other end of the sky ride was here, and then the pathway took you back into the Hill Country—home of what most people thought of Nashville with its bluegrass and traditional Appalachian folk music. Visitors to Dollywood have experienced what this area had to offer with local craftspeople working at their trade, real home cooking, and plenty of down home country music. An Arrow flume ride, the *Flume Zoom,* opened with the park along with the *Grinder's Switch* train station. As was the practice with Duell's designers, local references made for more personal theming, and *Grinder's Switch* was named after Minnie Pearl's fictional hometown on the Grand Ole Opry, which in turn came from an actual railroad switch nearby.

What set Opryland apart from other regionals was its emphasis on entertainment. Oh sure, all parks had shows, big and small. But this park took it to another level, essentially becoming one of Nashville's premiere training grounds for generations of future professional entertainers.[27]

A majority of regional parks around the country would endure a series of corporate ownership changes over the years, some for the better, some not. Opryland's parent company would be purchased by Gaylord Broadcasting in 1983,[28] and the entire Opryland USA complex would go public in 1991 as the Gaylord Entertainment Company.[29] Media expansion in television continued, along with the 1992 opening of their second park, Fiesta Texas in San Antonio.[30] By 1997, new management at the helm made a deal with the Mills Corporation, known for innovative shopping centers around the country. The thinking was that the seasonally-open park was not the best use of the property surrounding the successful hotel, entertainment complex, and media empire they had built. "Shoppertainment" was the new thing for a new generation, and a mega-mall promised to attract up to 17 million wallets a year, a far cry from the park's peak of 2.5 million in the 80s. Touting the new direction for the property, management pointed to declining attendance, which had fallen below two million, along with declining profitability. A mall, it was promised, was what Nashville needed to ensure the future of tourism.[31] As late as September the company was still publicly claiming that the park in some form, perhaps partially closed and transformed, would remain.[32] But at the end of the 1997 season Opryland's gates were locked for the last time.[33] Major rides were sold and shipped to Premier Parks, and most everything else was bulldozed and paved over, including most of those beautiful trees so carefully preserved over twenty-five years earlier.[34]

It appears that original intentions were to leave the upper corner of the park intact for future reimagining. This is probably why the remains of the Grizzly River Rapids could be explored as late as 2011, complete with concrete caves, hills, and the water trough. It was a beautiful area, fully wooded, and even featured a walking bridge over the area for guests of the hotel to explore. However, as of this writing only the walkway and a small corner of natural brush and trees are left with the remaining area completely cleared for hotel and event space expansion. The rest of the park site is all mall and parking lot, with a portion of the original Opry Plaza intact in front of the Opry hall. Gone forever are the beautiful trees and lakes, nostalgic shows, rides first shared with girlfriends or children, and a piece of Americana. Locals wonder why anybody thought Nashville needed yet another mall.[35] E.W. "Bud" Wendell, Gaylord's previous CEO before all the carnage began, was "surprised and mystified" at everything the new guy, Terry London, was doing to the company—and not just the park. Gaylord would become a shadow of itself in short order, effectively removing itself from the entertainment business.[36] Even Gaylord's own spokesman Greg Rossiter admitted in 2004 that "the closing of the park negatively affected the number of tourists that visited Nashville in the summer...The current management team has found no compelling reasons why the decision to close the park was taken in the first place."[37] And the knife is twisted deeper.

To be fair, there were critics who believed the park had not kept up with the times, had not managed to maintain its status as a first-class destination. There's surely some truth to this—the park didn't have that many rides and probably focused too much on country music in an increasingly eclectic tourism market.[38] Some pointed out what seemed obvious, that if the park was underperforming in attendance and revenue, why not, you know, make it better? That's how all the other places kept growing over the years. Who knows by now; the economics and trends seemed to point in a new direction at the time, and perhaps they were right.

Hope springs eternal and continuously teases us—in 2008 Gaylord and Herschend, the family-owned company that operates such properties as Dollywood and Silver Dollar City, were finalizing plans for a new Opryland park before the 2008 recession stopped them cold.[39] A grand water park was announced in 2012 before another change in corporate ownership killed the deal.[40] Gaylord finally opened *Soundwaves,* an indoor/outdoor water play area; it's nice, but comes nowhere near replacing what was lost. Opry Mills mall opened May 11, 2000, and actually did quite well financially over the years, gradually changing their tenant mix to feature more entertainment, such as Madame Tussauds wax museum.[41] It's not the same, though. Opryland was a gorgeous park, the likes of which will most likely never be rebuilt. As we have seen, once we lose parks like Opryland and Astroworld there is little chance of seeing new ones to replace them of the same scale and magnificence. And though many local families enjoy their vacations to Walt Disney World, Universal, and other destinations, they've lost something personal, something inseparably woven into their lives.

CAROWINDS

Everybody leaned forward a bit heading southbound on Interstate 77, ready to be the first to squeal with delight at the first sight of the *Skytower*. After the "Welcome to South Carolina" roadside greeting, you'd take the exit and turn toward the right; a short ways past the park sign the roadway was divided by the monorail beam, and what a lucky day it was to meet up with a monorail train as it glided silently overhead, eventually curving away and over the entry pond on its way back into the park.

The parking lot trams dropped you off in front of beautifully landscaped gardens, just a short walk from the columned, brick mansion representing the grandeur and formality of Southern antiquity. The message was clear—Welcome to the South: Come on in and make yourself at home. You'd purchase your ticket and walk through the ground floor level into Court of Carolinas. Looking around to get one's bearings, the usual guest services, restrooms, and shops were on either side, but then you'd look down and notice each paver was inscribed with the name of a county from either North or South Carolina. A bold golden line ran directly through the center of the plaza, North to the right, South to the left, leading you onward over the bridge towards unknown adventures. Here things generally got clogged in the middle with folks having their picture taken standing astride both states at the same time. Hearing a train whistle off to the right, take in the sight of the *Carowinds & Carolina Railroad* coming around the bend to stop at the station directly below. All of this was magic none of us had ever seen, and the newness of it all merely served to heighten our sense of fascination and awe, wondering what more lay just ahead.

Earl Patterson Hall settled deep into the luxurious black swivel chair as a filterless Lucky Strike burned in the ashtray, a Bloody Mary in one hand, the other unconsciously fiddling with the clip on his ubiquitous white necktie. His guest had to take a second look at the clip, wondering what on earth "YCDBSOYA" meant. But business came first, and to be honest the private railroad car—bearing the name *Carolina and Nowhere Railroad*—probably witnessed as much dealmaking as his regular office. Now permanently parked next to his latest dream project, the railcar was appropriately opulent with fiery red carpet, red velvet wallpaper, and a marble desktop with phones, lighting controls, and buttons to summon various employees. When not conducting business, he was often hosting social gatherings at the Carowinds lodge, a private affair a short walk from the park's administrative offices, decked out with zebra skin decorated walls, mounted animal trophies, and an inviting fireplace.[42]

The self-made multi-millionaire was known for 100-hour work weeks and major industrial development, including the nearby Westinghouse nuclear plant.[43] But his personal pet project, the one that would never make him any money, and the one he would lose within two years,[44] was a family entertainment center inspired by a trip to Disneyland some years before.[45] The thought of bringing a Disney-type experience to the region, scaled down a bit and adapted to the Carolinas, took several years to percolate, but when he made the public announcement on October 10, 1969 it sent shockwaves throughout the local community. A what? Here? And it wasn't just the park. The plan called for a staggering $250 million in total investment. "Carolina Center Industrial Park," consisting of the Hotel Carowinds resort and convention center, would be built next to the park and accessed via monorail. Commercial offices would support such tenants as General Motors. Phase II was to be an 1866-acre residential community along Lake Wylie.[46]

The next bombshell—the park was to be built straddling the state line, meaning everything just got way more complicated with planning, permitting, designing, building, and operating a complex theme park in two different states. But the concept was too good to pass up —a regional park that celebrated the rich heritage of both Carolinas, bringing them together in an experience designed specifically for Carolinians. As with his business deals, Hall didn't settle for second fiddle, hiring the A-team with Randall Duell and Associates. Only the best for his park, and so they set to work, breaking ground May 1, 1970 and targeting a 1972 opening. Weather issues pushed this back a year, but the gates swung open March 31, 1973 to a dismally small crowd trying to brave the rain.[47] By the end of the first year, however, attendance had reached 1,350,000 visitors.[48] His dream finally realized, there was no way to foresee the impending forces that would ultimately leave him with no choice but to find an operator with deeper pockets who could keep it alive.

Across the bridge, Plantation Square was the diminutive "main street" for the park with various treats and shops such as *Belk's Emporium*. Right smack dab in the middle of the road was *The Meeting House*, for information and customer service, and behind this was an honest-to-goodness, functional *Post Office*. A short line trolley wound its way through the Square, disappearing around the bend beyond the *Skytower*. This 262 foot tall Intamin Gyro-style rotating cabin was one of several major icons of the park.

Carowinds was roughly squarish in shape, laid out in the now-common, circular Duell loop. Moving off to the right we'd enter Contemporary Carolina. Unlike the "mod" areas of other Duell parks, this area featured then-current styling and attractions such as the *Carolina Speedway* Arrow sports cars, 1000-seat *Magic Theater, Sound Circus* outdoor show stage, and the *Monorail*. Since the hotel resort never made it off the drawing boards, there wasn't much to look at for a good part of the journey. But just riding the sleek, modern "highway in the sky" was good enough.

No park could do without some sort of western-themed land, and so next was Frontier Outpost. A tribute to the western North Carolina mountain frontier and the days of Daniel Boone, wood clapboard facades covered *Troubadour's Roost,* a circular cluster of structures featuring the *Blacksmith Shop* and *Jail,* along with an open-air theater hosting a popular puppet show. *Black Bear Train Station* provided a round-the-park journey with stops at Plantation Square and Country Crossroads. The *Skyway* soared out of the second story station over the walkway, touching down on the other side in Queen's Colony. Also standard fare by this time was an Arrow mine train family roller coaster, *Goldrusher,* featuring a well-themed station and custom layout. The sudden dip into the final tunnel was always a thrill.

Continuing counterclockwise along the Duell loop we found ourselves approaching Pirate Island in the upper-right quadrant of the park, featuring plenty of water, various flat rides, and *Blackbeard's Hold* pirate ship. Over the bridge and, aside from the *War Canoes* on the left that paddled alongside the *Carolina* riverboat and underneath *Goldrusher,* things began to gradually transition to a more rural setting with country architecture and the Arrow *Hillbilly Jalopies* car ride. Country Crossroads was the next land, featuring the *Harmony Hall* music theater, *Country Kitchen, General Store, Mule Go Round, Hay Wagons, Barnyard* petting zoo, and even a one-room schoolhouse complete with schoolmarm to intimidate the youngsters. Above all of this at the very top of the park was the pint-sized *Short Line RR,* which wound around the old *McClelland House,* the previous landowner's residence. E. Pat Hall's original agreement with the McClellands included the petting zoo, to represent the long history of farming on the property, and the *Chapel,* built in the far back corner of the park to showcase Gospel music performances and commemorate the family's Presbyterian roots.

Queens Colony reminded everyone that North and South Carolina were two of the original British colonies that got things started over here. You could take in a multimedia show in the *Heritage Theater,* projecting three centuries of Carolina history onto a 140-degree screen, grab a bite at the *Village Tavern Hamburgers,* then proceed to lose it whirling around in the *Oaken Bucket*. Look up at the *Skyway* buckets coming in for a landing from Frontier Outpost while you head down to the *Powder Keg Flume*, an Arrow flume ride with a unique coaster-like bunny hill on the drop.

To the immediate right of the flume exit was the beautiful *Nags Head Carousel*. This unusual double-decker model was built in Germany in 1905; the upper level featured boats that guests could rock and two spinning tubs that rotated around the perimeter. From here directly across the path was the majestic *Carolina* riverboat. This sternwheeler followed a submerged rail around the island in the middle of the park. Much like the early days of Disneyland, there wasn't so much to see on that side, but it provided a great view of the various park lands, especially from the upper decks. A Dixieland band livened things up on board from time to time. The *Carolina* was the premiere icon for Carowinds, featured on all their merchandise. And for good reason—not only was it a spectacular wienie to draw you deeper into the park, it provided a sense of kinetic energy as it slowly plied its course around the river.

And now we would pass the *Skytower*, step aside for the trolley, and find ourself back in Plantation Square, having covered Carolina history from settlement, pirate raids, western expansion, agricultural development, and into the current day. Even though Duell and his team recycled many attractions and elements throughout all their parks, they very effectively grafted local themes and culture onto boilerplate solutions. There was much that paid direct tribute to the Carolinas—it was, indeed, *our* park, and would always be a part of us.[49]

E. Pat Hall built Carowinds simply because he wanted to and thought the people in the region deserved it. "Let me be frank with you. I didn't have to build Carowinds. I built it for the people."[50] He never intended to make a lot of money from it, predicting it might break even in about ten years. "Even if Carowinds never made any money, if

I've helped make some people happy, if I've given families something they can enjoy doing together, then it's worth the effort."[51] Indeed, he was known as a positive force in the community, giving back any way he could.[52] Once the park got going he thought seriously about running for governor (for the second time in his career),[53] eventually serving as campaign chair for his neighbor and former Eckerd Drugs executive Ed O'Herron (they lost). A heart attack about a month before he died was hardly a speed bump to the fast-paced mover and shaker—cooped up in the hospital, he had several phone lines installed so he could keep right on going.[54] This included working on his Christmas shopping list—custom-made rag dolls with faces printed to look like his friends. He was always known as a practical jokester, getting in the last laugh as they received their unique gifts after he had passed on.[55] The fifty-seven year old Army veteran, industrialist, philanthropist, and dreamer was gone, having packed quite a bit into that short time span.[56]

Oh, and the tie clip? You can't do business sitting on your ass.[57]

WORLDS OF FUN

"I'm so sorry—I'm in the middle seat." Lamar shoved his carry-on into the overhead compartment and crawled over the aisle-seat passenger to settle in for the flight. Unlatching the catches on his briefcase, he dug in and tried to catch up on a bit of office work, first examining the current playoff standings for his Kansas City Chiefs, then the latest on his attempt to land a major league baseball franchise for the Dallas–Fort Worth area. Instrumental in bringing major league soccer to America a few years back, Lamar Hunt owned the Dallas Tornados while also holding an interest in the money-losing Chicago Bulls. He financed the touring World Champion Tennis operation run by a nephew. This on top of recently merging his American Football League into the NFL after nearly a decade of disrupting that sport.[58]

Business was his game, but sports was his passion. He collected athletic teams while the rest of us pored over our baseball cards. There were a couple of notable failures, such as the attempt to convert

Alcatraz into an amusement park and to establish bowling as a major league sport.[59] Legend and myth surrounded him, of course, contending he would spend anything for something he wanted. And he could have, but he carefully picked through his options, using the family oil income as a foundation and spending nearly all of his energies on his sports interests.[60]

Funny thing, though, you'd never know any of this by looking at the man. The unassuming, shy guy with a boyish face was surely the local banker or pastor who stood aside as you reached for the milk in the grocery store. He mowed his own yard, drove a five year old Plymouth, and yes, flew coach. Somebody who could just buy the whole airplane. Or the whole airline. In some ways he was just like his dad, a billionaire who made his fortune in oil and carried his sandwich to work in a paper bag, parking three blocks down the road to avoid the 50-cent parking fee.[61]

Back in the early 60s it had become clear Dallas wasn't large enough for two pro football teams. Kansas City was interested, it was an easy commute for him, and so off they went.[62] His renamed Kansas City Chiefs, then part of the old American Football League Lamar himself had founded, moved into Municipal Stadium alongside the Athletics baseball team. The situation was less than ideal, and since the merger between the NFL and AFL required a minimum stadium capacity of 50,000, the opportunity arose to do something far better. Lamar wasn't merely a business investor—he loved the sport, and this was his opportunity to design a facility that catered to both players and fans alike. Most athletic facilities at the time were multi-purpose, shared among a variety of sports. This made economic sense, but Hunt realized that to watch a football game, you really needed a football stadium, not a baseball stadium. The sight lines are different, the field is laid out differently, and so on. The plan called for two buildings, one baseball, one football, and the original concept was to connect both with a sliding roof. The roof idea never made it, but the debut of Arrowhead Stadium in 1972 set a new bar, ushering in a wave of modern facilities that continues to this day.[63]

Lamar became not only a notable sports promoter and enthusiast in that area, he also bought full-tilt into regional economic development to ensure locals didn't write him off as a meddling carpetbagger. His Mid-America Enterprises corporation purchased a large amount of land for industrial and recreational development; one tract had been the site of a long-running mining operation that dug an immense 1,100 acre underground cave. This was converted into SubTropolis, claimed to be the "world's largest underground business complex." It's still there today in case you want to store your spare space shuttles and Christmas merchandise.[64]

Deep into construction of Arrowhead, on August 4, 1971 Lamar Hunt stood before a luncheon crowd of over 200 business and civic leaders and unveiled plans for a completely new venture. This was no sports team, no arena, no athletic initiative of any kind. Phase one was an amusement park, encompassing 140 acres of the 500 set aside for the project. Motels and other commercial facilities would come later, or at least they would have had it not been for the looming gas crisis and economic downturn. Located seven miles northeast of downtown Kansas City, MO, along the bluffs of the Missouri River, the plan resembled many of the other post-Disneyland destinations such as Six Flags, Astroworld, and the currently planned Carowinds and Opryland. The project had been delayed for a year due to "uncertainties in construction labor and the unfavorable money market that developed shortly after our initial announcement," but things were now on track for "Kansas City's Worlds of Fun" to open in 1973.[65]

Lamar, who could have simply written the check for the entire project, looked for investors to raise $17M toward building the park. George S. Harkins, of HNC Realty Co, was willing to buy in for $7M, the remainder coming from Massachusetts Mutual. But as was customary for such deals, the lenders were looking for some sort of collateral. Hunt's offer? His Kansas City Chiefs football team. Harkin's response? Well, we normally go for tangible things like, you know, buildings and stuff. I need to know more. And so Lamar took him deep behind the scenes of the franchise with the condition that Harkin keep all of it under wraps; if players knew the inside details about the company's financials it wouldn't go well for contract negotiations. Harkin agreed, and with a letter of approval signed by Pete Rozelle, commissioner for the National Football League, the project moved forward.[66]

Breaking ground in November of 1971[67] and opening April 1973 at a cost of $20.5 million, Worlds of Fun was themed after Jules Verne's book *Around the World in Eighty Days*. Jack Steadman, Lamar's right hand man and in charge of the project, explained to the press "We chose the large, multicolored ascension balloon for our symbol because it represents fun, adventure and travel reminiscent of the movie, Around the World in 80 Days. These are the things we want Worlds of Fun to represent."[68]

In this spirit, Randall Duell[69] laid out the park to represent five lands: Americana, Europa, Africa, Scandinavia, and the Orient. But the first attraction started at the parking lot, located a quarter mile away from the front gate. Channeling a key design concept from Disneyland, the trams weren't merely transportation, but served to transition guests from the real world to a faraway adventure. And adventure lay just beyond the ticket booths over the gangplanks of the *S.S. Henrietta*, a recreation of the vessel from the movie that represented an around-the-world voyage to fun and excitement.

Typically, the centerpiece for a park's front hub or plaza would be a fountain or statue. Not so here. Following the park's theme, it was a compass that served as the focal point for families to meet and decide which way to go. Make a note to stop in at the end of the day for souvenirs at *Brims 'N Bonnets* or *Front Street Dry Goods & Electric Company*. Or for now grab a bite at *Manor Bakers Antique Bread Wagon* or *Donut Whole*, maybe candy from *Yum Yum Tree*, or perhaps an ice cream at *Fairmont Foods Dairy Dock*. However, the calling card over to your left was the majestic *Cotton Blossom* paddlewheel featured in the movie *Show Boat*. Bought by Lamar for $15,000 at a 1971 MGM backlot auction,[70] it majestically sat permanently docked in its charming pond, offering onboard gifts, shows, and dining at the *Paddle Wheel Cafe*.

From the hub, the park's Duell loop design gently guided you to go right, with larger pathways and the *Information Center* just over in that direction. This was Americana, set in the 19th century with appropriate frontier and barn-like architecture, split rail fencing, and so on. Across from the *Vittle Griddle* was the *9th Street Incline* funhouse; after your head cleared, consider hopping on the *Sky Hi* Von Roll gondola, a one-way trip over the park to Scandinavia, or instead send your little ones on the not-so-19th-century, kid-sized *Crashem Bashem* bumper cars.

Up ahead, *Union Depot* was the sole stop for the narrow-gauge *Burlington Northern Worlds of Fun Railroad,* which wound its way over numerous trestles and through the beautiful landscape. To this day, *Eli,* the propane-fueled, steam-powered locomotive manufactured by Crown Metal Products of Pennsylvania, continues to pull its passenger coaches around the one mile journey, in some seasons at risk of being held up by train robbers.

Since it's early in the day, skip the train for later; walk under the trestle to the left of the station and wander into Europa where the older ones can take out their frustrations bashing each other in *Der Fender Bender*. Grab the little tikes and bribe them to try the *Funicular,* a small Allan Herschell kiddie coaster, while you enjoy a drink at *La'Mars Libations*. Then everybody take the wheel of a taxi on an Arrow *Le Taxitour* car ride. Hungry yet? The *Le Poulet Bone Cafe* is across from the cars, and just beyond is *La Petite Toy Shoppe*. Before leaving Europa enjoy a can-can show at the *Moulin Rouge* theater.

Africa was next with the park's headlining coaster, *Zambezi Zinger*. This Schwarzkopf spiral lift model dominated the back corner of the park, following Duell's design principle of locating major attractions far from the entrance. The idea was to draw people deep into the park, ensuring they see everything along the way. It also provided more room to build these larger structures. Shop at *The Diamond Mine* and *Bwana's Bargains,* grab a quick burger at *Congo Clearing,* then cross over the bridge to ride *The Safari*. The park's second Arrow car ride featured safari-style jeeps that meandered back into the woods past menacing fiberglass African wildlife.

Passing under yet another railroad trestle, we would arrive in Scandinavia, the park's largest land. The major icon here was the *Victrix*, another full-sized vessel purchased by Lamar from MGM.[71] The four-masted schooner featured small cannons you could shoot at floating targets. This area was also home to *Tivoli Playhouse*, the park's major theatrical venue. Scandinavia offered numerous rides, shops, and shows, including the receiving station for the sky ride, *Ski Heis*. There were flat rides, such as *Finnish Fling, Scandia Scramble*, and *Kopter*, as well as the *Seitz Viking Voyager* water flume and *Schussboomer*, a compact Wildcat-type coaster from Schwarzkopf. The *Alpine Animal Village* petting zoo was in the back corner alongside the *Baltic Bazaar*, featuring artists demonstrating their craft. The park had a back gate here as well, closer to the parking lot and intended for buses.

Crossing over the scenic bridge past *Schussboomer* and over a stream, we found ourselves in the last section of the park, the Orient. This small land had a single gift shop, *Rickshaw Richard's Exporters Ltd*, the *Pagoda Soda* and *Rangoon Refresher*, the *Oriental Octopus* flat ride, and the *Fins & Flippers* dolphin show.

And that was it. The *Cotton Blossom* loomed ahead and drew us in for a final show, perhaps dinner, and then we'd be back at the front entrance for a last souvenir and tram ride back to reality. Worlds of Fun was a relaxing, beautiful escape in a natural environment. Duell's design team made good use of the existing landscape with extensive wooded areas, streams, and elevations perfect for railroad trestles and foot bridges. Unlike the fate befalling some regional parks, much of the natural areas remain intact, not quite overtaken by attractions, shops, and other additions over time.[72]

Sold to Cedar Fair in 1995,[73] Worlds of Fun has continued to survive over the years. Oceans of Fun, a tropical-themed water park, opened in 1982 on the other side of the railroad tracks from Europa and Africa. Lands evolved, such as reimagining part of Scandinavia into International Plaza and adding Planet Snoopy. But the big change came at the end of the 1998 season when the unique front entrance was closed forever. The parking lot trams had been retired, not uncommon among parks over the years. But in this case it brought up an interesting conundrum—the parking lot wasn't located near the main gate. The whole reason for the trams was to convey guests the quarter-mile from the lot, so when the trams went away you couldn't very well force people to walk that far. So the back gate was upgraded to the main entrance and the original entry was demolished, including most of the *S.S. Henrietta* (along with the original "gangplanks," which are still in use as footpaths, a section of the concrete bow remains, buried like some forgotten time capsule).[74]

Practicality and guest consideration must prevail, but the original design intent of the entrance, from the tram transition, the sailing vessel inviting you to begin your journey around the world, and the scenic *Cotton Blossom* sitting majestically off to the side was lost forever. As with the other Duell parks much of the vibe and sense of historical placemaking has faded with layers of paint, IP, and management changes. Worlds of Fun isn't considered a growth property for the company, so it doesn't see much in the way of big rides and attractions. But at least Kansas City still has their park.

Lamar Hunt, famous for his Chiefs, for transforming professional football, for bringing pro soccer to this side of the pond, and for being inducted into the Professional Football Hall of Fame, would always claim he was in the *entertainment* business, a notion further cemented by the nickname "Phineas T. Hunt" someone stuck on him along the way. His Barnum-esque, childhood dream-come-true was certainly fodder for a larger-than-life public persona. But that never seemed to change the man who would continue to cut his grass and fly coach.[75]

GREAT ADVENTURE

I guess growing up as the son of the guy who produced "The Wizard of Oz" and the woman whose dad was *the* Warner in Warner Brothers Studios, you can't help but be a bit different in your outlook on life. Warner LeRoy, born in Hollywood in 1935, grew up surrounded by movies, high art, and good living. Naturally thinking he'd go into the theater business, he finished up at Stanford, left for New York, and began writing and directing plays on and off Broadway. Life takes curious turns, however, and the theater got lost in his new quest to become one of the city's most notable restaurateurs. Famous for transforming Tavern on the Green and the Russian Tea Room, Warner's properties—like his personality—were high glitz and glamour. Perhaps too much so, as in the case of the $9 million, 850-seat Potomac restaurant in DC, which closed after only a year.[76] Dubbed "The Prince of Flash" in a Vogue magazine special feature, he dreamed big and spent bigger.[77] When he set his sights on building his own theme park it naturally had to be the grandest and most extravagant around.

In his mind, the 1500-acre Enchanted Forest and Safari Park would rival Walt Disney World. The initial plans were indeed expansive, but followed similar ideas that other park builders had envisioned. The complex would have been divided into no less than seven components: The Enchanted Forest (the primary theme park), Safari ("world's largest" drive-through animal park), Neptune's Kingdom (aquatic life park with shows), Dream Street (shopping and entertainment district), Over the Rainbow (small-scale picnic areas with small rides, playground, etc), Sports and Games (athletic facilities), and Wild Country (camping and outdoor recreation). The sheer scope and scale was enormous, and of course nowhere near feasible. Most of this never got off the initial proposal documents, much less the drawing boards. The scaled-back park, however, incorporated bits and pieces of these ideas.[78]

Considering LeRoy's extravagant spending on all his business endeavors, the park as it opened was ironically low-budget. Instead of stately buildings, porticos, and fountains, colorful tents greeted you as you passed through the turnstiles. Challenges with financing, land disputes, environmental impact studies, delayed construction...and arguments over whether zebras were or were not penned up on a couple of local dirt roads...resulted in only six months to get things built, and so funding as well as time constraints dictated what they were able to open by 1974's inaugural season.[79] To be fair, this wasn't just another fancy restaurant; acquiring thousands of acres of land and carving out a park of any size—in this case a theme park *and* a large drive-through safari—is in a different league.

Quite unlike the current park layout guests are familiar with, the original entrance was located next to the *Fort* and mine train coaster, providing a teasing view of the trains as they rushed by over the creek and back into the station. (A more stately, Colonial-style entrance would be built at its current location in 1976.) *Enchanted Forest,* not *Great Adventure,* was what the carnival-style banner proclaimed overhead as you handed over your ticket. Indeed, designers went to great lengths to preserve the heavily wooded environment; this, along with other natural features such as Lahaway Creek and Switlik Lake, contributed to a relaxing, get-away-from-the-city kind of day.

Once in the park, the main drag of Dream Street beckoned you to explore the various colorful restaurants and shops as you walked past the *Carousel* and fountain, the *Antique Cars* auto ride on your right, and farther along to the giant Ferris wheel straight ahead. Warner's imaginative brain wanted the restaurants to be designed just like the menus they served, so the *Yum Yum Palace* was architecturally decked out with ice cream cones and such (think Roller Coaster Tycoon). The *Garden of Marvels* was an elaborate walk-through of miniature world architecture, complete with waterways and railways. Souvenirs and other essentials were to be found along Dream Street.

At the far end of the park was Strawberry Fair, with the *Big Fury* Italian carnival coaster, *Traffic Jam* bumper cars, and the under-sized *Great Train Ride.* Head back toward the turnstiles, bear right, and you'd be in Great Adventure's old west section—Rootin' Tootin' Rip Roarin'. Of course, this would not be like any other, with a super-sized Conestoga wagon, *Super Teepee*, and *Fort*—the exact opposite of Disney's practice of scaling things down for charm. The park was situated along beautiful Switlik Lake, and the Neptune's Kingdom waterfront area was perfect for an aquatic theater. Surrounding the western section and entrance gate was Lahaway Creek, where you could take your scenic photos and hop on the Arrow flume ride.

True to his nature, much in LeRoy's new playground was bigger than anybody else's, including the longest flume ride, the largest Ferris wheel, the *Super Teepee*, and *Freedom Fountain*, the largest spray-fountain in the world at the time.[80] Also outsized from the get-go was attendance; the park was severely hampered in its capability for handling the crowds from New Jersey and New York, and plans were quickly put in place for major expansion starting the very next season.[81]

It was the Hardwicke Company, not Duell, that worked with LeRoy on the original project.[82] Duell & Associates was on hold with Marriott for their ill-fated third park in the D.C. area, so they lost out on the job.[83] Hardwicke's experience included a number of safari parks, and along with the Enchanted Forest, one of the original ideas that made it to construction was an expansive, drive-through safari. Wild Safari was the largest safari park outside of Africa when it opened. This was no mere petting zoo (although Enchanted Forest had one of those, too); it was a major nature preserve.[84] However, clearly they weren't in the theme park design business, and that first season was one of great trial and error. Too little of everything: rides, food, queue space, pathways, and so on.[85] Warner may have been the dreamer and visionary who brought the park into existence, but for the second year major changes were necessary. Bringing in industry professionals, management approved major expansion for 1975 along with necessary financial adjustments.[86] It's a business, after all, and you've got to clear some sort of profit in order to soldier on. Attendance soared for that second season, but LeRoy was beginning to tire of the less-glamorous side of running a complex place such as this.

For 1976 they called in the cavalry. Randall Duell arrived to provide his Midas touch, transforming the entry experience and improving the overall layout. Randall's designers were responsible for the impressive Liberty-themed front gate and plaza along with various enhancements around the park.[87] Management was trying, but finally decided to let Six Flags take a shot at it in 1977.[88] That company, getting revved up on their decades-long buying spree, had just acquired Astroworld two years before. The pattern of independent parks flashing bright out of the gate but quickly running into challenges was becoming evident.

With renewed investment by Six Flags, Great Adventure hung in there and began to find its footing. The Time Warner and Premier decades saw major upgrades with new theming (plus or minus) and attractions. Today LeRoy's dream is one of the biggest Six Flags parks in the chain. It may not look much like what he had in mind, but it's thriving and providing enjoyment for millions of guests each year.

And whatever happened to Warner? He kept at it with his over-the-top restaurants, some working out, others less so. He sold his remaining interest in the park in 1993. And he certainly outlived his dog—the original Toto from his dad's movie. That didn't work out so well either; he would always remember it as "that nasty little creature."[89]

SEAWORLD

Few people in the modern theme park industry were as revolutionary and game-changing as George Millay. Out of the Navy and in college, George bought an old truck and started a trash hauling business. After graduation he somehow got hired, then fired, in the brokerage business. The next venture was a very successful Hawaiian themed restaurant overlooking the harbor at Long Beach.[90] He learned as he went, always thinking ahead, and so the idea came one day to build an underwater bar at the restaurant where patrons could relax and enjoy the ocean wildlife. Early in the process, however, they discovered that the water was much too murky and you wouldn't see much of anything.[91] One of his consultants was Kenny Norris, the main fish guy at Marineland near Los Angeles. After Millay killed the project, Norris mentioned he'd always wanted to build a marine park on Mission Bay in San Diego, but he didn't know anything about business. George didn't know anything about marine life, but lots about business. Somehow not too long after that George received a mysterious package in the mail with all kinds of financial records from Marineland...enough to convince him it was worth taking a look.[92]

The land where SeaWorld would be located was actually public property along Mission Bay. San Diego was bidding for proposals specifically for a marine mammal park, and Millay's team was awarded a long term lease over the competitor's plan for "Sealand."[93] And so with a total investment of $3.5 million dollars[94] the 40-acre park opened on March 21, 1964.

The original SeaWorld did not quite fit the concept of a theme park as we currently think of them. There were no separate "lands," distinguished by some time, place, or subject. Being such a small park, it didn't have much room to build out such areas. The overall design motif was mid-century Polynesian; the unifying theme was marine life, though it was hardly the first park to fall under this umbrella. Although we've just explored the progression of several Duell-designed parks through the early 70s, we have to remember that SeaWorld came from an entirely different direction early in that process. Few major parks were yet open at that time; Disneyland had opened almost a decade earlier, but Six Flags Over Texas was only in its third year, with other parks like Knott's slowly morphing over the years. So the familiar pattern of what many of the upcoming regional parks would look like, almost all of which were designed by Duell and his team, was yet to be seen.

SeaWorld had no rides other than up-charge hydrofoil boats out on the bay. There was no train, no antique cars, no flats, nothing. But that wasn't the point. Millay's park designer, architect Ben Southland from the famous Victor Gruen Associates, created a beautiful, natural oasis of landscaping, ponds, rocks, and waterfalls.[95] The pathways meandered throughout, providing peaceful vistas enlivened with ducks and swans. With only forty acres for the entire complex, there was less need for a hub and spoke or loop layout to keep people oriented. You couldn't get lost, especially with the park's central icon, the Polynesian Pop-styled *Theater of the Sea* show building, visible from pretty much everywhere.

From the parking lot, a large Polynesian structure beckoned you toward the entrance. Once inside the gate you could go left toward the guest services building, right toward a playground and the *Japanese Village,* or straight ahead to the dominating *Theater of the Sea*. With steeply raked rooflines that flowed downward like waves, the building's shape resembled a big top tent; inside was a 15 foot deep water tank with seating for 1200 looking through the glass walls. The park's main show was here, featuring a fairly significant production of women "sea maids," dolphins and seals, music, and lighting.

On the right side of the park, the *Murata Pearl Japanese Village* featured almost-Japanese-like architecture and a large pool in the center where Japanese women would harvest oysters, searching for pearls to sell. Opposite this on the left side was the *Sea Grotto,* featuring more sea maids swimming with sharks, and the *Seal and Sea Lion Show*. Facing the bay at the far end of the park, take in the *Lagoon Show* or relax at the *Hawaiian Punch Village,* a Polynesian structure featuring films of the exotic Pacific. That's pretty much it, although of course it would grow over time.[96]

What was SeaWorld's draw? Why would people pay to go somewhere with no rides or games? People have always been drawn to animals of all kinds, and in the 1960s the sea was a mysterious wonder. Few people had any idea about ocean life beyond the goldfish in their bowls, so it was all new and wonderful.[97] And to see those cute creatures doing tricks and such just made it more memorable.

The first two years were tough; it took a bit to fully develop shows and get the park situated in the community's mind. Over time three more SeaWorld parks would open, all of them offering increasingly sophisticated shows, rides, and other standard park fare.

MAGIC MOUNTAIN

After the San Diego park found its footing, George and his staff considered getting into the ride park business after one of SeaWorld's executives, Dave DeMotte, told the others how well Cedar Point was doing. They just needed some land, and they found it by partnering with the Newhall Land and Farming Company. Newhall owned extensive tracts of land in the Valencia area, an undeveloped region that they hoped to put on the map with an elaborate planned community. The agreement was an even split for a $20 million dollar project with construction beginning in 1969.[98] Eighteen months later Magic Mountain opened on May 29, 1971, to a very rocky start.[99]

For starters, Gene Wade, the construction manager, was shoving unpaid bills into a desk drawer, claiming everything was proceeding within budget. By the time these were discovered the project was $5 million in the hole.[100] A press preview the week before opening, benefitting the Reiss-Davis Child Center of Los Angeles, was less than impressive for all concerned.[101] For another special event on May 28, the park invited employees from Chevron, a major sponsor. It was a total disaster after a staffer at Chevron issued family tickets, not individual tickets. Expecting about 10,000 guests, over 40,000 tried cramming into the park, an eerie rehash of Disneyland's Black Sunday. The media slammed the new venture as "Tragic Mountain"—the park was simply not ready for showtime, with a barren landscape and few operating rides.[102] It would take a couple of years of significant reinvestment and hard work to get things into shape.[103] But its distinctive location was one of the keys that ultimately contributed to a family-favorite destination. During a helicopter reconnaissance, Randall Duell selected the site specifically because of the mountain. The topography would make building much harder and more expensive, but would provide a more interesting place.[104]

Duell and his team set to work applying what they knew at that point. So far they had worked on the Universal Studios Hollywood tour, some C.V. Wood parks, Six Flags Over Texas, Six Flags Over Georgia, and Astroworld. The Duell loop concept had started to take solid shape, and the pathway for Magic Mountain clearly wound around the landscape leading guests through the various attraction areas. However, the left side of the park was steep enough they originally planned to tunnel through the mountain. After money fell short a funicular cable car system was installed to close the loop.[105]

A true theme park this was not; there were no themed lands, history, or backstory. Standard attractions such as Arrow's auto ride and mine train coaster were prominent along with the *Eagle's Flight* sky ride and *Metro* monorail, both of which provided welcome transportation around the park. An Intamin *Sky Tower* provided a panoramic view of the entire area. The layout was well done and on par with Duell's other projects. Attraction names came not from history, but were generic such as *Sugar Shack, Kaleidoscope, Circus Wheel,* and *Beep Beep.* Even though the richness of theme was not present, Duell's design touch gave it an advantage over other amusement parks.[106]

Over time management got better at running the park, capacity and guest services issues were resolved, and attendance stabilized. The 1978 season saw about 2.7 million turnstile clicks, a hefty number. But in 1979 Newhall, a large company with a variety of business interests, decided it wanted to redirect resources toward real estate and other ventures that offered a better return. SeaWorld had already bailed from the partnership in 1971. We will see this pattern again with large corporations discovering over time that the parks just didn't deliver what they were hoping for. Willing to sell, Six Flags was willing to buy, and so for $51.3 million Magic Mountain became the next member of the growing chain family.[107]

George would eventually leave SeaWorld, under duress, and then go on to shake up the industry yet again by developing the modern waterpark. Wet 'N Wild was the first water playground that featured various types of water activities bundled into one admission charge. He wasn't interested in theming, and he wasn't a designer. But he certainly was one of the most game-changing and colorful characters in an industry which suffers no loss for personalities.[108]

OLD DOMINION LINE
(LIFE OF VIRGINIA)
REBEL YELL
POP'IN PUPS
SKY RIDE STATION
CAROUSEL
RESTROOMS
THE MELODRAMA
FLORAL CLOCK
AND DATE
NNER BELL
WHITE HORSE INN
OLD VIRGINIA
BLUE RIDGE TOLLWAY
VIRGINIA REEL
THE EIFFEL TOWER
RESTROOMS
SUNBEAM
ALPINE DELI
BANDSTAND

Chapter Six

DAVY CROCKETT TANGLES WITH...YOGI BEAR?

Surveying the muddy waters that had just submerged the park, again, Gary Wachs knew something had to give. It wasn't just the recurring floods, an inescapable penalty from building right up against the mighty Ohio River. The old, wonderful park was landlocked with nowhere to grow. And grow it had since its humble start in 1870 as a picnic retreat in an apple grove. Coney Island thrived as one of the most enduring and popular amusement parks in the country.

Perhaps more than a little of this can be attributed to its name, though of no relation to its more famous namesake. Not long after becoming a popular local amusement area, Coney, or rather Parker's Grove at the time, attracted the attention of a couple riverboat captains who, in a unique twist to the trolley park trend of the day, operated riverboats along the Ohio to bring folks to the grounds. The new park was now called Ohio Grove, the Coney Island of the West. Over the years and decades new amusements and entertainment would be added, including its first coasters in the early 1900s. 1913 saw the first of several floods that would, ironically, serve to propel the park forward through the necessity of rebuilding newer and better. Transfer of ownership from time to time also brought renewed investment, and the crowds swelled from the nearby regions.[1]

Unlike so many similar parks around the country that struggled, fizzled, and flamed out through the ups and downs of changing economic and social conditions, Coney stood its ground, maintaining beautiful facilities, quality attractions, and a reputation that brought no less a figure than Walt Disney out to see for himself as part of his early park research.[2] It was a booming place in the 50s and 60s. And then came the 1964 flood, fourteen feet high and covering most everything except the rooftops and spectacular hills of the *Shooting Star* and *Wildcat* coasters. As Gary grabbed a broom and shoved mud off the walkways, his mind raced in all directions. What to do? The park has survived this before; we can rebuild. But we're out of room; nowhere to grow. Can't accommodate bigger crowds. He also realized the park business was at the cusp of a major shakeup with the success of Disneyland and Six Flags Over Texas, representing a new concept of the regional theme park. That's the direction they needed to go in order to survive, and they couldn't do it here at Coney. And then the unthinkable solution—move the park. How on earth do you move an amusement park? He wasn't sure yet, but the more he thought about it the more convinced he became.[3]

That was the easy part. Gary was but a twenty-eight year old assistant manager, the president's kid who was helping run the company. So when he laid the idea out on the table, dad didn't take too warmly to it. Ralph had been there a long time and, understandably, none of the elder management team could fathom such a drastic change at a time when attendance was at an all time high. The park was performing as good as ever. Most companies look to a different direction when they're in trouble, not at the peak of their game. Young Gary kept at it, never wavering, but needing a break to help make his point.

He got it in 1968 when Fess Parker, known to all as Davy Crockett, announced Frontier World. The regional theme park would be built in Boone County, Kentucky, practically next door to Cincinnati. With a single headline, Coney's team realized Gary had been right and that such a project would most likely wreak havoc on their park. He was given the green light to investigate options, particularly finding a partner with a much larger checkbook to help finance such a major initiative.[4]

The white knight turned out to be Taft Broadcasting, owner of the Hanna-Barbera cartoon franchise and who was looking for new opportunities to monetize the brand.[5] Taft's interest in the project got a major boost after a long lunch consultation with Roy Disney, who ironically pointed out that it was Ed Schott, then-owner of Coney in 1953, who enthusiastically encouraged Walt to pursue his own park.[6] The final doubter was converted after seeing the skyrocketing stock value of the company that had just bought the first two Six Flags parks from Great Southwest.[7] Coney was purchased for $6.5 million.[8] Over twelve hundred acres were then acquired northeast of Cincinnati[9] and a deal struck to build a $30 million theme park along with a motel and golf course.[10] But the first order of business was to shut Parker down; Taft was powerful in that area and the financing well suddenly ran dry for Frontier World.[11] Funny how things go in the world of business. With no options left, Crockett laid down his musket and traveled west to try again in California.

KINGS ISLAND

Construction on the as-yet-unnamed park began in 1970.[12] Bucking an industry trend, the decision was made to keep all design work in-house; Duell & Associates would have no part of this new endeavor.[13] That didn't mean, however, that they didn't know what they were doing. One of the more prominent members of this team was none other than Bruce Bushman, a former studio artist and art director for Disneyland. He had overseen Fantasyland, designing the fanciful *Casey Jr. Circus Train* with its whimsical ticket booth and the ride vehicles for *Mr. Toad's Wild Ride*, among others. Bruce had moved over to Hanna-Barbera, developing designs for a couple of parks that didn't see the light of day, such as Hanna-Barbera Land. Since he was already in the family, so to speak, it was a given to bring him over for the new project. Bushman would be responsible for giving International Street its majestic, yet intimate look and feel, unfortunately passing away just before the park opened in 1972.[14]

While all of this was getting underway, Coney Island was gearing up for its final season with a new Galaxy roller coaster and lots of marketing. Taft had quietly left the impression early on that Coney would continue operations, presumably to deflect any backlash towards the new project. Investment in the old property had continued with an Arrow flume ride in 1969 and a Hanna-Barbera show theater the following year. For the 1971 season, however, promotional materials talked up the new park in an effort to persuade folks that, yes, things were going to be even better at the new place. Coney's final days were spectacular, with 2.75 million guests pouring through the turnstiles to say goodbye. Surely everyone in management was holding their breath, wondering and hoping they had made the right decision. What if people didn't take to the new park? Look how unbelievable this year has been—are we nuts?[15] They would find out in short order.

Meantime, over at the project site things were kicking into high gear. Wachs and his new team explored the nooks and crannies of their acreage, considering what to build and where to put it. Toward the back of the site was a wooded area and ravine—perfect for a train trestle and surrounded by what would become Rivertown.[16] The remaining lands would be arranged in a hub-and-spoke configuration radiating outward from International Street and the *Eiffel Tower*: Oktoberfest, Happy Land of Hanna-Barbera, and Coney Island. The *Eiffel Tower*, a $1.2 million, 1/3 scale replica of the original, would be the icon of the park.[17] The tower had actually been contracted earlier for installation at Coney. Once the decision was made to move, it was put on hold with Intamin, a major ride manufacturer in Switzerland. Several attractions from Coney would be transferred once that park closed at the end of the 1971 season.[18]

With ample acreage the designers had room to play, and for a group who for the most part had little experience designing theme parks the result was highly successful. Gary had spent a great deal of time visiting parks in the United States and Europe and had a pretty good idea of what he wanted to do.[19] Even so, it would take over 150 tries to figure out the park's eventual layout.[20] Taft stayed out of the way and let him figure it out. By now they had a name—Kings Island, a combination of Kings Mills (the previous property owners were the Kings; the adjacent town was Kings Mills) and Coney Island from, of course, its predecessor. An August 1970 naming contest had brought in over 15,000 entries with local resident Rebecca Richards coming out on top, winning a week-long trip for four to Hollywood.[21]

The front ticketing and guest services building effectively concealed what was in store for park guests. This was deliberate, the designers understanding that the cinematic reveal from guests walking through and seeing the *Eiffel Tower* and majestic *Royal Fountain* was a powerful, dramatic transformation. International Street was inspired from European parks and the recent New York World's Fair, with carefully manicured green spaces, fountains, flags, and colorful architecture. It also, along with much of the park, paid tribute to the various immigrant communities that settled in the area long before. It was a beautiful promenade with various shops and restaurants along each side all set to European themes, organized in "city blocks" according to country: Auld Suisse Haus, Geselleschaft Deutschland, Fiera Italiana, La Tienda España, and Bazaar Française. Grab lunch at *Kahn's Sausage Haus* or *Munchen Cafe,* let your kids pick out a stuffed animal at *Spielwaren,* don a shirt from *Hute-Hemden,* buy a bracelet at *Bijouterie,* watch a glass blower at *Cristaleria,* and don't forget your candles, available at *Kerzen*. Small details make a difference; the cobblestone pathways lining International Street were from Colerain Avenue in Cincinnati. The animal themed countertop of the Italian ice cream shop was hand-made tile, and a pair of original chandeliers from Cincinnati's 1878 Music Hall hung high in the Swiss chalet.[22]

And there was more, but branching off to the right of the Tower was the Happy Land of Hanna-Barbera—the main reason Taft got into this business in the first place. This was no mere kiddie land; it featured significant attractions such as the *Scooby Doo* wooden coaster, *Marathon Turnpike* car ride, *Gulliver's Rub-A-Dub* water raft ride, and, most interesting of all, the *Enchanted Voyage*. This $2 million boat dark ride was housed in a large show building designed to look like you're floating straight into a television set. The Arrow-designed flume system had a unique turntable load/unload platform outside of the main building. The show itself consisted of six scenes all filled with Hanna-Barbera characters, animatronics—all 100 of them—and elaborate music that was scored in Hollywood and reproduced in surround sound.[23]

The *Sky Ride Station* offered a cross-park hop over to Oktoberfest, passing directly in front of the *Eiffel Tower*. Unlike a pure hub-and-spoke layout, pathways connected each of the two lands on either side of the tower without having to return to the hub. Rivertown was next, paying homage to Ohio's rich history of river life and related trades. The Arrow flume from Coney was relocated here as *Kings Mill,* and the *Kings Island & Miami Valley Railroad* offered a steam-powered excursion off into the woods. The two narrow-gauge locomotives, modeled after the Civil War *General,* departed *Losantiville* depot, the original name for Cincinnati, and set off for staged train robberies and live-action fights between frontiersmen and Native Americans. Rustic, frontier architecture and water features set the scene in this area. Kings Island would not have a *Jungle Cruise* look-alike, but here in Rivertown there were two canoe attractions, *Shawnee Landing* and *Kenton's Cove,* the latter of which would last only the first season before being replaced with an Arrow hydroflume. *Great Rivers Outfitters, Columbia Palace Dining Hall,* and a *General Store* provided places to browse, eat, and shop before heading toward the back of the *Eiffel Tower*. Here was another car ride, actually two of them intertwined —*Les Taxis* and *Ohio Overland Auto Livery*. One load station faced Rivertown, the other opposite toward Coney Island.

Coney Island. Of course there'd be an area dedicated to remembering where it all came from. The midway, pretty much like it was at the old park, was lined with green planters and gingko trees shaped kind of like corn dogs or something (actually the same trees transplanted from old Coney).[24] Whereas Disney and Six Flags had deliberately avoided any resemblance to the amusement parks of yesteryear, Kings Island would pay tribute. And why not? Coney was nowhere near the typical, disreputable, carny sort of place and held fond memories for the locals. Games and amusements lined either side, including a few classic flat rides brought over from the other park, but the big attraction was what commanded attention running the length of the midway and beyond. *Racer* was a magnificent dual-track wooden coaster built by famed designer John Allen. Pursuaded to postpone his long-deserved retirement, the task was to bring the spirit of Coney's *Shooting Star* while taking it to a new level. It spawned two similar rides at Kings Dominion and Carowinds and helped launch a renewed era of wooden coasters, something that had nearly died away completely.

The final themed area of the park, Oktoberfest, was a tribute to the significant German heritage of the region. It was the smallest land, with a drunken barrels flat ride, found in most parks of the time, and a Galaxy coaster, *Bavarian Beetle,* also relocated from Coney. The oh so very German-named *Sky Ride Station* connected with Hanna-Barbera Land. The *Der Alte Deutsche Bier Garten* was an expansive, well-themed structure situated on the lake with scenic outdoor seating.

Just off the hub toward Rivertown was the obligatory dolphin show, and connected directly to the *Eiffel Tower* was the *Carousel* and a bright red inflatable structure that was used for shows. The rather pretentiously named *Kings Island Theater* didn't last too long, giving in to heavy snows after a few years. Cheap to build at the time, it got the job done, but certainly the park's aesthetic value rose a few ticks after its demise. Most of the park's entertainment was not housed in show buildings, however, but situated outside all around the park. The individual hired to run the shows department, Jack Rouse, would go on to establish JRA,[25] one of the most successful themed design companies in the world.[26]

In addition to the park, the designers borrowed the concept of a resort destination that other parks had incorporated. The alpine village-themed Kings Island Inn, Kings Island Campground, and even the Jack Nicklaus Golden Bear Golf Courses completed the package, particularly important for an area that had very little development at the time. There was simply nothing there, but of course that was about to change.[27]

It may not have had the Duell touch, but it was a beautiful park and an immediate success for its owners. Somehow management had come up with a first season attendance prediction of two million, a staggering number at the time that no other park outside Disney had approached. By the last operating day of 1972, attendance had clocked in at two million twelve thousand.[28]

KINGS DOMINION

Taft Broadcasting lost no time looking to expand their new venture. Even before Kings Island opened as an unqualified success, the company sought locations to build more parks, first settling on 1500 acres of land just north of Richmond, VA, alongside Interstate 95. Land was cheap at the time, the climate was right, it was close to major population centers, and the Interstate provided easy access. $60 million was allocated for construction, the largest spent on any park outside of Walt Disney World which had opened just a couple years earlier.[29] After the first season wound down in Ohio, Gary Wachs moved east to oversee construction, bringing along a young up-and-comer named Dennis Speigel to help out and manage the park once it opened.[30]

The public announcement in 1973 included an artistic "map" of the property. The "Kings Dominion 800-acre development plan" showed Lion Country Safari, the theme park, golf course, "motor inn," camping, and future expansion plots.[31] Taft had worked with Jack Nicklaus on Kings Island's golf course, and they were entering into an agreement with Lion Country Safari, Inc. to open a drive-through safari at the Ohio park. Lion Country already operated locations in

Florida and California; the Virginia safari would open in 1974, one year before completion of the park.[32]

Lion Country was initially a drive-through experience with guests cruising through the animal preserves in their personal cars. This was a mixed bag, with lions, elephants, and other aggressive creatures chewing, ripping, and clawing everything that passed by. After constantly shelling out for new tires, fenders, and paint, the park finally installed a monorail that snaked around the compound in air conditioned comfort.[33]

Meantime, an experienced team exported from Kings Island was frenetically working to get the park open. Hundreds of daily decisions had to be made in a project of such a scale as this, usually on-the-spot with little time to think about any long-term consequences. Lucky for them there were few major hurdles along the way—no opposition from the locals, no environmental snags, no financing drama. The company had already done this before, and that invaluable experience provided a roadmap throughout the process.[34] Rising inflation in the 1970s didn't help, however, dramatically increasing construction costs and threatening to blow the budget. Half of International Street, the promenade that ran along the central fountains from the front gate, cost twice as much to build as the other half. In spite of all this the park opened on time and under budget. The folks from Kings Island were fairly young, ambitious, and ready to tackle anything. Sometimes it pays to be just a bit unaware of the enormity of the task.[35]

May 3, 1975—opening day. By 6am the lines were out into the parking lot, with traffic ultimately backing up for miles on the Interstate and local roads in every direction. The park gates were opened early... and by 9am closed again after tens of thousands of people rushed in.[36] Thousands more were turned away that day. The following week the park placed ads in the local papers apologizing for the madness and reassuring guests that they were working hard to keep it from happening again. Changes included limiting the number of visitors in the park each day and encouraging people to come during the week "when you'll have the park more to yourself."[37] In fact, the state had to pitch in with Taft to improve the I-95 interchange in order to prevent cars from backing up on the highway.[38] The team had successfully established the message and brand of Kings Dominion in an area of the country that was as yet unfamiliar with the concept of a theme park. Busch Gardens would open one week later just down the road near Williamsburg, but for the moment KD was the new thing in town. Projected attendance for the season was 1.85 million,[39] and they were well on their way.

The park's name is a mash-up from Kings Island and Old Dominion, Virginia's nickname. Perhaps reusing Kings Island to maintain a consistent brand would have been logical, but it really didn't seem to matter once the park was open. From a thematic perspective it actually makes better sense to localize it for the area, and this probably made for a better choice in the long run.

Borrowing heavily from its older sibling, the park's design was pretty much the same, greatly streamlining the design and planning process. Other than the Safari, there would be one less land; all but one of these would be themed the same as at Kings Island, the exception being to convert KI's Rivertown to Old Virginia. In both cases this was a nod to local history.

The entryway opened onto International Street and the fountains, just like in Ohio. The *Eiffel Tower* again served as the central icon at the end of the Street, branching off into the various lands. The architecture and layout of International Street was somewhat different, however, but still retained the international flavor. You could pick up a plush at *Toys Internationale,* find fudge at *Coffelt's Swiss Treats,* score a sandwich at the *Sunbeam Alpine Deli,* and on the way out sit down for an evening meal at the *Casa Del Sol Restaurant* after getting those last minute souvenirs from the *Italian Emporium* and *La Piñata Gifts.* At both parks, International Street was a beautiful center of activity with sculpted landscaping, dancing fountains, and the inspiring *Tower* rising above it all.

In the upper-right quadrant was Old Virginia, heavily wooded and themed to represent simpler times. After crossing over a mountain stream, to the right was the *Shenandoah Lumber Company*, an Arrow-built flume ride scenically nestled in the trees. To the left, the *Blue Ridge Tollway* auto ride wound its way around the countryside. Take in a show at the *Mason-Dixon Music Hall*, then all-aboard the *Old Dominion Line* steam railroad for a mile long journey deep into the woods through Moonshine Valley and Harmony Junction. Ida Lou, who's back from the city after failing to find her a man, has her sights set on the train's conductor. If he doesn't do her right, Pa's awaitin' at the end of the line with his shotgun.

Soon's the train stops, scoot off the platform and turn right out of the station, heading over toward *Lake Charles* and the intimidating racing coaster *Rebel Yell*. This younger brother to Kings Island's *Racer* was similar, but with the turnarounds pushed together in order to accommodate the Safari. For the first season, this area was named Coney Island and laid out very similarly to Kings Island with its midway flavor and gingko trees (it became Candy Apple Grove the following year due to negative connotations with the original New York Coney, the locals not having any connection with the more wholesome Cincinnati Coney).[40] Grab a candy apple after riding the *Galaxy* coaster and take in the *Wachs Bros. Mecham & Runyan Circus*, situated on a spit of land jutting into the lake.

At the far end of Coney Island lay the Happy Land of Hanna-Barbera, dominated by the *Scooby Doo* roller coaster and *Whacky Wheels* turnpike. If the kids would sit still long enough, they had a choice of either the *Flintstone Follies* or *Scooby's Magical Mansion* magic show. Journey into *Yogi's Cave* and explore the famous bear's colorful, animated world, carefully crafted at a cost of $1 million. Inside you'd ooh and ahh at the "precious gems" of "Rooby Falls" and listen as "The Genuine Rock Bandorgan" echoed among the intricate concrete rock-work. Then grab the handrail as you tried walking through the ranger's cabin, tilted at 18 degrees with water flowing uphill.[41] Now say goodbye to Yogi and head back, either following the pathway to the right which took you back to the *Eiffel Tower* or jumping on the

Sky Ride, offering an aerial hop back over Coney Island to land in front of the *Rebel Yell.*[42]

The *Safari* tour served as the park's fifth land. The "motor inn" was added later in the front section of the parking lot, but no Jack Nicklaus golf course. Strangely, to this day there's not much development around the park other than a few small hotels, a Burger King, and the old truck stop that was there long before Taft showed up. Nevertheless, Kings Dominion was wildly successful and has remained steady over the decades in spite of various changes in ownership.[43]

CANADA'S WONDERLAND

The third park in Taft's strategic plan took awhile to get going. By this time Taft had partnered with Family Leisure Centers (Kroger)[44] and was looking north for this one, in 1973 acquiring land in the region of Toronto, Canada, specifically the village of Maple (in the town of Vaughan).[45] But the idea of an amusement park—and especially an American-based one—didn't sit too well with the locals.[46] In a scenario that would become all too common for park planners over the decades, it was going to take serious politicking and education to convince them it might actually be good for them. Locals banded together as SAVE (Sensible Approach to Vaughan's Environment) while regional cultural centers such as the Royal Ontario Museum worried about competition. "For God's sake, Disneyland isn't the real world. We don't need a place like this. We have everything we need in Metro Toronto...It's an abomination and I don't want my children exposed to more of this kind of hucksterism," said an enraged Margaret Britnell, mayor of King Township.[47]

Taft realized none of these people had any idea what such a park would be like—there was nothing else in Canada for comparison. So they hosted a tour of Kings Island for the folks to get hands-on with what they had to offer. Reaction was somewhat mixed, but overall the group came away with a new perspective.[48] The mayor of Vaughan was an enthusiastic supporter. "That was a great public relations thing for them to do." "All this anti-American feeling is baloney.

Building this park is no different than watching American television."[49]

Opposition to the idea, however, was just cranking into high gear. Toronto city councillor John Sewell insisted "we should do everything possible to discourage this proposal."[50] Other local officials chimed in, and SAVE kept up the pressure. By 1978, however, enough of these individuals had a change of heart, and in March the Ontario Municipal Board issued a 32-page report approving the project, including a key stipulation that the park emphasize Canadian culture in the design.[51] Not all came away happy. Local councillor James Cameron rued to The Star "You could say Yogi Bear won and Maple lost."[52] "Resignation has been the real response of the people," SAVE told the Star in 1980. "It means we'll be living between two dumps." Dumps? Oh yes. The park...and the Keele Valley Landfill.[53]

Ground was finally broken for Canada's Wonderland in 1979, with the park opening two years later. True to Taft's expectations, the park was a hit, with first year attendance nearly breaking 2.2 million.[54] It has since gone on to shine as one of the most attended regional parks in North America with nearly 3.8 million guests in 2018.[55]

To their credit, Taft initially set out to design a park that was identifiably Canadian, rather than merely copying from the other two blueprints. The overall layout and entry concept remained, including International Street, the central fountains, and the park's towering icon at the far end. But in this case it wasn't a tower—*Wonder Mountain* with its majestic, cascading waterfall signified Canada's beautiful, rustic landscape and provided not only a visual centerpiece for the park, but also a vantage point for viewing the surrounding area. *Wonder Mountain Pathway* wound up and around the mountain toward the peak, which did nothing for preserving forced perspective of height, but provided lots of Kodak camera moments. International Street resembled the ones at Kings Island and Kings Dominion in its colorful, international architectural style. Interestingly, instead of indicating specific shop and food locations, the first year park map simply labels the *Alpine Building, Scandinavian Building, Mediterranean Building,* and *Latin Building.*

Off to the right through a well-themed portal lay the land of Medieval Faire, where everything was spelled accordingly: *Dragon Fyre, French Fryes and Shrymps,* and *Yee Ribb Pytt* give you the idea. An impressive castle facade led into the *Canterbury Theatre,* while the *Sea Septre* sailing vessel dominated the small lake as part of the pirate stunt show. Moving to the upper-right quadrant of the park we of course found the Happy Land of Hanna-Barbera, complete with an Arrow auto ride, carousel, dolphin show, and *Yogi's Cave.* With Canada's Wonderland opening later than the earlier regionals, roller coaster technology had developed and therefore the park featured several coasters, including the family-friendly *Ghoster Coaster,* complete with a wonderfully detailed station building and graveyard.

Returning back behind *Wonder Mountain* found us in the lower-left quadrant where everything reflected the Grande World Exposition of 1890. Rides, food, and shops were styled and named in international flavor, such as *Ginza Gardens, Moroccan Bazaar, Swing of Siam,* and *Persia.* Now, sitting on the upper-left edge of this land was the *Mighty Canadian Minebuster* roller coaster. If you happened to notice, we skipped an entire quadrant on our journey around the park, seeing only three lands spread around *International Street* and the mountain. Remember that caveat for approval from the town? The bit about emphasizing Canadian culture? Well, it didn't happen. As construction developed and budgets were updated, it became clear something had to go—Canadian Frontier…or the Happy Land of Hanna-Barbera. You can guess which way it went. "You could pick this thing up, lock stock and barrel, and move it to Pretoria and call it South Africa's Wonderland. There is nothing Canadian about it at all."[56] The *Minebuster* was about all there was for thirty-eight years before the park finally added a small section shoehorned between the mountain and the water park.[57]

AUSTRALIA'S WONDERLAND

And there was yet a fourth park in Taft's plans, this time in the land down under. Australia's Wonderland opened in 1985 as a joint venture[58] and, while sharing similar concepts from the Canada park, was nowhere near the scale of its sister. Missing was International Street and a park icon dominating the skyline. Guests entered the turnstiles, looked up the path, and saw *Bounty's Revenge,* a standard swinging pirate ship flat ride. It consisted of three lands, Happy Land of Hanna-Barbera, Medieval Faire, and Gold Rush, with many borrowed attraction concepts from the other Taft parks.[59]

Unlike its siblings that continued to expand and survive to this day, Australia's Wonderland never really connected with the locals[60] and went through ownership changes that eventually led to its demise in 2004. Then-owners Sunbury Group blamed the economy, 9/11 terrorist attacks, the Asian bird flu, and pretty much everything except their own doing.[61] In a pattern that's all-too-familiar to park enthusiasts, the site has been converted into an industrial park. But scattered around the periphery are the rotting remains, still haunting the grounds to ever remind us of what we once had. [62]

KINGS WORLD

Did we say Taft had four parks? Not so fast—there was a fifth property, this one in the works while they were building Kings Dominion and negotiating a (failed) merger with Cedar Point.[63] 800 acres had been optioned at the intersection of Route 47 and the Northwest Tollway, near the town of Huntley in Kane County, just outside Chicago.[64] Kings World[65] was announced in 1973 while Marriott's Great America was getting into gear; both companies recognized significant opportunity in a virtually untapped market.[66] Taft's proposal called for a Kings Island-type park, a 200-room hotel, golf course, campgrounds, trails, and exposition halls.[67] As part of the company's site studies, a height test was run to determine visibility of the iconic 450-ft tall *Eiffel Tower* (it would have been seen from four or five miles away). A twelve foot high earthen berm was planned for the two sides of the park facing Route 47 and the Tollway to contain noise and eliminate visual intrusion. Retention ponds would hold run-off from rains, and water studies determined no negative affects on the area supply. Taft even planned to build their own sewage treatment facility and pay for improvements to the highway intersection leading to the park.[68]

No matter, the plan immediately ran into all sorts of local opposition. In spite of the promise for jobs and positive economic impact on the region, many could only envision the traffic, congestion, noise, skyrocketing land values (and the associated property tax increases) and whatever else came to mind.[69] A local group even banded together as the Rutland Environmental Protection Association and filed a complaint with the Illinois Pollution Control Board against Family Leisure Centers (Taft). Their beef? That the park would deplete and pollute the ground water supply.[70] To be fair, both sides have legitimate issues. Building a major entertainment facility brings with it a slew of good and bad stuff. Did Chicago lose out by sending Yogi back to Cincinnati? No telling, but this scenario would be played out more than once as we shall see.

Gary Wachs could never have dreamed of the far-reaching legacy he'd leave. After all, he was just trying to plot a survival strategy for old Coney. But three out of four parks born from his crazy idea have thrived, survived a few ownership changes along the way, and thrilled millions of guests over nearly half a century.

Arcade
Barney Oldfield Speedway
Souvenirs
Hat Shop
Games Gallery
Sideshow Shirt Shop
Restroom
Sky Whirl
Farmers Market
Yukon-Yahoo
Northwest Shooting Gallery
Blue Ribbon Barbeque
Elm Street School
Lost Parents First Aid
Tot's Livery
Lady Bugs
Red Barron
Tradewinds Import Co.
Puppet Show
Restroom
Matinee Jewelry
Opera House Sweet Shop
Brown's Boarding House
HOME TOWN SQUARE
Grand Music Hall
Restroom
Willard's Whizzer
Hometown Grill
Hat Stoppe

Chapter Seven

MASTERS OF THE FRANCHISE

Perhaps the pinnacle of the Duell design era was revealed to the public when not one, but two nearly identical parks opened in 1976 over 2100 miles apart.[1] The Marriott corporation, known for its worldwide hotel chain, wanted to diversify and get into the booming leisure and park business. Big companies think bigger than everyone else, and so it wasn't *just* the two Great America parks. Marriott intended to develop yet another location between Baltimore and Washington, D.C. This was to be their flagship property, and the announcement on January 26, 1972 promised a $70 million, 850 acre complex that included a theme park, wildlife park, marine life park, hotel, and other entertainment options.[2] The idea was to promote the "mini-vacation," as Marriott put it.[3] As they would soon discover, the real idea was actually finding a way to get it done. As was to be the fate of a similar Disney proposal in the mid-90s, the plan continuously ran afoul of powerful local residents who wanted no part of it. Challenges with local officials over water, sewage, and highway access dogged the project. Land was first purchased near Laurel, MD, then sold as they switched gears for a scaled-down property in Manassas, VA, then back to try again with an even smaller park of 65 acres near the first location at Guilford, MD. It would prove to be quite a ride for the company.

First up was the 850 acre site in Howard County situated near Interstate 95 and Route 32, south of Columbia. Taking the exit from I-95, the old Guilford Methodist Church came into view, resting peacefully on one of those acres as it had for decades. And that's pretty much it other than the tiny graveyard and lots of trees. Two rural communities, Guilford and Savage, had been quietly going about their business for a long time, but that was expected to change dramatically. The marine life park would feature trained whales, dolphins, seals, and the usual assortment of sea creatures in a 2400-seat theater. Visitors could wander around and even underneath massive aquariums to see various sea life up close. The 200 acre animal park took you on safari among hundreds of animals; two amphitheaters would host animal and bird shows. And then there was the theme park, divided into areas representing a place and time from America's past. Concept art depicted a mighty sailing schooner docked in a Cape Cod New England harbor, a classic Midwestern county fair with rides, slides, and games, the *Gold Rusher* runaway mine train coaster in the Klondike, as well as a visit through the old Southwest, New Orleans, and the pre-Civil War South.[4]

Reception to the plans was mixed, to say the least. Citizens on both sides banded together in a clash between the CCC (Concerned County Citizens) and the much more creatively named CHAMPS (Countians Happy About Marriott's Park). It was the usual back and forth—economic growth and jobs versus a changing landscape that would alter their homes and communities forever.[5] A research analyst for the Department of Economic and Community Development wrote a confidential memo blasting Economics Research Associates' feasibility study performed on behalf of Marriott. ERA, of course, was Buzz Price's outfit, which was busily engaged doing this sort of thing for nearly all of the regional parks at the time. But this individual found their study to be far too biased toward the company, not providing sufficient details on how things would impact the community and local government.[6] The state of Virginia, developing its own response to Marriott's proposal, ignored the memo and promised a favorable outcome for the project. Governor Mandel, enthusiastic over the potential growth in the area, also saw no issues that couldn't be overcome.[7]

But as the long months of 1972 wore on circumstances were beginning to shift. Marriott, among a flurry of politicking and PR, had offered to send local officials on a three-day, expenses-paid visit to other parks so they could see for themselves what this business was all about. Not interested. CCC kept up the pressure.[8] Percolating from May onward, in late summer the Howard County planning board finally slammed the door shut in a 13-page report, declaring the project "completely inconsistent" with the county's general plan and a "serious threat" to the county's "physical and environmental amenities."[9]

Moving on, Marriott tried next for a 513 acre site off Interstate 66, near Manassas Battlefield. This time it was for a scaled-back, $35 million theme park that would cover about 80 acres. The thematic concepts were the same, such as the Longboat ride in the Cape Cod region and the *Gold Rusher* mine train. Entertainment offerings would be a multi-media presentation on *Our American Heritage*, a children's cartoon character theater in the round, Dixieland band, barbershop quartet, and Mardi Gras parades. 250 full-time jobs were promised along with 1,500 seasonal positions; the park would be open approximately 140 days each year. Water and sewage questions loomed over the project, as did the request for a new interchange off I-66.[10]

But after five months of effort, Marriott was awarded zoning and site plan approval from the Prince William County Board of Supervisors in April 1973. Nine months later everything changed—the county was rescinding their approval due to a "legal error." Apparently there was a discrepancy with the exact number of days required for public notice of a proposal hearing. The issue? What exactly is meant by "two weeks notice"? It seemed logical at the time to consider this to mean two consecutive, five weekday periods. A recent Virginia attorney general opinion on a different matter defined it as two full seven-day weeks. On such trivia are great matters in life often determined, and this effectively killed Marriott's second attempt in the region. The company would have to start completely over from scratch, and even though the county encouraged them to do so, they decided to look elsewhere.[11]

"Elsewhere" was close to where they tried the first time in Howard County. Although other sites were suggested to the company, they had a pretty good idea of what they needed, and so they screwed up their courage and tried again at the place that showed them the door a few years prior. By now it was late into 1977, five years after the initial announcement.[12] But the third time wasn't the charm as they were soundly rejected by those same officials again on Oct 3 by a zoning board vote of 3 to 1. Stated concerns were "lack of safeguards" for community impact, water issues, traffic congestion, and so on.[13]

January 1978 found them talking with officials in Anne Arundel County,[14] and as late as March 1978 Marriott still held expectations for getting a park built *somewhere* in the region, fielding numerous offers from other municipalities interested in their business. But at some point it just wasn't worth it, especially with potential construction costs now over $100 million.[15] Meantime, throughout all of this drama, sites in Gurnee, IL and Santa Clara, CA had been acquired, planned, opened, and were already in their third season of operation.

GREAT AMERICA

The Santa Clara property had originally been conceived of by Fess Parker, who had turned to real estate development and wanted to build his own park. He, of course, had originally tried in Kentucky, only to have the Taft Corporation out-draw him when they decided to build Kings Island. Frontier World would of course have a western themed area, but also space, history, and interestingly, an area with rides based on farm and industrial machinery. "I always wanted to ride an oil well pump, you know." Randall Duell and his team was helping Fess with ideas, traveling the country showing him various parks they had designed. At one stop, the perhaps overly-enthusiastic owner of Carowinds, thrilled to have such a celebrity visitor, tossed him into the riverboat's waterway. Twice. The patience of Job was evident not only here, but time after time trying to meet with Santa Clara officials to get their approvals. After a potential partnership with McDonald's founder Ray Kroc fizzled, Parker finally had enough and sold the property to Marriott.[16]

By now Randall and his team had over a decade of experience, with some members of the company going back as far as the C.V. Wood projects in the late 50s. They had worked through lots of refinements for park layout, people movement, attractions, services, and operations, and all of this would be realized in the Marriott masterpieces. The complex puzzle of determining park scale, pathway routing and size, quantity and design of necessary services such as food and restrooms, and thousands of other details took a great deal of trial and error back then. Today's park designers benefit greatly from their work as much of this information is found in tables and other resources. How many restrooms do you need? How long should the queue be for a major coaster? Or a kiddie flat ride? How do you plan for expansion? How many shows and attractions are necessary? None of this is based solely on preference; it's a careful balance of budget and satisfied guests. Too little to do and lines get long, people get bored, they're not spending money, and they don't come back. Too much and you've probably blown the budget and might never recoup the expense. Although the Marriott projects were not low-budget affairs, there were certainly financial constraints the designers were obligated to meet. Herb Ryman, legendary artist for film and Disney parks, once advised a young Imagineer working on EuroDisneyland: "Eddie, bad taste costs no more."[17] His main point, a bit tongue-in-cheek when referring to mediocre work, was that instead of just designing a nice structure, make sure it's got historical authenticity, which doesn't cost anything but a little time at the library. We can also take away the notion that quality comes from an experienced artist who knows how to put together a good idea.[18] Duell's designers were at the top of their game in the early-mid 70s, and so they brought a quality standard many other companies simply couldn't match.

Both Great America parks would follow almost exactly the same design; it's quite surreal comparing side by side aerial photos from opening year. Due to higher attendance projections, the Gurnee park was slightly larger with a few more small rides,[19] and the front entrance plaza had more room before transitioning into the parking lot. The Duell loop weaved in and out of the various themed areas, featuring nooks and crannies that provided a sense of exploration. Unnoticed by guests was a masterpiece of a solution for park services and maintenance. Over time Duell's designers learned that large bodies of water, while beautiful, should not be placed in the park's center. The most effective and efficient way to service a park's restaurants, utilities, and other facilities was directly in the center, behind everything that faced outward toward the loop. Great America featured a service corridor right down the middle, a spine that supported the functions of the park. This eliminated the need to cart supplies, food, and trash along guest pathways. If a utility problem arose it could be dealt with immediately, out of sight, without having to close off a public area and dig up the pavement or lake.[20] Water features were prominent, including numerous streams and ponds beautifully integrated with rides and walkways, but located out of the way of these essential support operations. With larger acreage to work with, each themed area was a fully-developed mini-park and not just a couple of buildings as was the case with some of the early Duell parks. Architecture, signage, entertainment, and even the food was representative of each theme and was elaborately executed. The park clearly had the stamp of a Marriott property in terms of quality, beauty, and emphasis on customer service. And of course building two nearly identical parks followed the company's long history and expertise in perfecting and franchising a brand experience.

The most fondly remembered detail of Great America is the *Columbia Carousel*. The entrance to the park is exquisitely grand and elegant; resplendent at the far end of a glistening reflecting pool, the double-decker carousel serves to this day as the park icon. As a visual wienie, it calls you to come explore the grandness of the park. But this is no typical, garden-variety merry-go-round. The ornate structure is 100 feet tall (the California version is actually 101 feet and the tallest in the world). The carousel's designer at Duell & Associates, John DeCuir, had actually come up with a three-decker ("But three levels are better than two!") only to be talked down a bit by Randall simply because it would cost too much (the final version still cost over a million dollars).[21] No loss, because this is truly one of the more magnificent pieces to be found at a regional park. A good thing they changed their minds from the original idea—a 300 foot tall Ferris wheel. Sure wouldn't have been the same.

As at Carowinds, a trolley wound its way through Carousel Plaza, with turnaround loops at Orleans Place and Home Town Square. The overall theme of the park was a celebration of America; this seemed especially appropriate for a park opening in 1976, so each area was dedicated to a different region of the United States. Walking past the right side of the *Columbia,* we would pass underneath the railroad bridge, the station prominently positioned up to our left behind the carousel. This was Home Town Square, taking you back to small town America and featuring a central green park and gazebo surrounded by the trolley tracks. Facing the square from each side was the train station, *Engine Company #1* ice cream shop, and the *Hot Shoppe*—a tribute to the original root beer shop where J. Willard Marriott and his wife Alice first got started in business. Enjoy one of the park's premiere shows in the *Grand Music Hall* before getting in the queue for *Willard's Whizzer,* a Schwarzkopf Speed Racer coaster, featuring a unique spiral lift hill (yes, it was a family name—the privilege of building your own park). Ride first, then eat, so next get a down-home chicken dinner at *Maggie Brown's Boarding House.* Just up the pathway, a children's section with pint-sized rides was in a cutout to the left before crossing over the bridge and into Midwest County Fair.

Ferris wheels are a signature feature of all fairs and carnivals, and Great America upped the ante with *Sky Whirl,* a gigantic custom-designed Triple Tree Wheel sold by Intamin. Though there were a few carnival games, few parks had extensive game midways such as would be added over time. It's as though parks shunned such activities in the effort to get away from the negative carny stereotype that plagued Walt Disney during his planning. Over time it becomes more of a vintage thing, an historical throwback that gives it a fresh, wholesome attribute. A *Farmer's Market* food court and bandstand, the *Big Top* circus shows, and a small merry-go-round contributed to the fair atmosphere. The main attractions were the *Turn of the Century*, a state-of-the-art Arrow corkscrew coaster, and the *Barney Oldfield Speedway*, featuring custom Arrow 1920s race cars traveling on no less than three tracks. The *Eagle's Flight* sky ride station provided an aerial view of the park, touching down below Orleans Place, and *Fairgrounds Junction* serviced the railroad, making its second stop at Home Town Square.

Working our way back around the other side of the loop, we'd cross over the covered bridge that cleverly hid the central service corridor roadway and into Yukon Territory. (An interesting side note regarding the thousands of details involved in park planning—it was discovered too late that the bridge wasn't positioned high enough to accommodate an ambulance driving along the service road underneath, making it impossible to reach anywhere in the park without traveling on the main guest pathway. There's always something that slips by.)[22] The great logging traditions of that rugged northwest region of Canada were represented here with pole climbing, totem pole carving, and log rolling in the lake. Although Canada is most assuredly not part of the United States, presumably the idea was to showcase life in the upper-west regions that shared similar characteristics. Dolphin shows were all the rage in the 70s, and the capacious *Wilderness Theater* was located just around the corner from the bridge. Arrow Development had scored big with their water flume rides, and Marriott again went all-out with a custom dual-flume configuration. *Logger's Run* was the side stationed in Yukon Territory, where guests boarded log-shaped boats.

Crossing yet another bridge over a stream, Yankee Harbor was evident from the lighthouse, New England architecture, nautical theming, and lots of water. The other flume station, *Yankee Clipper,* featured clipper-style boats instead of logs. After enjoying a parade by the authentically-garbed Continental Militia, grab a bite at *Capt. Morgan's* or *Dockside Sandwiches,* pick up a unique souvenir at the *Nautical Shop,* or watch a glassblower at work in the *Glass Schooner.*

Orleans Place, celebrating New Orleans and the deep South, featured a small park and gazebo similar to Home Town Square, with the other end of the trolley tracks looping around it. Architecture, including its signature wrought-iron filigree, distinguished this area along with cute French names such as *Maison le Crystal, Lafitte's Treasures, Chapeau Chateau, Rue le Dodge,* and *Alle Mistique Magic.* The *Delta Flyer* sky ride station provided transportation back to the County Fair area.[23]

Overall, the Great America parks were a showcase of design and presentation. Years of experience were reflected in the layout, theming, operations, services, and detail. Marriott wanted to build a first-rate park, and while not being extravagant and trying to match a Disney level of sophistication, the attention to quality was evident. They were of the last built-to-purpose parks from the golden age of the regionals that started with Texas. Unfortunately for the Marriott company, attendance figures didn't meet their expectations and the parks became a burden on the company's bottom line. They also remembered they were in the hotel business, so they decided to concentrate on that.[24] Both parks would be sold off in 1984, the Gurnee property to Six Flags,[25] the Santa Clara park to the city itself.[26] Six Flags Great America would go on to several changes in ownership and management with a few ups and downs, but overall would come out performing quite well.

The California site has an interesting saga after the Marriott sale. A local developer wanted to bulldoze everything and build an office complex.[27] The city wanted to preserve the park, first of all because it's generally a good thing for the social fabric of the area, but secondly because it provides thousands of jobs, particularly for young people, and stimulates economic activity. The city won the bid,[28] a few years later selling the park itself, minus the land, to Kings Entertainment, which operated several other parks including Kings Island, Kings Dominion, and Carowinds.[29] Paramount bought the entire chain in 1992 before eventually selling to Cedar Fair in 2006.[30] The property is landlocked and has had to make aggressive changes in order to add new attractions. In 2011 the park was slated to be sold, again, to the owners of the 49ers football team.[31] Cedar Fair was looking to reduce their corporate debt and had been sparring with the team for several years over a proposed stadium to be built right next door. In the end Cedar Fair kept the park, made an arrangement with the 49ers to solve the parking issues,[32] and has focused attention on developing the property. Unlike the tragic endings of Opryland and Astroworld, Great America has gritted its teeth and survived to go on making memories for new generations.

In the end, Marriott got the last word in Virginia. Late in 1978, as the company was shaking the dust off their boots after the long ordeal, a regional Howard County historical group asked to borrow a "Tom Thumb" replica steam engine that was on display at the Gurnee park. The original locomotive was locally famous for an 1830 race against a horse-driven stagecoach between Baltimore and the Ellicott City terminal. The replica had recently been on-site at the local railroad museum as promotion for the planned park. The response?

> "Unfortunately, the people of Howard County expressed their belief, through their elected officials, that Great America would be an unsatisfactory neighbor—on not one, but two occasions. I hope you can understand, then, our reluctance to share the fruits of our labor by way of providing our Tom Thumb replica. It was to have operated daily, carrying people, had we been able to build our park in the county."[33]

24.
26.
11.
13.
12.
7.
6.
5.
4.
10.
9.
8.
1.
17.
3.
2.

Chapter Eight

ADOLPHUS PLANTS A GARDEN

In 1903 Adolphus Busch, the millionaire co-founder of Anheuser-Busch, bought a sizable plot of land along South Orange Grove Avenue in Pasadena and built a magnificent mansion. Landscape architect and horticulturalist Robert Fraser was hired to craft a lush, beautiful garden setting with terraces, lagoons, arbors, glens and glades. Extensive underground plumbing was installed for irrigation, fed by a new water pumping station. It was an oasis for Mr. Busch and his wife, Lilly, during their annual visits from St. Louis;[1] it also quickly became a hot spot for curious visitors, occupying one of his gardeners nearly full-time just keeping folks off the grounds. In 1909 Adolphus approached the city with a proposition—they pay for a policeman to keep an eye on things, and the family would open the gardens with no charge to the public a few days each week.[2] The "Busch Gardens" formally opened in 1912, quickly becoming a major tourist attraction in Southern California and pulling in a staggering 1.5 million guests in 1915.[3]

By 1919 Adolphus had been dead for six years, and on June 19 Lilly finally pulled the plug, closing the gardens in an attempt to move on. Annual costs for maintaining the sixty acres was a hefty $40,000, and with prohibition in force the family business was going to have a rough time of it.[4] But the following year she decided to put the gardens to good use, turning them over to the Pasadena Hospital Association. The new 25 cent entrance fee was donated for a hospital building campaign.[5] Then in 1921 management was transferred to the Busch Gardens Fund for Disabled and Needy Veterans; the Busch estate covered all operations and upkeep, all gate proceeds were donated directly to the charity. This lasted until 1928 when the gates were again locked, only to be reopened in 1933 by a local organization who wanted to use the gardens for hosting civic events.[6] Two years later they began working with the American Legion, again as a benefit for veterans, even entering a float from time to time in the Rose Parade branded as the Pasadena Busch Gardens.[7]

The famous Busch Gardens were closed for the final time in 1938, to be subdivided for residential development. But even though old Adolphus' beautiful oasis is long gone, you can still discover a few remaining pieces here and there while taking a stroll along Busch Garden Court, Busch Garden Drive, and Busch Place.[8]

BUSCH GARDENS TAMPA

With the end of prohibition the Busch empire continued to expand and prosper, building new breweries around the country. In 1957 the company announced plans for a new $20-25 million facility in Tampa.[9] But this would not be merely another bland industrial site. Busch wanted to try something different, as August Busch Jr. shared during the plant's dedication in 1959: "The company wanted to do more than build just another plant...it should contribute its attractiveness and add to the beauty of the community."[10] Recalling his experiences as a young child at his grandfather's gardens in Pasadena, he instructed the project's landscape architect to do something similar.[11] About seventeen acres would be dedicated to a hospitality center and surrounding gardens, featuring subtropical landscaping and exotic birds, with another 117 acres set aside as a retirement farm for the company's famous Clydesdale horses.[12]

The new Busch Gardens and brewery were dedicated March 31[13] and opened to the public in June. There was no admission fee, the idea being the gardens would promote the company and their product in a favorable light. Free samples and a tour of the brewery proved an effective marketing tool, and the beautiful gardens attracted visitors by the thousands. One month later operational hours were expanded to handle the crowds, and the local city planning engineer was busy figuring how to deal with parking issues that left guests abandoning their vehicles along residential streets in the area.[14] Within ten months 800,000 visitors had come to see what the fuss was all about,[15] many following the map published by the Tampa Bay Times in response to readers asking how to find the place.[16]

The focal point in the gardens was the *Hospitality House,* a unique heptagonal-shaped structure with a "floating roof" and cantilevered balcony overlooking one of the lagoons.[17] Guests enjoyed refreshments while listening to music in "stereophonic sound" provided by Altec speakers.[18] Three interconnected man-made waterways were surrounded by meandering footpaths bordered by thousands of tropical trees, plants, and flowers. *Devil's Island* served as home to "incorrigible" birds with clipped wings, and exotic bird shows were performed several times daily in a sunken theater. *Dwarf Village* was similar in concept to Disneyland's *Storybook Land* with miniature hand-carved figurines from Europe; five fairytale scenes were depicted with Snow White, Red Riding Hood, Hansel & Gretel, and so on in a forest setting. The *Stairway to the Stars,* an outdoor eighty-six foot escalator and one of the world's longest at the time,[19] led to an upper floor of the brewery for the tour.[20]

BUSCH GARDENS LOS ANGELES

Busch seemed to have hit upon a magic formula. The Tampa property saw continual expansion over the years, including a bird aviary in 1960 and the Serengeti Plain in 1965, a vast 70-acre free-roaming animal preserve.[21] Their experiment an unqualified success, the company decided to try the same approach at their brewery in Van Nuys, California. Adapting the design concept from Tampa, 17.5

acres[22] from a former cabbage patch[23] was converted by Bill Morgan[24]—Disneyland's landscape designer—into another beautiful oasis of gardens, full of subtropical flora and fauna, a wide variety of exotic birds, and of course the free tour of the brewery.

Opening May 26, 1966 at a cost of around $4 million,[25] Busch Gardens Los Angeles was similar to the Tampa property with free admission, immersive pathways, a bird show, and colorful birds flying everywhere. But for 50 cents you could board a 34' fiberglass canopied boat[26] and enjoy a 20-minute cruise through the wonderland. The electrically powered craft rode a submerged rail that wound through three areas. First was *Palm Island,* a cluster of islands with palms, subtropical foliage, exotic birds, and lots of flowers. After proceeding underneath a couple of overhead foot bridges, the waterway turned and passed by *Michelob Terrace,* an open platform for guests to relax and sample the company's products while gazing at the rich scenery (and passing boaters). Next was the *Central Lagoon,* an open expanse of water with waterfowl and *Flamingo Island*; on one shoreline stood the *Budweiser Pavilion,* facing it across the lagoon was the 450-seat bird show amphitheater. Continuing onward the path started to get twisty; you could hear the thundering waterfalls and look up at the towering crags of the *Gorge*. This mountainous region was fashioned from tons of volcanic foam rock extracted from a local lake, being much lighter and easier to work with than regular rock.[27]

Arrow Development, the can-do upstart manufacturer of coasters and other amusement rides, produced the *Skyrail,* a suspended monorail that provided an elevated tour of the brewery facilities. Which, after all, was the main purpose of the exercise. These were promotional facilities, offered at no charge to the public and intended to push the brand. Over time, however, the need for expansion at both the California and Florida properties and the resulting increases in operating costs forced the company to reconsider the business plan. In June 1970 Busch announced their intention to convert these hospitality centers into entertainment business ventures, essentially gated theme parks. Tampa, flourishing with 2.5 million guests in 1969, would again be the prototype with a $12.6 million expansion and a new entrance fee of $2 in 1971.[28] The Van Nuys park added amusement rides along with an adult ticket price of $2.75 for the 1972 season.[29] The beer, as always, would remain free.

Meantime the company was planning two additional locations in Houston and Williamsburg, VA. The formula would be roughly the same, with a gardens park area adjacent to the brewery. But these would be pay-at-the-gate attractions from the get-go, with the property in Texas being the first up.

BUSCH GARDENS HOUSTON

Busch Gardens Houston was announced in 1969 and opened May 1971.[30] Twenty-seven acres[31] next to the brewery had been transformed by R. Duell & Associates into an $11 million park.[32] The theme here was Asia, where the "Far East meets West," nicely implemented in the architecture, landscaping, and selection of animals.[33]

Towering over the park was the ornate *Pagoda of Chin-wa-shwe*; climb the stairs to a higher level for a panoramic view of the park. Head over to *Hospitality House* to sample the company's products while your kids run ahead to the children's area. There were few rides for kids (or for anyone, for that matter), but there was a *Tree House* that looked like it was from *Bridge on the River Kwai*, with two slides, one a bit smaller for younger children, along with a (short) swinging bridge. A tiny, unique Ferris wheel, built from thick wood-like beams and iron brackets, fit the theme quite well.

Circling this section of the park was the small scale *Orient Express*, chugging by *Hidden Harbor*, *Sherpa Slide*, and *Rhino Land*. The locomotive, designed to mimic 19th century steam trains used by the British in Asia, pulled beautifully detailed passenger cars featuring ornate iron work. The cheerful steam and whistle sounds could be heard throughout the park.

Houston was a bit more of a zoo than a garden, and so the animal enclosures were designed to reflect their native, natural surroundings as much as possible. The Bengals hung out in ancient Indian *Temple of the Tiger* ruins while the *Ice Cave* was home to polar bears, penguins, and sea lions. And there was lots more, with *Orangutan Island, Elephant Compound, Macaque* (monkey) *Island, Camel Compound, Onager and Yak Compound, Flamingo Island, Bear and Tiger Cub Area,* and *Deer Park.* A petting zoo got you up close and personal with a variety of fun creatures such as goats, lambs, and llamas, and the company's trademark horses relaxed in the *Clydesdale Stables.*

All of this could be seen either from the footpaths that meandered around the property or by boat. These water-powered craft floated through the *Ceylon Channel,* cruising past the various animal islands and structures, through the *Ice Cave* and the bird aviary, and stopping along the way at the petting zoo. Don't miss the bird show in the amphitheater, complete with oriental stage design, then pick up an Asian rice hat before heading over to the brewery for the tour.[34]

The Duell touch was prominent in the beautiful architecture and thematic touches, and everything was nicely integrated. The architecture was certainly, for the most part, more thematically interesting and detailed than in the other Busch parks up to that point. Company officials had reason to be optimistic, basking in the success of their properties in California and Tampa. And so the gates swung open, ready for whatever was to come.

What that was, however, was unexpected. Although the Tampa park was an unqualified success as a gated attraction, the other two properties were already in trouble. Houston, opening from the get-go with an entrance fee of $2.25 for adults, never came close to expected attendance of 800,000 for 1971. The following year was no better in spite of their efforts, and so during the 4th financial quarter of 1972 they announced the park would become a promotional facility, like what Los Angeles had started out. Busch admitted the park was never profitable, and with the significant costs of maintaining the animals it was too much to bear. After only two seasons the gardens in Houston closed for good, incurring a $5 million accounting charge to do the conversion.[35]

Meanwhile, over at Los Angeles things were also beginning to unravel. The conversion to a gated park in 1972 included a $6 million, five acre expansion across the railroad tracks,[36] then in 1975 a second major upgrade saw an *Old St. Louis* section and an elevated monorail that toured the park (the original concept art for the monorail was spectacular, designed to mimic an ornate turn-of-the-century streetcar...the *Sky Trolley* that arrived on property didn't come close).[37] For a short while the future looked bright enough, but the changeover to a gated park began to stifle attendance. Operating costs were fairly high with the rides, labor, and insurance, and the company never recouped their investment. So in 1977, after losing another $5 million the previous year, Busch gave up on the amusement side of things and converted the park back to a free-of-charge gardens promotional facility. This moved expenses over to the corporate advertising budget, allowing the entertainment division to flourish in Tampa and the new park in Virginia. With a reduced staff of 17, down from 45, the new Busch Bird Sanctuary focused on its famous gardens and tropical birds, becoming an officially sanctioned nature preserve.[38] And of course the free beer flowed as always.[39]

What went wrong with both of these properties, especially considering how well the Tampa park was doing? Were the gardens beautiful? Oh yes. Busch spent millions creating paradise in the middle of industrial zones. Were they serious amusement parks? Hardly, not with the likes of Disneyland, Knott's, Magic Mountain, and Astroworld close by. Both locations were seriously site-constrained with no more room to grow. Over time the allure of a simple boat ride and monorail tour of the brewery just couldn't compete. There were hardly any thrill rides in Van Nuys, none at all in Houston, and presumably families considered the ticket prices too expensive with not enough to do. Attractions must continually evolve in order to generate repeat business, something the Tampa location was able to do with ample land and a better connection with guests for whatever reasons. At any rate, not enough people showed up, and that was that.

BUSCH GARDENS WILLIAMSBURG

Once upon a time Williamsburg, Virginia was a sleepy little place. It had been that way since 1780 when then-governor Thomas Jefferson packed up the state government and hauled it away to Richmond. Things became so laid back the locals even forgot to hold an election.[40] Then came the Colonial Williamsburg restoration project, which stepped things up quite a bit and put their little town back on the map. Things would change yet again when Anheuser-Busch formally announced on September 17, 1969 that the company had acquired nearly 4000 acres in James City County for a state-of-the-art brewery, large-scale residential planned community, and a "Busch Gardens type" recreational attraction. No further details were provided at the time.[41]

Interestingly, most of the land was purchased from the Colonial Williamsburg Foundation, which saw Busch as a good neighbor and just the ticket for "clean industry" development of the region. Carlisle Humelsine, president of the Foundation, made great efforts to explain to the community why they were so supportive of the venture. Along with a much-needed increased tax base for public services, Busch would bring an orderly, harmonious development by working closely with the Foundation, as opposed to a piecemeal, helter-skelter encroachment of the beautiful landscape over time. The sales agreement required Busch to coordinate design plans with the Foundation, instituting a three-person review board comprised of nationally recognized experts, and in fact an early example of this involved the proposed brewery facility. Paying homage to the local heritage, Busch's architects had imagined colonial-style structures with appropriate brickwork motifs. But the Foundation said no, being opposed to any "pseudo-colonial style in commercial buildings." Busch also agreed to allow scenic easements along the James River and for a planned stretch of "country road" through their property that would eventually connect Colonial Williamsburg with Carter's Grove, a working 18th century plantation made financially possible from the sale of land to Busch.[42]

One plot of land Busch needed in order to organize everything into a neat, contiguous package was not controlled by Colonial Williamsburg, but by the Federal government. Camp Wallace was an army facility located in the southern region of the planned sites for the park and residential areas. It just so happened that Busch, previously looking at property in Newport News before deciding on Williamsburg, had optioned 193 acres adjoining Fort Eustis. So they offered the Feds a good deal—we'll take Camp Wallace and you can have our chunk of land directly adjoining your facility. The swap served everybody's interests and all parties walked away happy.[43]

In January 1970 Busch announced that the gardens component of the overall project would open in 1973. The brewery was already under construction, and no specific theme for the recreational area was mentioned. "It is quite likely" said Richard J. Bender, vice president for corporate affairs, "the gardens will be animal-oriented. Our strong point is how to display and handle animals."[44] Later in June the project planners met with local officials just to introduce themselves and get to know everybody they'd be working with over the next several years.[45]

By 1972 it was clear that the opening date wouldn't happen until 1975. A year's delay seems to have come from a change in master planners for the entire property, with the company rejecting the first consultant and hiring Sasaki, Dawson, and Demay Associates of Watertown, MA.[46] The pause also came from Busch taking a hard, second look after the debacle of their Houston Gardens, which had just closed in the middle of all this after only two seasons.[47] But so far the Los Angeles property hadn't yet tanked, and Tampa was off the charts, falling only to Walt Disney World in 1971 as the state's most popular tourist attraction.

Pushing forward, the company announced in January 1973 that they indeed planned to "open a Busch Garden adjoining its Williamsburg brewery." Though there was as yet no description or name for the recreation area, they promised it would not be a colonial theme so as not to conflict with Colonial Williamsburg.[48] April brought the news that construction on the gardens would begin immediately with a $30 million budget.[49] But still no theme or name; local sources rumored that the project would feature several foreign villages representing countries where most American immigrants hailed from. And it seemed pretty clear that animals of some type would be involved, possibly North American to match the theme of the Asian, African, and tropical settings of the other Busch parks. At some point in 1973 a physical model of the plans was built in St. Louis, but that wasn't made available to the public.[50]

An interesting historical aside to all of this involved Busch funding an archaeological team to investigate 17th and 18th century plantation sites at the Kingsmill residential area. Working over on park property, a college student discovered a brass and steel saber made for grenadiers in the French Army in 1767. Most likely it was lost during the Revolutionary War, but it could have been from a Confederate soldier in 1863, since that army often suffered from a lack of modern arms. The region, of course, has seen numerous battles from multiple wars, so there are undoubtedly countless treasures and remembrances yet to be unearthed.[51]

Finally in May came the details everyone was looking for. For $5 guests would be able to visit villages from England, France, and Germany. The overall theme would be "America's pre-colonial heritage," and in order to complement Colonial Williamsburg, architecture and details would be styled to represent each country from around the 16th century. Promised attractions included a river cruise, an English castle with drawbridge, a French Canadian trapper's village, toyland, fairytale land, an outdoor theater for the now-standard exotic bird shows, and a field for the Clydesdales. A monorail would whisk guests over for a tour of the brewery. Also planned in addition to the Kingsmill residential area were several hotels, including an immediate joint project with Marriott, and a campground. Clearly park developers understood the concept of a resort destination by this time.[52]

Also evident was the idea that this "garden" would not be merely a hospitality center. The Virginia property was planned as a major theme park from the beginning. But what that was to be exactly was unclear to the company early on, as can be seen by examining an evolving string of logos for the upcoming park. First was the standard Anheuser-Busch Eagle prominently perched over "Busch Gardens" with Williamsburg, Tampa, and Los Angeles underneath (Houston was apparently dead at this point). This connected the new project with the company's brand and entertainment lineup. Further thinking, however, led to the idea that maybe this park, being much bigger and most likely quite different from the others, deserved its own identity. So the other location names were dropped and a different font style was adopted. As a medieval theme began to emerge, the "Friendly Eagle" didn't quite say the right thing, so out that went. At this point the formal name was "Busch Gardens at Williamsburg: The Old Country." Park plans continued to distance the project from the other Busch properties, so gradually emphasis was placed on the theme of the park. The name was flipped to "The Old Country" in a large, modern typeface with "Busch Gardens, Williamsburg, VA" in much smaller print below. Bill Francisco, marketing manager at the time, pointed out there was no medieval "e" in "Old," a deliberate decision to indicate the park was a modern interpretation of old Europe.[53]

As with any major development there were hiccups along the way. Busch sent a request to the state legislature to revise regulations allowing them to sell Busch-branded merchandise in the shops. But then Virginia beer wholesalers got their barrels in a twist over the idea of being thrown into the "novelties" business. They lost, for whatever difference it made in the end, and you could happily buy a Bud shirt or Michelob something-or-other in the park.[54]

James City supervisors attempted a cash grab by threatening a 1% admissions tax on park tickets. An avalanche of corporate lobbying and personal letters from August Busch himself squelched that.[55]

The very month of opening—May 1975—local officials were preparing their review in order to issue a certificate of occupancy for the new park. They discovered that Busch had not filed numerous building permits for various structures and rides. It caught everyone by surprise, with Busch's marketing manager Bill Francisco exclaiming it to be something "we flat overlooked!" Some of this was certainly due to the urgency and chaos of building a major park like this, but the company also said they weren't aware permits were required for certain items such as large rides, railroad bridges, and small buildings. Everyone agreed it was simply a matter of having so many people involved with changing lines of communication during the course of construction, but the county stood their ground. File the paperwork or you won't open. And then you'll have to tear that stuff down. Busch filed. Quickly.[56]

Opening day was delayed due to weather interfering with construction, so they missed the original April 15 deadline.[57] A preview for employees' and construction workers' families was held Sunday, May 4, just to work out the kinks and get things in gear. Saturday, May 10 was the big day, and the Busch Friendly Eagle welcomed the official first family through the gate. John and Betty Rose from Bel Air, MD and their two children received passports to the park. But before they could run on to see what was in store, one of the kids took a few moments to outdance the demonstrative Friendly Eagle. You can't buy better promotional material.[58]

The big marketing push leading up to opening day was that you could visit Europe for only $6.50. Few Americans had been there, and the idea was that this was just about as good as the real thing. "Introducing Europe. On this side of the Atlantic."[59] Park your car in the French, German, or Hastings lots, then hop on an English double-decker bus for the brief trip to the ticket booths to begin the journey across Europe. Once through, the pathway led up the hill, through the entrance turnstiles, and into Banbury Cross. Here...

> "It's as if time had stood still. You see cobbled streets. Old-world shops. Castle courtyards. There's even a replica of Shakespeare's famous Globe Theatre. The year is 1603. London. And you are there."[60]

The as-close-as-we-wanna-get reproduction of the real *Globe* housed one of the three major live shows in the park. Next door was an actual branch of the United Virginia Bank of Williamsburg, just in case you forgot to stock up on cash before leaving home.[61] Brave the "brooding moors" and make your way to Heatherdowns, Scottish home of the Clydesdales. Visit their stables and take photos while they relaxed in the pasture. Then hop on board the standard-gauge Prussian or English-styled steam train at *Tweedside Station* for a trip around the park with beautiful trestles and views of the wildlife. If you completed the round trip without disembarking at New France, hop off and head across the bridge toward Hastings, passing through the castle gate and...

> "into the land of parapets, canopies and bright flags flying in the breezes. This is the scene for knights of old, princesses in flowing gowns, tournaments and kings' rewards. Styled after late Medieval Scotland, Hastings is the mood that legends are made of."[62]

This was the "land of fast-paced adventure" with carnival games, a fun house, and *The Catapult*, an indoor scrambler ride with unexpected run-ins with knights of old. *The Reynolds Aluminum Theatre* presented the Sid and Marty Crofft show *Camelot Revue*. Hastings was where you could catch the *Eagle One*, an ultramodern, completely automated monorail from Westinghouse that cruised silently over to the brewery for a tour and free samples.[63]

Continuing counter-clockwise we reach Aquitaine, where "You'll feel like an American in Paris. At the turn of the century." The open-air market of street vendors, sidewalk artists, and cafes set the mood before strolling over to enjoy the famous *Anheuser-Busch Bird Circus* at the *La Jolie Plume* outdoor amphitheater. Afterwards get away from all the hustle and bustle with a relaxing car ride through the French forest in a not-so-fast replica *Le Mans* antique race car.

Up the path and into the woods, we've crossed the Atlantic and find ourselves in New France. Everything was frontier here, with a trapper's outpost, bluegrass music, and pioneer artisans at work on various crafts. The park's premiere thrill ride, which wasn't quite ready for opening day, was an Arrow-designed water flume. *Le Scoot* was an original for sure, with a spectacular drop after nearly getting sliced to bits by a seven foot buzz saw. After drying off, head over to the park's final section:

> "Welcome to a simpler, lustier era: Germany of the 19th century. The hub of the hamlet is the *Willkommenhaus*. Stop in and enjoy gemütlichkeit while oompah bands and folk dancers entertain... There's a thrilling German steel roller coaster. And a fleet of river-boats to carry you across a 60-acre waterway...And it's all nestled in a centuries-old forest where more than 500 head of wildlife roam free. Come soon. Everyone should visit a once-upon-a-time place. At least once."[64]

The park's designers, PGAV, took full advantage of the 300-acre natural landscape, full of ravines, hills, and beautiful trees, plants, and flowers. And of course there was plenty of wildlife, some cleverly contained within fenced habitats, others just local creatures making their way in life. The guest brochure emphasized this, pointing out the various types of trees, animals, and so on to be discovered while also entreating guests to help preserve the environment and keep it clean.[65]

The varied elevations and dense forests provided a natural, free way to apply Disney's practice of avoiding visual intrusion between lands. The idea is to not see anything from another section in the park, which would destroy the illusion of where you're supposed to be at the moment. Busch was selling the idea that you were visiting countries in Europe at a different point in time, and the park's layout made this possible in a way few others could take advantage of. There was no way a regional park could have accomplished the same immersive feeling if built in an industrial center...such as, say, downtown next to a Los Angeles brewery.

The geography brought its challenges, of course. It's much easier to build a park on a flat lot, and helping guests get around takes on a higher urgency. Attractions such as the train and sky ride gondolas were not only fun rides, but essential modes of transportation to ensure visitors had an enjoyable experience.

Another highlight of this park was the crafting of period-authentic items by skilled artisans. Sure, you could buy the standard cheap stuff, but there was a richness and added kinetic energy with such live demonstrations immersed among authentically-detailed architecture and settings. Buildings were trimmed with rough stone, wood, brick, and even small touches like ceramic chimney tops. No plywood cutouts and drywall here. They acknowledged that many guests wouldn't even notice, but the belief was that it made a difference and contributed to the park being "a very special place."[66] August Busch himself spent time walking around the park taking notes of things he wanted to see, insisting on making things better and with quality. He "got it"—just like Walt.[67] It does indeed make a difference when you go the extra mile. Or dollar.[68]

Whether they "got it" or not, people came in droves and packed the park that first season.[69] By fall Busch already had plans for Oktoberfest, their Germany expansion for 1976.[70] Italy would come four years later. Like the runaway success of Kings Dominion, opening just the week before, Busch Gardens seemed to validate the theory that even during financial recessions people want entertainment and viewed the parks as a reasonably priced option for their families. Buzz Price from Economics Research Associates backs this concept up—with lots of data, of course.[71]

The Virginia project was a significant departure from previous Busch properties due to its conception as a resort destination with a planned series of hotels and campground. This idea wasn't new, having been pioneered by Disney in Florida and several of the regionals such as Astroworld, Opryland, and Kings Island. But for the first time Busch had plenty of land to play with, just like what Walt had dreamed with his Florida Project. The park would not be butted up against the brewery; that facility was out of sight down the road. The park was set off from the outside world, buried in the trees and countryside. And a majority of the development was the upper-scale Kingsmill residential community, beautifully situated away from all of this (mostly). Such a large, comprehensive design from the get-go is extremely rare and expensive, and it was a bold investment decision by the company.

Of course there were naysayers. As we have seen, there are always pros and cons to such a large-scale intrusion into people's neighborhoods and cities. A couple local residents, outraged at the notion of a beer manufacturer running such a place, called for a boycott that first year because of the rowdy, drunken atmosphere Busch was bringing to the area. Others fired back, pointing out the family-friendly atmosphere of the park and how wonderful the place was. The question was posed: "Mr. Moore, have you actually visited Busch Gardens or met Mr. Busch?" Of course not.[72]

And then there was the self-appointed culturally elite, such as the good Edwin Wilson in "These Groans are from Shakespeare":

> "...I'm afraid if we opened Shakespeare's grave this summer we would find not just that he had turned over, but that he was spinning wildly, a conclusion based on seeing an entertainment at the new Busch Garden amusement park...The Busch version (*of the Globe Theatre*),

> which The Old Country brochure calls an 'authentic replica of Bard's famous Globe Theater' is twice too big and seats fewer people; it has a roof, no seats on the side tiers, and movie seats where people used to stand. The distortions of the building are nothing, however, compared to the show itself: a 30 minute fable about a group of actors who cannot put on Romeo and Juliet because the actress playing Juliet is ill...Shakespeare himself would have difficulty plumbing the paradoxes of this production...Perhaps the saddest commentary of all is that we have been so bombarded with amplified sound and become so accustomed to the mechanical reproduction of the human voice that many in the audience may not realize that the actors on stage are not speaking their own words (*apparently the show was all lip-synced*)."[73]

Mr. Wilson's worry was that too many people who have not actually seen Shakespeare will be damaged for life by believing this is it. There's no telling whether this gentleman ever returned to the park to try again, but odds are slim.

The same thing was happening up the road at Kings Dominion, as so eloquently put by one of the long-time locals who lived half a mile from the park:

> "This used to be a pleasant, provincial sort of county," said Katherine Myers, whose home in Hanover was built in 1703. "All of a sudden—ta-dah—we're catapulted into the 20th century. This is the place where (*Kentucky Derby winners*) Riva Ridge and Secretariat were foaled. They're sort of local heroes to us. We all felt that sort of thing was a whole lot neater than living near an amusement park...It's like modern day carpetbagging. They figure, 'those suckers, they need the money.' It's what they did to the South 100 years ago and it's no more attractive now than it was then."[74]

Apparently Ms. Myers just couldn't stand the loud elephants, the "fat ladies" screaming on the roller coaster, and of course that "herd of buffalo"...tourists staring down at her from the *Eiffel Tower*. Bruce English of the Hanover County Citizens' Federation agreed. What he saw was a "hasty, ill-conceived adventure in development that has raised taxes, thrown the county's sewage treatment plans into chaos, plagued the park's neighbors and threatened local thoroughbreds with nervous breakdowns." Certainly a total fiasco.[75]

To be sure, the sewage plan was controversial in that the local government rejected Taft's offer to build their own plant, deciding instead to install their own, anticipating enormous growth in the area after the park opened. That didn't happen, and the plant operated at one-fourth capacity at an annual deficit of $50,000.[76]

Sewage, water, taxes, traffic, visual intrusion, tourists...all of these are legitimate concerns when something such as an amusement park comes to town. There are no clear answers and somebody is certainly going to lose in the end.

BUDS OVER BIRDS

By 1979, two years after reverting back to a promotional attraction, it was all over in California. Busch Bird Sanctuary closed completely after a turbulent 13 year run to make room for a $250M brewery expansion.[77] As someone quipped along the way, apparently a bird in the hand wasn't worth a Bud in the can.[78] Most of the exotic bird collection (1200) was relocated to Tampa and Williamsburg, along with a few zoos.[79] The only remnant is the old bridge over the railroad tracks, still sitting there and completely disconnected on either end. Most folks have no idea what's up with the "bridge to nowhere," but to those in the know, it's a silent reminder of a time gone by.

Chapter Nine

MUNCHKINS, BERRIES & HERSHEY BARS

The parks designed by Walt, Woody, Randall, and Taft were planned from the ground up as theme parks. Disneyland created a new template for outdoor, immersive experiences that showed the way beyond mere amusement enterprises. But there were others that followed the basic template of a theme park, many that arguably fit the loose definition of a theme park, and still more that transformed into "legitimate" theme parks as owners looked to Disney's model as a way to move their properties forward. Here is a sampling of these in no particular order.

SANTA CLAUS LAND

In 1856 the new town of Santa Fe, Indiana was informed there was already a Santa Fe in the state, and that they would have to think of something else. During a magical Christmas Eve meeting, inspiration struck and they came away with the name of—what else?—*Santa Claus*. Over the ensuing years thousands of letters poured into the local post office searching for the big man himself. How could you have a place called Santa Claus, yet not get to meet the jolly fellow? And so a few enterprising souls tried to remedy the problem, such as

Santa Claus Park in 1935 and Toy Land Enchanted Forest in 1936.[1] But in 1946 Louis J. Koch changed the local landscape forever when he opened a small fun park and named it Santa Claus Land.[2] He wanted a place where families could enjoy time together, cater to children, and celebrate the magic of Christmas.

A 1/8 scale railroad was the first ride in the park, providing scenic views of the growing number of attractions over the years. A repurposed stage coach offered another option for touring the land, then later the rather modern *Pioneer Land Train* (actually a tram). Over time a *Deer Farm, Hall of Famous Americans* wax museum, *House of Dolls,* various kiddie rides, an Arrow auto ride, *The Greatest Miniature Show On Earth* mini-circus, and ski shows were added, themed to Christmas of course. In 1984 the park decided to branch out and diversify, hiring Duell & Associates[3] to transform the place into a more comprehensive theme park. Adding the new themed lands of Halloween and Fourth of July begged for a more encompassing name, and so the park became Holiday World.[4] Averaging about one million in attendance over the past decade,[5] the park defies all feasibility studies as to why it's been so successful. There is no population in the surrounding region to justify such a large operation, and yet people come from all over. As with Disneyland, this just goes to show if you build something from the heart that resonates with people, they'll appreciate it and support you.

Many argue that Santa Claus Land was the very first theme park, as it was a park that did in fact have a clear theme. It was a very different kind of experience from Disneyland, and so one can get lost in the semantics of what exactly a "theme park" is. What's the answer? We could say it was the first themed park in the country, while Disneyland introduced a new concept of immersive, themed experiences. Everyone wins and can share the spotlight for how each made their mark on the American dreamscape.

KNOTT'S BERRY FARM

"America's 1st Theme Park" originated as a simple road-side berry stand in the 1920s. Walter and Cordelia Knott began buying land, and by 1934 were successfully producing their unique Boysenberries. In debt and unable to pay their bills, they started frying chicken and serving it on their wedding china. Soon the line waiting for a table was so long Walter began searching for ways to keep them entertained. Over time he would add gardens, shops, shows, and other items of interest, and in the 1940s began building Ghost Town, transplanting authentic structures from old western towns. The *Butterfield Stagecoach* was the first ride at the park in 1949, then the *Ghost Town & Calico Railroad* began operations in 1952. 1968 saw a fence erected around the park and a front gate admission charge for the first time—Knott's was officially a modern theme park. It was a long process, and though areas of the park took on various thematic overlays, clearly the most themed section was Ghost Town. After being sold to Cedar Fair in 1997, the park began turning more toward standard amusement rides, though recently has seen much love from the company in restoring some of their historic, highly themed attractions such as the *Calico Mine Train* and *Timber Mountain Log Ride*. Disney it's not, having more in common with the regionals, and it wasn't designed from the ground up as a theme park. But as with Santa Claus Land, it doesn't really matter—Knott's will always hold a very special place in park history.[6]

TWEETSIE RAILROAD

For nearly a half century the sweet "tweet, tweet" reverberated through the hills as the twelve locomotives of the East Tennessee and Western North Carolina chugged and clanked along the 66 mile narrow gauge line. Nobody called it that, of course, not even ET&WNC. It was just *Tweetsie*, fondly known for its distinctive whistle. But by 1950 the line had dried up and everything had to go.[7] One of the locomotives was No. 12, a Baldwin 4-6-0 built in 1917.[8] First moved to Harrisonburg, VA as part of a small tourist attraction, the owners were forced to sell after hurricane Hazel swept through. Actor Gene Autry bought it, then apparently saw the bill for shipping it to California. So Grover Robbins, local to the mountains of North Carolina, took ownership along with other rolling stock and started laying rail not too far from where No. 12 used to haul iron ore, lumber, and passengers.[9]

Tweetsie, as No. 12 was now known, was shipped to Hickory where the Carolina and Northwestern Railway shops lovingly brought her back to glory, decking her out with the ET&WNC's trademark green coat and gold trim.[10] Moss Trucking of Charlotte somehow wrangled everything up the mountain to its new home,[11] and on July 4, 1957, Tweetsie made its first run on top of Roundhouse Mountain near Blowing Rock, N.C. That first run was about a mile to a picnic clearing, then literally backwards to the station.[12]

Over time the three mile circuit would be completed around the mountain, and a western-themed small park gradually emerged. *Main Street* features the depot, general store, bank, and shops. Off to the right are the roundhouse and steam locomotive shop, which is kept busy servicing steam engines from all over the country. Catch an old-time show at the *Tweetsie Palace,* then ride the chair lift up to Miner's Mountain where you can pan for gold and ride the mini *Mouse Mine* train. Halfway up the mountain is the *County Fair,* with small flat rides and the *Turnpike Cruisers*. But the main attraction, of course, is riding the rails around the mountain, listening to the signature whistle that gave the railroad its nickname oh so long ago. Once over the trestle and through the woods, bandits board, looking for loot.[13]

Tweetsie was an immediate hit both with the locals who fondly remembered the original railroad as well as with tourists who began making their way to Blowing Rock. Robbins needn't have worried, but from the start it really was just kind of a hobby for him. "We hope Tweetsie will pay for herself, but I don't really care. I'd be just as happy driving her around and around this mountain all by myself."[14] One poor woman probably wouldn't agree with that plan; she had been anxiously pacing around the station for a long time when the staff finally asked if they could help. "When's the train for Boone leave...my husband's gone over there to wait for me."[15]

As one of the earliest theme parks in the country, architecture, activities, the steam train, and character actors are all part of the show. While it may not be as immersive and extravagant as Disneyland, Tweetsie showed us how we could play the part in our own small corner of the country.

DOLLYWOOD & SILVER DOLLAR CITY

In 1961 Robbins took his rustic, railroad-themed ideas westward to Pigeon Forge, TN. Rebel Railroad celebrated the centennial of the Civil War. At the *Rebeltown* depot Confederate uniform-clad youngsters would help you aboard the train pulled by *Klondike Katie*,[16] a full-size coal-burning steam locomotive. (For train enthusiasts, #192 *Klondike Katie* is a twin to Tweetsie's #190 *Yukon Queen*; both served the army in Alaska during WWII.)[17] Journey five miles through the mountains, surviving an ambush by Union soldiers before becoming embroiled in a bitter fight for control over *Fort Agony*. These were no simple animatronics, but real life actors running about on foot and horseback. After being inducted into the Confederate Army, your little ones were issued toy rifles before boarding so they could help fend off those pesky Yankees. If your train made it back to *Rebeltown*, check out the wartime goods at the *General Store*, order a simulated gold horseshoe with your initials at the blacksmith shop, then finally take a moment to relax and unwind at *The Lady Gay* saloon.[18]

The buildings were simple, the landscape nearly barren apart from the surrounding mountains, and the attractions were slim, but it was a new and exciting adventure for a region that was as far from Disneyland as one might imagine. Upon Robbins' death in 1970,[19] new ownership decided the Confederate theme wasn't appropriate and operated the park as Goldrush Junction for about six years,[20] when it was sold again to a family that would go on to make an indelible mark on the park industry—Jack and Pete Herschend.[21] The Herschends, who had operated Silver Dollar City in Missouri since 1960, renamed their new property Silver Dollar City Tennessee. The park couldn't help but have a fabulous theme; set in the beautiful Great Smoky Mountains of Tennessee, it was pure local living, representing simple life in the mountains. An operational grist mill, local craftspeople making all sorts of mountainy things to buy, and musical shows to match were an irresistible draw for tourists. One pretty successful local lady took notice, and in 1986 Dolly Parton bought an interest in the park, to be renamed Dollywood. The park has since expanded greatly with several themed lands beyond the early fair and Craftsmen's Valley. And of course the railroad is still there, still featuring their beloved *Klondike Katie.*[22]

Back to the Herschends, who got their start in 1950 when their father, Hugo, took out a lease on Marvel Cave, a long-running tourist attraction in the Ozarks near Branson, MO. An old traveling salesman by the name of Charlie Sullivan happened by one day in 1954 as they were working on the property.

What are y'all trying to do over here? You aren't trying to rebuild the old town, are you?

What old town are you talking about?

The gentleman proceeded to tell them all about the tiny mining town that existed in that very location during the 1880s. 1884, in fact, was when the town of Marble City was registered, soon thereafter changed to Marmaros (Greek for *marble*—the adjacent cave was originally known as Marble Cave). This wasn't a gold or silver mining operation—their fortunes derived from tons of guano that had accumulated over the centuries. Guano, a somewhat pretentious name for bat droppings, was used for manufacturing gun powder. A dirty business for sure, and when it dried up the town drifted off. What was left burned to the ground shortly afterwards.

Charlie had actually been born in the original general store and remembered where most of the old buildings were located. Intrigued, they proceeded to dig through the underbrush and—what do you know, he's right—there were the original foundations. And so the idea was sparked to recreate the old place, a perfect complement to their cave tour business. Hugo would not see this come to fruition, having a final, massive heart attack and passing away in 1955. But his wife Mary, a force to be reckoned with, was not about to throw up her hands. Pushing forward to carry out her husband's dream, she hired Russell Pearson, a carnival guy who had overseen Frontier City park in Oklahoma. Pearson came up with designs and built a model to show what it ought to look like.

The family took over in Herschend fashion, handling everything themselves and figuring it out as they went. No architects, no blueprints. They just followed the model, but with one caveat. Pearson suggested putting up simple buildings and dressing them up, like what most parks did. Mary had other ideas, insisting on authenticity for everything. They researched construction methods from the 1880s, following their eye and instinct. Andy Miller, art director and set designer, stepped in to lay out the details. The idea was to create a charming place with a sense of discovery just around the corner. And that's how they built their new/old town of...what? Ozark Mountain Village? Nah. *Silver Dollar City*, proposed Don Richardson, a publicity dynamo serving as the Herschend's press agent in 1959. His rationale? Because we're going to make change in silver dollars. They'll take them home and everybody will ask where they got them, and they'll tell 'em all about the park.

In a day and time when most transactions were handled in cash, it was brilliant marketing. Word of mouth (and silver dollars) spread far and wide, obviating any need for paid advertising. The new park officially opened May 1, 1960 and was a runaway success. Essentially twins, Silver Dollar City and Dollywood share similar themes, attractions, and overall vibe. And as with Knott's, both parks gradually transitioned over many years from simple road-side attractions into highly successful themed destinations.[23]

LAND OF OZ

Grover Robbins, years after successfully getting Tweetsie Railroad and Rebel Railroad rolling, hired a designer from Charlotte, NC and dragged him to the top of Beech Mountain. It was no easy trip, being a rugged, undeveloped region. "We want to put something on top of the mountain," Grover and his brother told him.[24] Something that would attract people but interfere with nature as little as possible. Jack Pentes explored the nooks, crannies, and amazing twisted trees that had been standing sentry for, well, centuries. "He walked the property on his knees on a dirt path so he could design everything from a child's perspective," explains Sean Barrett, the park's artistic director.[25] And then it began to dawn on him. The trees seemed to reach out and grab him, seemed so familiar. And then he turned a corner and there it was—the Cowardly Lion's cave, placed exactly as in the movie. "There was no question that this was Oz. It was over the rainbow—part of another world."[26]

Pentes' design director, Joe Sonderman, took charge of the project from concept to final construction.[27] The goal was to fit the park elements into the natural surroundings without disturbing anything. "We had to lay Oz into the set."[28] In the end they wound up chopping down only a single tree of any significance.

Land of Oz opened in 1970.[29] Just getting there was an adventure, driving up steep, winding roads deep into the mountains, then taking a ski lift from Beech Tree Village up to the top. No earthen berm required here to keep out the real world. Explore Dorothy's house and hold tight as the tornado ripped you from Kansas, then step out onto the yellow brick road, passing through the miniature setting of Munchkinland. The ultimate destination was Emerald City, where you could shop and witness the Wizard presenting a heart to Tin Man, courage to the Cowardly Lion, a brain for Scarecrow, then joyfully watch Dorothy lift off in a hot air balloon on her way back to Kansas. As a child I remember floating over the park in one of those magical balloons (a modified gondola), basking in the breathtaking views of the surrounding Smoky Mountains.[30]

It was a magical, quirky kind of place. If Land of Oz had been built most anywhere else it wouldn't have had the charm and emotional connection it did. The combination of physical setting and emotional attachment to the movie was a powerful effect. But the 70s were a difficult time for vacation destinations, and a combination of Robbins' death,[31] financial difficulties at his company,[32] increased competition, and a major fire that destroyed a large portion of Emerald City helped bring about the end.[33] New owners tried for a few years, but with attendance dwindling down to almost nothing, finally gave up in 1980.[34]

The park has found a bit of new life in a limited role by opening certain weekends during the year. After sitting abandoned for decades, with decaying buildings and trespassers snatching pieces of the brick road, the owners are gradually trying to rediscover the magic.[35] You never know—maybe someday, somewhere over the rainbow, the dream will come true.

PACIFIC OCEAN PARK

"Well, then I guess we don't have a deal."[36] The meeting between Walt, Roy, and Charles 'Doc' Strub was intended to negotiate a joint venture to build Disneyland. The Disneys would contribute $10 million with Strub's company, Los Angeles Turf Club, pitching in another ten. But the catch was that Strub insisted it be located on the coast and operated by his people. Obviously that didn't sit well, so Walt moved elsewhere and Strub, still interested in building a park on a pier, moved forward on his own.

The region around Santa Monica and Los Angeles had enjoyed decades of amusement piers. As they burned down, others rose from the ashes, bigger and better. These were typical amusement enterprises, with dance halls, standard carny games and rides including roller coasters, and of course the beach. One of these, Ocean Park Pier, would serve as the foundation for a new type of coastal entertainment—a nautical themed park inspired by the ideas Disney had developed for his venture.

Pacific Ocean Park opened in July 1958 and was an immediate hit. Much of the original pier had been demolished and reimagined, with several structures and rides being repurposed. As at Disneyland, art directors from the movie industry were hired who knew design, including the park's supervising art director Fred Harpman, who had worked on Disney's Main Street with Wade Rubottom. They frantically worked to translate their creative ideas into practical attractions that would open on time. The park was very loosely divided into themed "lands," the bulk of it located along the coast with a long pier extension out over the ocean.

Visitors entered into Neptune's Courtyard, featuring a 60' high Googie-style arch with rotating seahorses on top. Water was everywhere, and pathways took you over and around on the way to the various attractions in the park. It was an impressive first scene that set the stage for how this park would be quite different from what had been there before. Beyond lay *Neptune's Kingdom*, where an elevator took you "deep underwater" to a walking exploration of animated sea life, real sea life, and Neptune himself. The *Submarine Diving Bells* would pull you underwater, then suddenly release for a rather explosive jump back to the surface. The *Ocean Skyway* was a standard Von Roll skyride with beautiful, "Jetsonian" style bubbles that soared over the ocean, off to the side of the pier, giving you a great view of the park and ocean beyond. Running alongside was the *Ocean Highway*, an auto ride similar to the Arrow attractions at most parks. This one, however, was not from Arrow; it used cheaper cars and had no center guiderail. The route took you through the park along the pier before turning around and heading out over the ocean for the return trip. As with most parks in those days, some sort of space travel attraction was all the rage, and so *Flight to Mars* took you to the red planet where you could see where Martians lived, including a peak into their home. If you didn't throw up along the way, the return to Earth via the cleverly designed "Matter Transmitter" ensured that you were intact and had survived the alien encounters. *Magic Carpet* featured ride vehicles suspended from an overhead track and sailed over various fairy tale scenes.

Ports O' Call was the old pier's midway area and retained many of the carnival rides and games, though re-dressed to match the park's theming. The old coaster was renamed the *Sea Serpent* and a classic "pretzel" dark ride became *Around the World in 80 Turns*. A number of ambitious dark ride attractions were added to varying degrees of success. The tame *Jeep* ride took youngsters through a jungle safari, and the *Sea Tub Adventure* floated you in a tub through various seaside scenes, narrowly avoiding an octopus attack. The *Flying Dutchman* was a two-story dark ride through the world of pirates (another popular theme of the day). Many of these were quite impressive in design and rivaled those of other parks.

The beckoning Polynesian architecture of *Mystic Isles* drew you toward the far end of the pier. This was tiki-heaven, with the towering longhouse on the other side of a waterfall leading the way to the *Mystery Island Banana Train*. This was the signature attraction for the park; guests boarded beautiful banana trains designed by Arrow Development, with locomotives that pushed the short trains through the active volcanic mountain, over the water, and past lush jungle scenes.

Pacific Ocean Park opened the same year as C.V. Wood's Magic Mountain, but followed a similar trajectory as Pleasure Island. Year one was incredibly strong, and the park closed over the winter for major upgrades and additions. Year two, however, saw a dramatic decrease in attendance that stopped everyone cold. Management experimented with a risky idea for season three—implementing a pay one price that included nearly everything in the park. It worked, at least at first. The trouble was that all the attractions and concessions weren't owned by the park, but by individual operators who previously sold their own tickets. Now the front gate had to be split among all operators while covering ongoing costs such as maintenance, payroll, insurance, and lease payments on the property to Santa Monica and Los Angeles. It was not sustainable with the attendance figures coming well short of projections and requirements. On top of all this Santa Monica decided the surrounding area needed to be redeveloped, so construction fences hindered access to the front gate. Changes of ownership resulted in the gradual ouster of the park's artistic designers and original visionaries, and so the park suffered a long, slow decline. By 1967 it was all over. Pacific Ocean Park declared bankruptcy and the pier was left to rot.[37]

DOGPATCH USA

With the turmoil of the 1960s nearly inescapable in the daily news, Americans sought refuge in a steady stream of rural, down-home television shows. Feel-good fodder such as *Hee Haw, Mayberry RFD, Green Acres, Petticoat Junction,* and *The Real McCoys* were set in simpler times and places, reminding many of what the good ole days must've been like and restoring hope for an anxiety-ridden society. Long before these scripts were written, however, people opened their Sunday papers each week and turned to *Li'l Abner*. The strip by Al Capp showcased a hillbilly clan in the fictitious small town of Dogpatch. Immensely popular for decades, it was one of the early comics set in the South, and it had a good bit to do with how everyone perceived folks from down there.[38]

In 1966 a local realtor named O.J. Snow had just listed an old trout farm in Arkansas for a family. Walking the property, it struck him as a scene right out of *Li'l Abner*. After seeing the place, Al Capp enthusiastically agreed, even claiming he would adjust his drawings accordingly. Announced in 1967, the concept immediately drew harsh criticism from many who felt it played upon the negative stereotype of people in Arkansas, an image they were desperately trying to move away from. But in that day and age those voices weren't enough, and so the park opened May 18, 1968.[39]

Only partially completed for the first season, it was essentially a small hillbilly town with many original structures—such as log cabins and the old mill—restored either in-place or carefully moved and reassembled. *Jubilation T. Cornpone's* cartoony statue in the town square was surrounded by typical frontier-land types of attractions like the general store, shops and restaurants, and the *Kornvention Hall*. All signage and attractions painted a picture of a dumbed-down, backwoods population.[40] Over the coming years the park would add various rides and attractions, such as a railroad, water slide, and even a few coasters, most not fitting at all with the original story concept.[41]

For a few years the park did well enough, though not coming anywhere close to projected attendance. Two or three hundred thousand was enough to pay the bills at first,[42] but trouble was brewing from a variety of angles. Profits from the successful first season were not poured back into the park, but distributed as dividends to shareholders who demanded a return on their investment.[43] They built a second destination, a resort centered around a ski lift,[44] but its limited operation was a major financial drain on the company. Dogpatch wasn't doing well enough to support two properties, and the idea of a ski resort probably wasn't the smartest. You can't make artificial snow in Arkansas and expect it to last through the day. It flopped, and soon after closed.[45]

Undercapitalization is one of the primary causes for failure in themed attractions, and this certainly became an issue with Dogpatch. The entire project was conceived and rushed to opening by businessmen who knew nothing about the park business and for most of whom this was merely a quick investment opportunity. Future development was hindered for the same reason—you need creative people who know the ins and outs of the industry and are willing to spend sufficient capital. Al Capp's son was on-site to keep an eye on things and reported back to his father that "this is a mistake."[46] The park was in the wrong location, nowhere near an Interstate and difficult to get to. Nearby Silver Dollar City and the growing music show scene in Branson, MO, was dominating the tourism industry in the region. There was simply not enough reason to make the trek to Dogpatch.[47]

Then came the "rural purge." In 1971 America and the television industry had had enough of all this hick charm; every major TV series of this ilk was cancelled. Finally, Al Capp retired in 1977 and died two years later, effectively removing the park's entire story from American society.[48] After a long series of complicated ownership changes and bankruptcy proceedings,[49] the park managed to continue operations in one way or another until 1993. At that point the park had drifted far from the original vision, essentially a theme-less amusement park set in a beautiful location.[50]

The remains of the park have been largely overtaken by nature, a series of new owners taking stabs at doing something productive with the land.[51] So far nothing's worked out, including an interesting proposal to develop another theme park and resort.[52] For now, Dogpatch lives on in the memories of those in the area who happened to grow up nearby. It was an interesting concept from the beginning, and is now a fascinating tale for the rest of us who never even heard of the place.

LIBERTYLAND

Memphis, TN. Home of Sun Studios, Stax Records, and Elvis. Sam Phillips, B.B. King, Jerry Lee Lewis, Otis Redding. The first rock 'n' roll record, "Rocket 88." Visitors today can still step inside this rich history and relive the impact on American culture.

There's another town icon, however, that you cannot visit. There's nothing to see, and yet when Libertyland opened on July 4, 1976, it was the pride and joy of the city. They were finally in the big leagues along with the other newly built theme parks around the country. Libertyland's origins date back to 1897, when a portion of the old Deaderick Plantation was used for various public activities, including thoroughbred racing. In 1912 the city of Memphis bought 168 acres for use as a fairgrounds and a park. Joy Plaza park came about in 1923 and included a Dentzel carousel and the John Miller-designed *Pippin* wooden coaster (some believe *Pippin* was originally built in 1912 and was relocated from the old East End Park, but there is no evidence to confirm this was the same ride).[53] Over time additional rides would be added to the renamed Fairgrounds Amusement Park, but by the late 60s it was clear things were changing for outdoor amusements.[54] A new generation of park concept was sweeping the nation, and so in 1971 officials from the fair approached the city to propose a $15–30 million theme park,[55] complete with a monorail, sky ride, and expensive animatronics.[56] This proved overly optimistic; Economics Research Associates was brought in to perform a feasibility study[57] which redirected them toward a more realistic, scaled-back $8.3 million endeavor.[58] Randall Duell, of course, was hired to help them take their park to the next level.[59] Knee-deep in planning for the Marriott properties, Duell took 22 acres[60] of the old fairgrounds and transformed them into a beautiful piece of Americana.

Everything from the old park except for the coaster and carousel was demolished. In its place rose a charming, colonial-themed retreat based around three lands: Colonial Land, Frontier Land, and Turn of the Century Land. Colonial Land was first after entering the front gates, taking you back in time to those early days of the new nation. Beckoning you into the park, the full-size Frisco #1351 steam locomotive and caboose stood majestically beside *Independence Station,* inspired from the original Philadelphia site where the Declaration of Independence was signed. Catch the miniature gauge *Casey's Cannonball* train for a 3/4 mile trip around the park, gawk at the full-size Liberty Bell replica, stand to the side while the marching band filed past, and hear the town crier as you browsed the *Tailor's Thread* and *Colonial Chest* for souvenirs. The park's only indoor entertainment venue, the 200-seat *Bell Tavern Theater,* was located here.

Walking toward the center of the park, the *Zippin Pippin* coaster roared by on the left as it negotiated the turnaround. Directly in front was the *Grand Carousel,* serving as a hub of sorts as the Duell loop started its journey around *Tom Sawyer's Lake* in the middle of the park. To the right was the *Turnpike* antique car ride, then off into Frontier Land where the architecture was straight from the pioneering 19th century. Cool off on the *Old Hickory Log Flume,* shop in the authentic log cabins, and take a seat with your honey on the 110' foot *World's Longest Love Seat*. Paddle around *Tom Sawyer's Island* in *Injun Joe's Canoes,* then cross over the suspension bridge to play on the island. See the animals at the petting zoo, take in a show at the *Fort Liberty* outdoor stage, then keep circling around the lake and back into Turn of the Century Land. Here was the *W.C. Handy Amphitheater* and many of the park's flat rides such as the *Little Dipper* coaster, *River Round-Up,* and *Spinning Spider*. Take in a game at the *Skeeball Palace,* then hop on the *Zippin Pippin,* hoping you got a seat next to Elvis. The king of rock 'n' roll was a big fan of the coaster and brought the park untold value in free publicity.[61]

The park was lovely, with great care taken for its extensive landscaping. Original trees from the site were preserved as much as possible, and two artificial waterfalls added kinetic energy to the scenic surroundings. At first the grand experiment of a mini-theme park seemed to go pretty well, but over time attendance began to trail off. As usual, continued reinvestment was a must for garnering return visits, and so the park added more thrill rides over the years. It didn't help that the fair board insisted on opening the park free of charge during fair season, thereby lowering the perceived value of the place in the public eye.[62] 2005 saw an attempt at rebranding with a new logo, bright colors (that had nothing to do with the original thematic intent), and marketing campaign.[63] Turns out new paint wasn't enough to satisfy fair officials, however, and on Nov 3, 2005 they voted to close Libertyland permanently.[64] October 29 had been the last day of operation for a private event.[65] Locals rose up in protest, organizing the Save Libertyland campaign in a desperate attempt to get the park reopened.[66] They succeeded in delaying the nearly-inevitable, forcing the city to re-examine legal ownership of park property and contacting outside developers known for reinvigorating failing parks. In the end, though, it wasn't enough.[67]

Over time all the rides were auctioned off and relocated to various parks around the world. The *Pippin* and *Grand Carousel* were owned by the city, not the fair, and were handled separately.[68] By the time someone tried to move the coaster it was too far gone to be saved, and so the ride plans went to Bay Beach Amusement Park in Wisconsin where the Gravity Group designed a near-replica.[69] The 1909 *Grand Carousel* has had a long saga: saved from auction, placed into storage for years, it is now beautifully restored and spinning once again at the Children's Museum of Memphis.[70]

All that's left of the charming park is a historical marker and the Creative Arts Center, a red brick building dating back to 1922 (it was originally called the Women's Building for fair displays such as cooking, arts, crafts, and so on).[71] This large structure sat to the left of the park's entrance. The rest of the site is nothing but trees, grass, and dirt. Satellite views are eerily similar to that of the former Astroworld property, which also remains vacant today. Plans have been announced to redevelop a portion of the old fair grounds next to the park,[72] but yet again, a piece of Memphis history and the source for untold numbers of fond memories is gone forever.

HERSHEYPARK

They say third time's the charm. Must be so, because after failing twice at making candy, first in Philadelphia, then in New York, Milton headed back to Pennsylvania to make another go at it. The Lancaster Caramel Company did the trick, becoming so successful he couldn't pass up the buy-out offer of a million dollars...in 1900. All of forty-three years of age, Milton wasn't about to head for the golf course, and so he began buying land in a tiny village called Derry Church. Hershey didn't just build a factory, he built an entire town for his workers.[73] And on May 30, 1906 he officially dedicated a park for "the use of anyone who may desire to avail themselves of the pleasure it offers."[74] Located across the railroad tracks from the factory, Hershey Park was a beautiful, serene retreat with picnic tables, a band stand, and Spring Creek gently winding its way through the grounds.

Before long others began taking the Hummelstown and Campbelltown Street Railway Company's trolley to enjoy the park. (Thankfully for all involved, the name was soon changed to the more palatable Hershey Transit Company.)[75] Milton quickly realized the tourism potential of his widespread chocolate sales, and so each candy wrapper featured postcard images from the park. The story goes that Mr. Hershey would walk through the park, picking up litter along the way. But if it was a Hershey wrapper, he would make sure the company logo side was facing up and leave it on the ground.[76] Thanks to the park's popularity and Hershey's resources, growth steadily continued over the years. A six thousand seat Convention Hall was completed in time for the Church of the Brethren conference in 1915,[77] and a one million gallon Spanish Moroccan-style swimming pool facility, complete with nearly five thousand lockers, opened in 1929.[78] Small rides were added here and there, with the Herbert Schmeck-designed *The Wild Cat* becoming the park's first coaster in 1923 (the original name was *The Joy Ride,* mercifully short-lived).[79]

Changes in American society through the 1950s and 60s forced parks to consider difficult decisions. The old go-to standards were no longer valid, such as the large ballrooms, and the grand swimming pool was falling apart. Violence and unrest increased, and the park had great difficulty dealing with it. Hershey Park was an open park, with no surrounding fence and no front gate for admission, and any incident, whether at Hershey or other parks, caused families to reconsider visiting. Maintenance and upkeep fell by the wayside, and things were looking fairly bleak for the once-beautiful, carefully landscaped picnic grounds.[80]

When Walt opened his magical playland, everybody saw it on TV. Shortly afterward other regionals such as Six Flags Over Texas and Astroworld picked up the ball and signaled a new era in this concept called a theme park. With the company founder long gone, in 1968 the park assigned J.O. Hershey to figure it out. After visiting Disneyland and other parks and asking them what Hershey should do, he presented his report to the board of directors. The choice was clear, and so they brought in the big guns: Economics Research Associates would do the financial feasibility studies while R. Duell & Associates would be tasked with reimagining the amusement park into a full-fledged, modern theme park.[81]

Leading off the five-year, six-phase plan in 1971 was a new name, *Hersheypark,* the distinctive pinwheel logo, and a fence around the place.[82] The main gate was moved to the other side of the park where the Hersheypark Arena is, but there were also four other entrances in various locations.[83] It look awhile for locals to swallow the idea they could no longer saunter through the grounds whenever they felt like it, but the new image gradually took root. 1972 reduced the gates to one (at the arena), and saw the addition of *Der Deitsch Platz* (Pennsylvania Dutch-themed retail and foods) and *Carrousel Circle,* featuring Philadelphia Toboggan Company's #47.[84] The company, while committed to the new plan, insisted on proceeding in stages as they couldn't afford, nor stomach, attempting to rebuild the entire park at once.[85]

1973 was the breakout year with record attendance and a brand new entrance area. Modeled after a 17th century English village, Tudor Square set a high standard for regional parks. Emphasis was on quality, with elaborate cut stone, slate floors, and lead glass windows employed for authenticity. Duell insisted on doing it right, making it beautiful and designing it to last. Guests strolled across the moat over a stone bridge, past various retail and food beautifully themed for the setting, and paid their fare at Tudor Castle.[86] The pathway from parking lot to ticket gate very effectively transitioned you from the outside world into a different place; you were already immersed in the magic before you even took out your wallet, something few parks did quite so well.

To be a theme park you've got to have themed lands, and so by this time the park had various labels such as *Tudor Square, Rhineland, Der Deitsch Platz, Carrousel Circle,* and *Minetown*. There would be more, but the other major enhancement for 1973 was the introduction of the Hershey candies as characters and marketing icons. Hersheypark is actually part of a separate company from Hershey Foods, but they have collaborated over the years, and in fact the park's ride height categories are identified by candy, from Jolly Rancher and Twizzlers down to Hershey's Miniatures for the little tikes.[87]

It took a lot of faith and a sense of "we really have no choice" for Hersheypark's management to jump into the deep end. It paid off beyond their expectations, and now the park boasts the highest annual attendance for an independent park (about 3.4 million in 2018).[88] However, that beautiful Tudor entry area is no more. A victim of their own success, that narrow, winding pathway created a logjam on busy days. A more modern "arrival experience" has been the trend with today's parks, providing more efficient processing and accommodations. And so the park went big with *Hershey's Chocolate-town,* themed on the town of Hershey and its rich, milk-chocolatey history. Oh, what would Milton think now of his little picnic spot?

Phonehenge Stage
The Kitchen Below
Magic Mushroom Garden
Queen's Head Pub
Malibu Beach Party
Gibson
Les Paul Sunburst Icon
Gibson
Vegas High Roller Plaza
The Whammy Bar
Cool Country Stage
The Wheelhouse Canteen
Amp'd Coffee
Muddin' Monster Race
Just A Swingin'
Rockabilly BBQ

Chapter Ten

WHO SAYS WE CAN'T BUILD A THEME PARK NOW?

After the 70s boom fizzled out, there wasn't much in the way of new regional theme parks. While Disney, Universal, and Legoland have steadily developed their properties, few others have found the formula (or guts) to attempt building a park from scratch. It's mostly economic; real estate values often render parks less desirable than housing or commercial use. It also just plain costs a whole lot of money, which is why most of the activity revolves around acquiring existing properties and rebranding them. It's not unheard of, however, and two examples demonstrate that you just don't know. It might work. And it might not.

FIESTA TEXAS

Gaylord Entertainment, the conglomerate who owned the Grand Ole Opry, Opryland park and hotel, The Nashville Network, Country Music Network, and much more, was at the top of their game by the early 1990s.[1] In the late 80s they had joined forces with the USAA insurance company to investigate building a park similar to Opryland in the San Antonio, TX area. Realizing the stiff competition from SeaWorld, Six Flags Over Texas, and Astroworld in Houston, they realized any new park in the region must be different and offer something unique. And so the concept of a music show park was finalized, something Gaylord was certainly comfortable with after operating music-focused Opryland since 1972.[2] Following a positive feasibility study by Economics Research Associates, FORREC International was contracted for concept design and master planning, a process that took about a year. Master Plan #11 was officially greenlit, construction began in 1990, and $100 million later the park opened for the 1992 season.[3]

The overall theme was Southwest music traditions. Guests would enter through the gates into Los Festivales, featuring appropriate entertainment and the usual shops and guest services. The park's primary theatrical facility, *Zaragosa Theater,* was here and featured two shows: *Festival Folklorico* and *The Heart of Texas*. But what would draw your attention and pull you around the winding pathway was the *Rattler* roller coaster, nestled in and along the steep sides of a former quarry on the far side of the park. To get there you'd pass the small water park, *The Ol' Waterin' Hole,* cross the railroad tracks and enter Crackaxle Canyon. Of course this was a 1920s western boomtown, complete with outdoor entertainment venues and appropriately themed dining, shopping, and rides. The *Gully Washer* raft ride spun and tossed you between the *Rattler* and the train tracks with a beautiful view of the waterfalls gushing down the quarry walls.

Spassburg was next, reflecting early German heritage in Texas. Take in dinner and a Festhaus show in the cavernous *Sangerfest Halle Stage* and enjoy the Bavarian architecture while hopping on various rides, including the park's carousel. Step into the 1950s in Rockville and go to school...Rockville High School, that is, where the *Rockin' at Rockville High* 50s show was sure to keep you hopping. If you decided to play hooky instead, go driving on the *Motorama Turnpike* or take in a round of mini golf.[4]

Fiesta Texas was popular with guests from day one, hitting just over two million in attendance the first season.[5] Quality live entertainment from over 400 performers set it apart from the competition.[6] The park was well-planned and well-organized, benefiting from owners who knew how to run a theme park.[7] USAA would become the sole owner in 1996, bringing in Six Flags (Warner) to brand and run the place.[8] By 1998 the park was sold to the Six Flags chain (by then purchased by Premier Parks),[9] and was well on its way to becoming a thrill ride park. Skillful execution based on solid information is the lesson learned for others looking to build their own dream destination.

THE PARK THAT ROCK BUILT

It's nearly impossible to fathom there hadn't been a park themed around music before. Oh sure, Opryland and Fiesta Texas were designed to showcase American music, but they still looked and felt an awful lot like the other regionals that sprouted up in the 60s and 70s.

In the early 2000s, Jon Binkowski was looking for a way to capitalize on his ice skating show theater in Myrtle Beach, SC. His company, Renaissance Entertainment, had been highly successful producing shows and attractions for major parks and destinations, but the post-9/11 era was tough for this sort of thing. With a local investor ready to jump in, the idea for a theme park began to emerge. Acquiring land adjacent to his theater, including the old Waccamaw Pottery outlet, *Fantasy Harbor* was intended to celebrate the four seasons. Four seasons? It's a free theme. No IP, no licensing, lots of creative ideas. Funding was available to begin infrastructure and other improvements, and concept art was developed. Then things began to stall out with the death of his partner and difficulty finding other parties willing to support the project. It needed something a bit more interesting than the changing of the calendar. Thoughts of a movie-based park came and went, primarily because, well, that idea had already been done. Several times.

His new partner had done work for the Hard Rock franchise, and when Jon discovered one of the vice presidents was his next-door neighbor, he began the pitch. Hard Rock ultimately agreed to license the brand, and over time the park was able to gather some pretty remarkable music icons to sign on.[10]

Hard Rock Park featured six themed areas, starting with the All Access Entry Plaza. Through the ticket gates and front courtyard, you continued under a brick archway with a spoof of Michelangelo's famous *Let There Be Rock* painting of rock-star Adam lounging with nothing but a guitar on. The "Main Street" shops and restaurants bent toward the right, offering a tremendous cinematic reveal of the central lake and the park's icon—a 70 foot tall Gibson Les Paul guitar towering over everything. The layout was essentially a Duell loop, simply circling around the lake from land to land. First on the right was Cool Country, with the Eagles' *Life in the Fast Lane* coaster. Amazingly, the park successfully negotiated deals with such artists as the Eagles, Led Zeppelin, and The Moody Blues for branding various attractions. The Eagles jumped on board, willing to edit their song to match the ride. Jon's original theater was home for an edgy country ice skating show, *Country on the Rocks*. And who could forget *Rock-Cow-Billy*, a bronze Elvis-impersonating cow statue that cracked jokes (via off-stage performer) and shot water out of, well, everywhere?

Moving along, you'd pass through the *Heavy Metal Graveyard* sculpture garden. The idea here, other than the funky tribute to rock, was to be an in-park access to a future resort hotel. Nothing else to see for now, though, so continue to Born In The USA. Symbolized by the Statue of Liberty wearing sun shades and holding up the eternal flame (a lit Bic), this was home to *Alice's Restaurant*, a tribute to Arlo Guthrie's famous song and chock full of music history details. The park was plastered with this sort of stuff, some of it authentic items, much of it outrageous puns and nearly-inside jokes. A Premier-designed suspended coaster, *Slippery When Wet*, got riders soaked from ground-based water cannons...but they could retaliate by pushing the green button, triggering shower heads over the people on the ground.

You know you're in Britain when the pavement directional arrows cross you over to the left side. British Invasion gave a taste of London with the *Magic Mushroom Garden* (Huss Airboat flat ride), the *Punk Pit* inflatable play area, and *Phonehenge,* British phone booths laid out to resemble its namesake. Step into a booth and it would ring; answer and listen in on various conversations. Coaster fans marveled at the innovative and oh-so-short *Maximum RPM,* featuring a ferris-wheel type of lift that rotated each car up and over to the main track. But the highlight in British Invasion was one that remains legendary to this day—the *Nights in White Satin* dark ride. The Moody Blues completely re-recorded the title track for one of the most interesting and talked about dark rides ever made. This psychedelic trip was a result of Jon telling Sally Corporation "No animatronics. They're expensive. Do stuff with lighting and whatever." The result was nothing short of remarkable.

The final themed land, located to the left of All Access Entry Plaza, was Rock & Roll Heaven. Gaze at more music artifacts in *Taste of Paradise Grill,* soak yourself in *Reggae River Falls,* or sit a spell for the *Malibu Beach Party* show. Towering over all of this was the park's iconic coaster, *Led Zeppelin: The Ride.* This beautiful B&M took off from a unique zeppelin-shaped station with the band's *Whole Lotta Love* blasting you through onboard speakers. The condition for getting the band to sign on, though, was that the *entire* song—all five minutes and thirty-four seconds or so—had to be heard by guests. So the queue was designed as a pre-show, getting people into the "story" and starting the music before jumping onboard.

Of course music was the foundation for everything, and they very cleverly divided the park into acoustically isolated sound zones, where music from one section would not leak out into the next. Instead of hiding speakers in the bushes, big Peavey-branded monitors were hung on poles just like at a concert. They even went as far as recording different flavors of a song that matched the attraction. So you'd hear a pop song strolling along the walkway, but head over to a kiddie ride and you'd hear it transform into a calypso or played by a calliope without skipping a beat. Live entertainment stages were everywhere, featuring a wide variety of styles to fit each land.[11]

Hard Rock Park soft-opened April 15, 2008. Five months later the music died. Cause of death: lack of attendance. The park was 100%

private—it was Jon's project to do as he liked. The downside of this is that he had no parent company to run to when times got tough. No sugar daddy to bail them out and provide desperately needed funds. Undercapitalization, again, is one of the most common causes of failure for themed attractions.[12]

But there are others, and they seem to have found most of them. Being one of the most notorious failures in modern theme park history, Hard Rock's story has been the subject of endless speculation. Most often heard is that the park didn't market adequately and that ticket prices were too high. Probably true; few people knew about the place, and fewer were willing to spend $50 for a day at the park when they were really in town for the beach. And that's the main point. Myrtle Beach caters largely to a certain demographic, most all of whom are there for family vacations to enjoy the ocean. Golfing is popular as well, and so it's difficult to get people to give up any of that to see a park that's nowhere close to where all the other action is. Hard Rock was off the beaten path, the site selected primarily because Jon already owned his Ice House property. Wrong location, wrong demographic, too little to offer for too high a price, and so on. Too bad, really, because the core concept was pretty cool; the lesson learned is to never forget fundamental principles when thinking about a new venture.[13]

MGM GRAND ADVENTURES

While we're at it, there's yet another "whatever happened to..." story that's too good to pass up. In December 1993 MGM opened their $1 billion Grand Hotel and Theme Park.[14] Some of you may find it difficult to believe, but for a very brief blip in history Las Vegas was actually trying to rebrand itself as a family-friendly destination.[15] They soon regained their senses, but in the meantime a beautiful 33-acre theme park sprouted up just outside the MGM hotel and casino.

Designed by Randall Duell,[16] the $110 million MGM Grand Adventures was built around the concept of a movie backlot, paying homage to the parent company's long cinematic legacy. Or at least the concept of the legacy—no MGM movies would actually be found in the park in order to save licensing costs. Guests could explore eight lands, starting with the Moroccan-themed Casablanca Plaza. Next was New York Street, the largest section of the park, alive with street performers and the indoor, *Space Mountain*-style *Lightning Bolt* coaster. The designers made clever use of building facades and other structures to reduce visual intrusion, and off to one side was a fake, but impressive-looking elevated train parked at the station. Architecture was authentic and detailed, creating believable environments.

Taking the Duell loop toward the right, we'd find ourself in the Asian Village. First up was *Deep Earth Exploration*, a moving-vehicle, motion simulator ride (think *Indiana Jones* at Disneyland). Guests could take in the action through a video screen in front and windows that opened whenever the vehicle passed physical sets on either side. Take a right out of this building and head down the pathway to the *Backlot River Tour*. This *Jungle Cruise/Jaws* descendent took you on a floating backlot tour through "active" movie sets. See swamp creatures pop up out of the lagoon, blunder into a Civil War ironclad battle, escape the volcanic Temple of Gloom, then get caught in the crossfire of the Jungle Storm helicopter attack. (The family connection to *Jaws* is more than just concept. Park designer R&R Creative was involved with Universal's original *Jaws* ride in Orlando, and when that attraction was shut down due to mechanical issues MGM was able to get the boats on the cheap.)[17]

French Street was next on our trip through the movies, with retail, food, and the *Parisian Taxis* bumper cars. Salem Waterfront ran alongside the central lagoon, complete with quaint New England architecture, lighthouse, and the *Haunted Mine* dark ride. Crossing the beautiful stone bridge toward the left, we could grab a bite to eat at the magnificent *Cotton Blossom* riverboat (the actual *Cotton Blossom* from the movie *Showboat* was permanently docked at Worlds of Fun in Kansas City).

At the far end of the park lay Tumbleweed Gulch, the Wild West area. Cool off on the *Over the Edge* water flume, then become part of the magic in *You're in the Movies*. Here you jump into costume, grab a script, and become a part of celluloid immortality. New Orleans Street was another example of the wonderful detail and theming in the park, sporting a non-functioning, but awfully real-looking steam train parked at the station. Over to the left as we work our way down was *Dueling Pirates*, a stunt show set against a castle facade. Over to the right, however, was the gem of the park. *Grand Canyon Rapids* spun and churned riders through rich scenery, past wonderfully detailed structures, and inside show buildings. You'd find yourself in the crossfire of a bank robbery shootout, coming face to face with Marshall Rick. (Most people dream of having a cardboard cutout of themselves; attraction designer Rick Bastrup got his own animatronic!) Kinetic energy came from animatronic figures, overhead rolling mine cars, a water pumping station, and of course the water itself. And for the finale, narrowly escape the mine blasting tunnel!

The last small bit of the park was Olde England Street, a short thematic section that completed the Duell loop back to New York Street.[18]

By 1996 it was clear the park wasn't meeting expectations. The following year saw it chopped nearly in half, with MGM building a pool and conference center on the property.[19] By 1998 the operating calendar was shortened, then in 2001 it was renamed The Park at MGM. No longer open to the general public, the park, such as it was, only operated for groups and special events. One year later it was all over.[20]

What happened this time? The autopsy of Grand Adventures probably suggests several causes of death. The park was well designed and executed, but limited in size and located far in the back of a casino. Guests had to find their way through the sprawling facility just to get to the park entrance.[21] Ira West, one of the park's designers, once got a call from a friend who had been trying in vain to find the place due to insufficient signage.[22] Ticket prices were rather steep at $25 for adults; kids were $20, making it a hefty outlay for families (which were the target demographic, after all). A thrill ride park this was not, disappointing teens and young adults.[23]

Las Vegas' family-friendly experiment was quickly fizzling out, and so the land became much more valuable for gaming, conventions, and the like. It's all gone now, replaced by the casino, Cirque du Soleil theater, and The Mansion, a 4-star hotel. Interestingly, there's an old directional sign listing various destinations in the resort that still includes "Grand Adventures."[24] This is about the only bone left over from the special little place that ought to have made more of an impact than it ever did. Too bad.

The Anchor
The Creel H
Pier 4
The Gangplank
The Gold Rusher
The Golden E
Gem and I
Bottoms Up
Shangri-La Station
Four Winds
Four Winds Station
Valencia Falls
Whitewater Lake
Log Jammer
Painted Pullet
Sugar Shack
Top Treat
Dance Area
Mini Bar
Mini Pree
Mini Bike

Chapter Eleven

EVOLUTION

Many of these regional parks flourished for a number of years, changing relatively little at first. Economies are always in flux, however, along with social interests, technological development, and so on. These forces gradually introduced major disruption at the local level, seeing many beloved parks swept up by chain operators who for the most part had no interest in regional heritage. With few exceptions, original story and theming gave way to the latest money-making innovations. No one was around to remember why the buildings were painted a certain color or were built from specific materials. New management needed to expand and attract attention, so old stuff was disbanded and demolished. Story, theme, and detail was "something that Disney did," and there were no Imagineering departments or creative executives who cared much about it. Slowly the original thematic underpinnings of the regionals were eroded away, largely transforming them into iron parks featuring as many rides, shops, and shows as they could cram into every nook and cranny. So what happened? Let's take a look at some of the factors involved in transforming these beloved retreats into near-homogenized corporate brands.

ADEQUATE FUNDING

Sufficient capitalization is crucial to get a park off the ground (and keep it there). Regionals built by smaller companies were susceptible to economic conditions; many were highly leveraged for initial funding and simply didn't have a reserve to weather any storms until they set solid roots. The majority of these parks opened during the 70s when the country was racked by recession and the oil crisis; with skyrocketing interest rates and gas rationing, families stayed closer to home. When Carowinds opened in 1973, the park provided a "Gas Information Center" with the latest updates on which gas stations were open in order to help families make it home. They even placed ads in local papers that featured driving distance maps, assuring guests they would be able to make the trip on one tank if they lived within a certain radius.[1] They survived year one, but by the end of the second season Carowinds Corporation, suffering declining attendance and unable to pay their short-term construction loans, was forced to sell out to Taft Broadcasting, a company with bigger pockets to keep things afloat.[2] Many of the grand ideas, such as the resort hotel, shopping complex, and NFL stadium never saw the light of day.

Others ran into similar issues. Money-losing Astroworld, minus Hofheinz's dreams for a monorail, museum, race track, and sea-themed park, was able to hang on for awhile as part of his Astrodomain complex. However, the judge's entire empire was crumbling around him due to soaring interest rates, exorbitant debt, and a debilitating stroke; Six Flags rescued the park in 1975.[3] Great Adventure had no chance whatsoever of building all of Warner LeRoy's vast ideas and couldn't even manage what they did get done; the park was in foreclosure by the First Bank of Chicago.[4] Magic Mountain amusement park in California, a joint venture between SeaWorld and Newhall Land & Farming, opened before it was ready and with insufficient capital. It didn't help that the construction manager kept hiding the real costs for getting it built; faced with this and the need for more cash to make it work, SeaWorld bailed.[5]

The most recent example of undercapitalization (and other problems, as we have seen) was Hard Rock Park in Myrtle Beach, SC—highly leveraged, barely enough cash to build what they needed for opening, and no parent company to run to. And then they ran smack into the 2008 financial crisis.[6] On the other hand, Angus Wynne had negotiated a sale of Six Flags Corporation back in 1966 to the Pennsylvania Railroad, retaining operational control and bringing a much bigger checkbook that not only made the Georgia and Missouri properties possible, but enabled the entire chain to survive.[7] Kings Island and Kings Dominion were brought to life by media giant Taft, while Opryland also benefited from a financially sound parent and solid tourism market in Nashville.

LACK OF EXPERIENCE

A few independent operators simply had no idea how to design and run a theme park. The dream sounded good, but when push comes to shove you've got to know what you're doing. Great Adventure, scaled down considerably from Warner's unrealistic dreams, was struggling when Six Flags bailed it out in 1977. The company who designed it wasn't experienced in theme parks—they built safari parks. New management brought in industry professionals, including Randall Duell, to implement necessary changes to get it on solid ground. Operators such as Six Flags had built up years of experience by this time and had a pretty good idea of what needed to be done from a business standpoint, regardless of the impact on theme.[8]

SATURATED MARKET

By the late 1970s the theme park business in the United States had largely matured. Regional parks of some sort had been built in the most likely spots around the country, leaving little room for growth in numbers.[9] A typical indicator of a mature industry is an increasing consolidation of control, which certainly happened with large chain operators acquiring parks and even other chains. The benefits are deeper pockets for investment, a distribution of risk in case unexpected events at one site negatively affects returns, and the potential for hiring specialized skills, such as creative design, that smaller parks might not be able to afford. The downside, of course, is that every ownership change takes you yet another step away from the original dream.

REINVESTMENT IN PROPERTIES

Capital reinvestment is key to a healthy themed attraction. People don't return in sufficient numbers unless there's a reason, such as a compelling new attraction or ride.[10] When the regionals first opened, everything was new and amazing, especially since few visitors had experienced the high bar of Disneyland. Over time, however, fake cannon shots splashing in the water and crude animatronics didn't measure up to increasingly sophisticated tastes and expectations. Many families eventually made it to a Disney park, and it became very difficult for a local enterprise to keep up. Theming a new ride can add anywhere from 5—20% to the budget, something few operators can justify. Economy of scale was possible with a large chain, where attractions and other offerings could be replicated across parks. Designing a new ride, land, or marketing campaign once is far cheaper than starting from scratch multiple times, so in some ways it's simply a smart business decision. Parks are, after all, a business. They must do whatever it takes to bring in guests and keep the gates open. As designer Ira West put it, "The manager lives or dies on attendance. If the numbers aren't there, he's gone."[11]

Many chains discovered that underneath the glamour of running a theme park lies the hard work of spending time and money—lots of money. Many ownership sellouts for regional parks were due to corporations deciding they just weren't worth the trouble. For the large conglomerates such as Taft, Viacom/CBS (Paramount), and Busch, the parks division was a tiny fraction of total income, and often, such as with Marriott, the extensive operational costs and reinvestment necessary for driving attendance was seen as a drain on their resources and a diversion from their primary focus.[12] As a result they bailed, forwarding these poor parks to yet another corporate owner who would drape their brand and way of doing things over everything.

Along the way, however, most of these operators recognized that at least some level of reinvestment was necessary to keep them viable, even if it wasn't in the spirit of the original design intent. To be fair, had a good number of these parks remained as-is, they most likely would not be in existence today. Part of Opryland's demise might be attributed to this. Decades of stagnation were unkind to many, including Disney for a time, where very little was added that would maintain, much less increase, attendance.

REAL ESTATE VALUES

Rising real estate values in certain markets placed parks on the endangered species list. More than once it was determined that the land was worth more with housing or a mall. That was the story behind the demise of Freedomland, Astroworld, Opryland, and very nearly Magic Mountain in CA.[13] Six Flags put it up for sale in 2006, but retreated shortly afterward.[14] The tragic irony of Astroworld and Opryland, however, was that the expected outcome didn't pay off.[15] There are many benefits of running a park in a local region far beyond ticket income. Opryland was a major factor in visitors planning a multi-day visit to the Opry complex, and its entertainment division fostered the development of generations of performers for Nashville and beyond.[16] It's difficult to imagine that the mall and parking lot now situated on the park's grounds have brought greater joy and economic benefit to the area. The former location of Astroworld is still a dirt lot, contributing nothing to its owner or the surrounding community. Great America in California was once up for sale, but the primary buyer wanted to demolish the park and go commercial. The city of Santa Clara stepped in to intervene, recognizing that the park provided thousands of jobs for locals, especially teenagers, and therefore bought the property to preserve it.[17] There are many factors, often intangible, that add toward the overall value of a theme park.

BUY OR BUILD?

Companies would rather buy existing parks than build their own from scratch. Building a comparable park today is considerable more costly than when this whole business got started. Walt's magical kingdom was extravagantly expensive at $17 million in 1955. Scaling the concept down for Six Flags Over Texas cost Angus about $10 million, while the next park in Georgia upped it a bit to around $12M. Mid-America in 1971 was reportedly more complicated to put together and jumped to $29M.[18] Taking advantage of design-once-build-twice, Marriott's bill for their two parks in 1976 rang in at $72,751,000.[19] By the time Canada's Wonderland came about in 1981 it had set Taft back $122M (Canadian).[20]

A mature market makes this even more challenging due to lack of opportunity and increased competition. It's not just inflation padding the bill, either; everything has become increasingly sophisticated and complex over the years, making it all cost more. Take a $5000 car in the 70s; a similar model might command $80k today. An "entry level" park can run $300 to $500 million, and that's just startup money; as we've seen, heavy capitalization is required to get a fledgling park through its early seasons.[21] So, aside from the Disneys and Universals (and the impressively large LEGOLAND currently being constructed in New York State), most new development in this country tends to be either purchasing existing parks, opening smaller family entertainment centers, or transforming abandoned malls into "retailtainment" venues.

SHORT OPERATING SEASONS

Many of the original regionals were located in geographic areas of the country that precluded year-round operating seasons. Even those in more moderate climates only operated during the summer, severely hampering their ability to pay the bills, much less move ahead. There's a reason Walt stuck to sunny Southern California and Florida. The recent trend is for regional park chains to increase their operating schedules throughout the calendar year, adding Halloween, Christmas, and spring events. This brings in additional revenue and helps offset any seasonal downturns due to weather impacts and such.

SOCIETAL CHANGES

Finally, demographic shifts in society play a major role in tourism. Families were on the rise in the 1950s, and the rapidly developing highway system provided the freedom to travel wherever they wanted. Except for the gas crisis in the 70s, increased mobility was key for attraction destinations. Over time, however, the baby boom slowed, and today fewer young adults are starting families due to anxiety over finances and student debt. This affects the types of places they want to go and what they want to do there. Social norms and trends are part of this as well; consumers demand increasingly sophisticated entertainment as is evidenced by the progression of television programming, movies, and so on. The rise of the "experience economy" has led to greater interest in immersive, participatory dining, shopping, and entertainment. Bass Pro Shops transformed the monochromatic aisles of fishing reels and tents into a thematic adventure. Instead of being shown to generic table #14 for lunch, Rainforest Cafe takes you into the jungle and surrounds you with an auditory and visual experience. Just sitting in a boat watching scenery go by is no longer the thrill it once was (of course, this depends on the level of design). People largely want to engage and enjoy an *experience,* and so all of these industries have tried to adapt accordingly. Reinvestment thus takes on a variety of twists and turns to meet demand, again not necessarily with the original thematic design in mind.

Due to all of these factors and more, consolidation began occurring not long after the first parks opened and rapidly increased over time. Once the original designers and owners were gone, no one was left who was there to know the reasons for the design nor particularly cared very much about any of it. The dream belonged to Angus Wynne, E. Pat Hall, Irving Waugh, Roy Hofheinz, and Warner LeRoy, not the corporate management that came after them. It was personal —for them as well as for the locals who grew up identifying with *their* park. The maze of buyouts and consolidation is complex, but let's trace the major changes as the industry reorganized from multiple independent parks down to a few major players.

LET THE BIDDING BEGIN: SIX FLAGS

Wynne's deal with the Pennsylvania Railroad allowed Six Flags to weather the 70s financial storm.[22] Once its Georgia and Mid-America parks opened, and with its new owner's resources, the company set course for aggressive expansion. No longer building parks from the ground up, they began a series of acquisitions—slowly in the early years, but a foreshadowing of what would transpire in the 1990s. First was Astroworld in 1975,[23] Great Adventure in 1977,[24] followed by Magic Mountain (California) in 1979.[25] Just a few years later in 1982,[26] Bally Manufacturing purchased the Six Flags assets from what had become the Penn Central Railroad, soon afterward adding the magnificent Marriott's Great America in Illinois to its portfolio (1984).[27] By 1987, however, the company determined that the parks were too much of a financial drain, largely due to expensive, seasonal operations and the need for significant reinvestment, and not where they wanted to focus their resources. They therefore sold the chain to the Wesray Corporation,[28] which held on for a few years. Time Warner slowly became interweaved into the various ownership splits, finally buying the entire chain outright in 1993.[29] Two years later they turned around and sold a 51% stake in the company to a finance entity, Boston Ventures, retaining partial control over management of the parks.[30] After establishing a management agreement to run Fiesta

Texas in 1996, that park became a Six Flags property two years later.[31] These years were generally good for the brand, with extensive reinvestment in the parks, though things gradually began to stagnate as part of the Time Warner empire.[32]

Meanwhile a regional real estate company in Oklahoma unexpectedly found itself trying to help a floundering park make another go of it. Frontier City was destined for the dozers in order to make way for commercial land development. When the deal fell apart, they had little choice but to fix the place up and see what it could do. That it did, enough to make them rethink their purpose in life. Over time TierCo Group would rebrand itself as Premier Parks and embark on a buying spree throughout the 90s and into the new century that would collect such properties as Wild World in MD, Geauga Lake in OH, Darien Lake in NY, and Kentucky Kingdom in Louisville, KY. There were lots more, but the big grab was the entire Six Flags chain in 1998—all eight parks. Add a bunch of international parks as well, and Premier became, well, the premiere chain for regional properties. Rebranding itself again in 2000, this time as Six Flags, the flags began flying over a multitude of parks around the globe.[33]

It was too much. By the mid-2000s the company was clearly in trouble, in over its head in debt and facing demands from shareholders and investors to do something about it. The massive sell-off and draw down commenced, including the infamous decision to demolish Astroworld.[34] The 2008 recession didn't help matters for anyone in the tourism industry, and so it was a slow climb from the bottom to regain their footing. However, the general good health of the park business in the second decade of the 2000s was largely kind to Six Flags.

TAFT BROADCASTING

Taft Broadcasting got its start when a brother of the President (the 27th, to be exact) bought a couple newspapers in Cincinnati. This was the late 19th century, and over time they would expand into broadcast media, first with radio, then television, eventually acquiring the

Hanna-Barbera studio.[35] When Gary Wachs made his pitch about selling old, flood-prone Coney Island and building a new place, Taft was looking for ways to expand the red-hot brand. After shutting down Fess Parker's proposed Frontier World in Kentucky, they got busy arranging financing and selecting a 1600-acre plot of land in Mason, OH.[36] Kings Island was a rousing success from the get-go, and they had already begun planning a second (and third) park in a joint venture with the Kroger Company. That partnership, Family Leisure Centers, was formed May 4, 1972, specifically for the purpose of building and operating parks.[37] But while they were busy opening Kings Dominion in Virginia, Carowinds was floundering, and so Taft/FLC agreed to acquire that unique, state-straddling property while also completing plans for Canada's Wonderland.[38] Perhaps influenced by all the trouble involved getting the Canada park moving, Kroger decided it didn't want to be in the amusement business after all. FLC was dissolved in February 1981,[39] just before Wonderland finally opened. After a reorganization of Taft's media properties, Kings Entertainment Company (KECO) began managing the parks in 1984, soon thereafter spinning off completely when Taft also decided it had had enough. The parks were draining company profits, from 22.4% in 1982 to 17.4% just two years later.[40] New to the portfolio was Hanna-Barbera Land in Houston[41] (a short-lived park that would eventually transform into a water park); Australia's Wonderland would follow in 1985. The big sell-out occurred in 1992 when Paramount Communications (Viacom) bought the entire chain, rebranding everything to *Paramount's Whatever*. The purchase of CBS by Viacom in 2000 made it the world's largest media company where the parks division became merely a footnote on the balance sheet, with earnings before interest, tax, depreciation and amortization of only $108 million in 2004. What was left of the parks was sold to Cedar Fair in 2006.[42]

CEDAR FAIR

In the late 1860s Louis Zistel built a series of bath houses along the shores of Lake Erie. He quickly began adding rides and other attractions, and over time the simple enterprise grew into one of the most successful amusement parks in the country. By the 1970s Cedar Point was on a roll, rapidly expanding and piling up the profits. But instead of considering numerous offers to purchase the park, they looked outward and bought a small park in Minnesota named Valleyfair. Now officially a chain, management took the company private in a venture renamed Cedar Fair Partnership. But it was a decade before they made their next move, acquiring Dorney Park and Wildwater Kingdom in 1992. Worlds of Fun in Missouri followed in 1995, then the big one—Knott's Berry Farm, finalizing the deal in December of 1997. They now had a major, year-round property to enhance their overall financial picture. Along with various water parks, they added Michigan's Adventure in 2001, and in 2004 got hold of Six Flags Worlds of Adventure in OH (the old SeaWorld and Geauga Lake properties). But the big catch, other than Knott's, was the entire Paramount Parks chain in 2006. This move further diversified their portfolio and brought Kings Island, Kings Dominion, Carowinds, Canada's Wonderland, and the former Marriott's Great America in CA. Cedar Fair has of late been generally considered one of the better regional operators, not merely investing in new attractions, but putting some soul and care into what they do.[43]

SEAWORLD/BUSCH

George Millay was not one to sit on the porch and stare into his iced tea. After he got the original SeaWorld up and running in 1964, expansion was the obvious next move. SeaWorld Ohio opened in 1970, while the Orlando park surfaced in 1973. But in the meantime George heard about a company who owned lots of land and wanted to build things to draw attention to their budding little city of Valencia. Newhall Land and Farming Company agreed to enter a partnership to build a ride park, and Magic Mountain stumbled into being in 1971. Things got tough, and SeaWorld's board wanted out before spending more money to fix the issues.[44]

Two years later, right in the middle of opening the Orlando park, George was kicked out of the company he had founded. Financially, it was a very difficult time with the gas crisis and skyrocketing interest rates. Worried about the bottom line, SeaWorld moved on without him. Soon afterward, Universal made an offer to buy the company, following up with an unsolicited takeover bid. Finding themselves in a vulnerable position, in 1976 they rather desperately sold the parks to publishing company Harcourt Brace Jovanovich for $52,241,000.[45]

In 1985 HBJ bought Cypress Gardens, a long-standing favorite from the 50s, then acquired Circus World before converting it to Boardwalk & Baseball. 1988 saw the addition of a fourth SeaWorld park in Texas. Things were going well, but the company was facing the threat of a hostile takeover and decided to sell the parks in 1989 to lower their debt load. Competing against Disney, Paramount Studios, a British entertainment magnate by the name of Robert Maxwell, and even a team of ex-SeaWorld execs pulled together by none other than George Millay, Busch Entertainment Company won the bidding to the tune of $1.1 billion.[46]

Busch had gotten into the tourism business with smaller garden parks that served as visitor centers to their breweries. Excluding the two short-lived locations in California and Texas, the Tampa park (1959) is the oldest surviving property, with the Williamsburg park opening in 1975. 1995 saw the sale of Cypress Gardens (part of the HBJ portfolio) to a partnership of that park's executives;[47] SeaWorld Ohio was handed off to Six Flags in 2001.[48] The big shake-up was in 2008 when parent company Anheuser-Busch was acquired by InBev. The parks division was suddenly in flux, with the giant brewer conglomerate now deep in debt and widely expected to sell off assets to reduce the burden; one year later Busch Entertainment was sold to the private equity firm Blackstone Group. InBev was most certainly not that interested in running a chain of amusement parks, as confirmed by CEO Carlos Brito when announcing the sale to Blackstone in 2009: Busch Entertainment Corporation was "not a core business for Anheuser-Busch InBev."[49]

With a new name, SeaWorld Parks & Entertainment, the company was on the rebound, leading to a decision to go public with an initial stock offering in 2013.[50] The renamed SeaWorld Entertainment almost immediately took a major hit with the *Blackfish* documentary, severely impacting attendance and their public image. Blackstone sold its remaining stake in 2017 to Zhonghong Group, an Asian real estate company that got way in over its head on multiple fronts; just two years later this deal began to crumble. Meanwhile, the parks division was showing signs of recovery with refocused priorities, pricing strategies (particularly in the busy Orlando market), and smart reinvestment in their properties.[51] But for now the drama continues with an endless rotation of CEOs, apparent conflict with the Board, and an uncertain future for some of the industry's most treasured properties.[52]

HERSCHEND FAMILY ENTERTAINMENT

Telling the tale of Herschend park ownership doesn't take very long. In 1950 Hugo and Mary Herschend decided to lease an attraction in the Branson region known as Marvel Cave, which was transformed into Silver Dollar City over many years. In the mid-70s they acquired their second park, Goldrush Junction—the original Rebel Railroad built by Tweetsie's founder. After a couple of name changes, Dolly Parton came into the picture as a business partner and the Pigeon Forge property became Dollywood. That's it. No corporate changes in ownership, no equity firms, no mass chain buyouts; the privately-owned company still runs everything. Over the years Herschend has expanded their portfolio with a variety of entertainment locations, including Stone Mountain, Wild Adventures, a couple of aquariums, dinner shows, and so on.[53] But keeping the list relatively short allows them to keep a close eye on things—not merely how business is doing, but more importantly helping their people learn about the values the company maintains and how this translates to management and operations. They are not a soulless corporate entity. They love what they do, they love the people who work with them, and the results are clear any time you visit one of their properties.[54] And that special story, that vibe where it all started? It's still there, and each new attraction or development is embedded in the original design intent.

IMPACT ON THE PARKS

Even though they shared common characteristics, attraction concepts, and ride systems, the original Six Flags and other regionals were very much individualized. Attractions and theming were adapted for each park, such as the variations on the *Jungle Cruise* concept. Off-the-shelf rides from manufacturers such as Arrow saved money and could be dressed uniquely to fit the local storyline. As the parks began to be grouped under the same corporate umbrella, it was a natural move to implement as many identical characteristics as possible. Slowly at first, this homogenization gradually increased to varying degrees for different companies. Kings Island, Carowinds, and others in the Cedar Fair portfolio are clearly distinct places today with their own charm and placemaking, but the corporate stamp is evident everywhere from logo and signage design, services such as FastLane, and even identical shows and parades. At the far end of the spectrum, today's Six Flags is the most notorious for overlaying a standard design and plan on their properties. It's difficult to tell which park you're in with nearly the exact same rides, shows, branding, characters, advertisements, and so on. They'll buy a handful of a particular ride and install them at various parks around the country, slapping random IP names on them. A ride labeled *Batman* means something completely different depending on where you are. Perhaps there's some business rationale behind this, but you'd never see this in the 70s. All three *Jungle Cruise*-type rides at the early Six Flags parks were named—and themed—differently. Same goes for their dark rides, where we went from *Tales of the Okefenokee* and *Spee-Lunker's Cave* to mass-produced *Justice League* shooters.

Having said this, it should be noted that Six Flags wasn't the first chain to pursue a McDonald's franchise strategy. When Marriott decided to get into the park business, they planned to build three nearly identical properties. They were, after all, in the hotel chain industry and were extremely successful in selling the concept of identical quality and experiences no matter where you stayed. The same would apply to their beautiful parks. In some ways this makes sense; it's unlikely visitors from one area of the country are going to travel long distances to see your other regional park. Disney maybe, but not these. And so more people can enjoy the same wonderful attractions and experiences if they're duplicated across the board. Perhaps this was a bit more palatable in the Marriott days due to the high standards those parks represented, as opposed to the cheap plywood and fiberglass facades plastered over many of today's parks. At any rate it's a smart business decision when you own more than one property; the trick is finding a balance.

Another challenge was finding brands and experiences that the public would relate to and pay to enjoy. As new attractions and expansions were planned, it became less viable to use an "old fashioned" theme like some of the historical references in the early parks. Nobody would presumably travel to see the latest history of the Carolinas show or hop into a boat to explore LaSalle's river adventures, but everybody loved Yogi and Scooby, Star Trek, and any other of the latest movie or television phenomena. Especially if it went really fast, so roller coasters were the hot thing, lightly themed to some IP franchise. It must be more thrilling to ride a coaster called *Hurler* in anticipation for what'll happen to your lunch than for the underlying, rather bland ride experience it actually was. Thrill-seeking was the rage and these parks delivered, knowing it would bring in the numbers. That's how we ended up with monstrous steel roller coasters dominating the skyline over Knott's Ghost Town. In some cases, however, the updates were well considered and implemented, such as transforming Six Flags Over Texas' *Spee-Lunker's Cave* into the excellent *Yosemite Sam & the Gold River Adventure*. Or Six Flags Over Georgia's *Tales of the Okefenokee* to *Monster Mansion*. As always, it's finding the right mixture. It's also the willingness to invest in creative design to give new attractions that extra thematic touch, something that was too often ignored along the way.

What did these changes actually do to the parks? A few examples will show the progression from a local-themed park to a corporate-branded, generic destination.

Carowinds was conceived to honor the heritage and people of North and South Carolina. For the most part it looked and felt like a Southern park, starting from the very first walk-up to the columned, neoclassical-style ticket gate. Ladies dressed as Southern Belles flitted and whirled about, and the lands were themed to represent various aspects or regions of state history: Plantation Square, Contemporary Carolina, Frontier Outpost, Pirate Island (yes, North Carolina has a history with pirates, most notably the infamous Blackbeard), and Queen's Colony. Agriculture and farming were represented as was down-home entertainment in *Harmony Hall.* There were glaring exceptions, of course, if you stopped to think about it. Monorails, sternwheelers, and *Goldrush* mine trains had nothing to do with the region, but they were part of the thrill and show. Mostly having nothing else to compare it to, guests took it all in and never thought twice about it. Of course it was a local park. And always would be.

The first corporate intellectual property showed up after Taft bought the park in 1975. Taft, owners of the Hanna-Barbera cartoon characters, had built Kings Island and Kings Dominion with dedicated lands for the franchise. Now Carowinds would get its own Hanna-Barbera Land with the junior *Scooby Doo* wooden coaster and a relocated, re-themed miniature train, now known as *Flintstone Express.* Scooby Doo, Yogi Bear, and others would walk the park and star in their own shows. Nobody complained, of course, because who doesn't like Saturday morning cartoons? Not everything new was Hanna-Barbera, with the magnificent dual racing *Thunder Road* based on the true story of mountain moonshine runners. (It was also based on the 1958 film

Thunder Road, a rare case of corporate IP coinciding with local history.) Even after the heart-breaking loss of the narrow gauge railroad that circled the property, the park was still identifiable as the original, thoroughly charming retreat we were growing up with. It was also still in business thanks to the sale and continued investment by Taft.

The park would get more love over the next several years from Taft and its successor, Kings Entertainment. A new outdoor entertainment venue, the *Paladium*, was an immediate hit for big-name concerts. Major rides such as *White Lightnin'*, *Carolina Cyclone*, and *Rip Roarin' Rapids* helped propel the park into the big leagues. Maintaining the Southern heritage of the park was still a thing, in spite of adding, well, *Smurf Island*.

Then in 1992 everything changed. Paramount Pictures Corporation bought the entire Kings Entertainment chain and immediately began its transformation into a movie-focused property. Star Trek shows and characters took over, and the unique state line spanning the center of the entrance bridge was plastered with pavers showcasing decades of Paramount movie history. Gone were the county names inscribed throughout the entrance plaza that had forged a personal connection for guests. Even the plaza itself morphed from Plantation Square to Paramount Plaza. We lost another of the park's icons, the monorail, in 1994. The park expanded, but with Wayne's World, a recreated scene from the movie which had nothing at all to do with the Carolinas. The feature ride, the *Hurler* coaster, was a carbon copy of the same thing at Kings Dominion. This had happened before, with the junior Scooby Doo coaster, but now the IP branding was becoming much more obvious and taking over anything to do with the park's heritage.

Perhaps the most emotional blow occurred in 2003 when the majestic *Carolina: Queen of the River* sternwheeler disappeared forever, replaced with the *Borg Assimilator* coaster. It wasn't even a new ride, having been transplanted from California's Great America with a simple Star Trek theme overlay. The small river that encircled the central island was filled in, another progression in the loss of original water features in the park and the latest victim to the desire to maximize space for stuff.

Presumably the entire park would have been rebranded and transformed into movie land if not for the sheer unfeasibility for rebuilding everything. Paramount clearly did the most damage to the park's thematic origins, but they also kept it current and fresh with new investment. At least they actually *did* theme their attractions and lands. Could it have survived if development had stuck to original design motifs? Hard to say. Movie IP, as we see all around us these days, is a powerful, emotional connector that resonates with people. It's a very effective option for story and thematic branding, but it's also been done ad nauseam. Maybe a clever, creative design of Carolina-focused ideas would work, something we're beginning to see again with Cedar Fair's renewed investment. Then again, maybe the public doesn't really care too much what the name of the ride is.

Some decisions are more difficult to criticize in spite of the emotional pain inflicted. The next-to-last remaining park icon, the antebellum-style ticket building, was demolished to make room for a more spacious and modern front entry area that is far more efficient and effective. The right decision? Certainly. It was dated, and more importantly, it sent the wrong social message. Could the new design have been better integrated into the Carolina theme? Possibly. Hersheypark made the same decision to tear down their beautiful Tudor entry area in favor of a similarly-conceived front gate and plaza. Was it needed? Something had to give as the original design wasn't intended for the large attendance numbers the park had been generating. Was the Tudor theme and style outdated? Matter of opinion, but the new Chocolatetown theme is far better suited to the company's heritage. And again, most folks really won't care too much either way. After all, they just want to have fun.

This story would be repeated at all the original regional parks. Six Flags Over Texas, the one that started it all, lost *LaSalle's Riverboat*

Expedition, *Skull Island*, *Astrolift*, the *Happy Motoring Freeway*, and many others. A visitor would be hard-pressed to recognize what "country" they are walking through as they roam the Duell loop, and the recent decision to cease flying the original countries' flags all but dooms any historical context. At least they still have their steam train, and for decades we continued to embark on an utterly charming journey through their re-imagined Yosemite Sam-themed dark ride (though its fate is currently in doubt due to recent floods). Six Flags Over Georgia also miraculously retained their dark ride, transformed into the delightful *Monster Mansion*. But the entire front entrance with the magnificent gardens, statuary, and Corinthian columns is gone, replaced with a generic retail corridor. The few remaining columns are largely hidden behind a performance stage. Guests no longer enjoy a spacious, distinctly Georgian/Southern welcome, instead stepping directly from the curb through a decidedly underwhelming entrance facade. It too, has lost its historical roots with the flags no longer flying; the only original land at Six Flags Over Georgia is Georgia. Everything else is Loony Toons or whatever. Six Flags Over Mid-America, now Six Flags St. Louis, has closed the coffin on any concept at all of themed lands—the current park map doesn't even pretend there's a Missouri, Illinois, or even Gotham City. It's just a bunch of rides, shops, and shows.

California's Great America, one of the magnificent Marriott properties, has undergone tremendous change over the years. Gone are the railroad, trolley, twin water flumes, the unique *Whizzer* coaster, and much of the American-themed vibe. The park was, after all, designed to pay homage to the United States. Few of the original lands remain, such as Yankee Harbor and Yukon Territory. The once-charming Orleans Place and Home Town Square are overrun by coasters on all sides. Residue from the Paramount years are everywhere. Its Chicago twin retains many of these attractions, but the Six Flags overlay makes it difficult to see much of what the designers brought to life back in 1976.

Many early attractions were removed because they took up large amounts of space, such as the various river boat and Arrow auto rides.

Six Flags Over Mid-America took out one side of the expansive dual Arrow mine train attraction, a wise decision as newer coaster technologies made better use of that land. *Skull Island* at Six Flags Over Texas was an easy target because it generated zero revenue, being essentially a large playground. From a management standpoint, space like that can be better utilized with food, games, and merchandise integrated into the land. In some cases, parks have no room to expand and must make difficult decisions, such as with California's Great America.

The *International Streets* at both Kings Island and Kings Dominion are still magnificent and certainly rank among the most beautiful "Main Street" segues into a park. However, instead of authentically themed shops and restaurants with delightfully intriguing names as *Kerzen, Spielwaren, Hute-Hemden, and Bijouterie,* we get yet another *Starbucks, Cinnabon,* and *Auntie Anne's*. I get it—it's easier to bring in outside franchises with powerful brands. It's just a bit of a downer, considering a theme park ought to provide more adventure than what you can find at your local shopping mall. Even the current park map downplays these *International Street* buildings, showing them in a very subdued way as nothing more than bland structures with facades on one side—a surprising artistic decision. The original maps were more intricately drawn with appropriate architectural features as if these industrial buildings were in fact small, quaint shops and restaurants. Victim to the Paramount years, both Kings Dominion and Kings Island lost some of their original themes and attractions, but yet retain the flavor of lands like Old Virginia, Candy Apple Grove, Rivertown and especially Coney Island (now Coney Mall).

Many of these parks featured lots of open space, largely due to lack of mature landscaping and limited number of attractions and facilities. Over time these were filled in with rides and other structures, maximizing use of space, but also losing some of the natural charm of walking the pathways. Transitions between lands generally got lost along the way with so many things crammed anywhere they could find. This diminishes the thrill of walking a path to see what's around the next bend and increases visual overload, what Disney designer John Hench referred to as visual chaos and contradiction. It all runs together, most of it isn't coordinated, and it has a negative affect on one's psyche. You get more tired and distressed, as opposed to Disneyland which is carefully designed to be a pleasing, restful, emotionally satisfying environment.

The Herschend properties have survived much of this turmoil thanks to everything remaining in the family, literally. The Herschends never sold out and have maintained control over Dollywood and Silver Dollar City, preserving each park's rich heritage, theme, and overall vibe. This might not have gone so well had the parks been merged into a larger chain's portfolio. Instead, they've managed to find ways to update, expand, and stay in business without losing their soul, such as with the recent opening of Dollywood's Wildwood Grove area. Beautifully designed to reflect nature and Dolly's love of butterflies, this new land is a natural extension of what the park is about. Even the thrill rides around the park are creatively themed and situated to fit into the story and surroundings, such as the B&M wing coaster *Wild Eagle*, featuring a gorgeous crafts-style station and promoting natural preservation. There's something authentic about walking around Dollywood and Silver Dollar City, much more than just seeing old frame buildings, water wheels, and hearing bluegrass music across the way. It is what it is, the real deal, and the glue holding all of this together is the loyal staff who love the park and what they do there. The company is run like a family, not a corporation; it makes a difference, and one wonders whether some of the other chain operators ever make the trek to see firsthand what all the fuss is about. Much of this is adaptable to any location; it just takes awareness and effort from management to care enough and make it a priority.

Longtime fans of each park can spend hours, if not days, scouring around looking for original buildings and other remnants from their childhood. One feels like an archaeologist digging through the layers of great societal change to uncover the original bones. Much of this is a sad trek, wistfully recalling the good ole' days when the park was really *their* park. It once told a story, however lightly, about their heritage and where they lived, and that meant something. Much of that is long gone, covered up and trampled by ever-newer thrills and experiences. Might it have been different? Probably not. Too many factors made such change inevitable, and most of us can at least be thankful we have a park to enjoy. Some are not so fortunate, and so in the evenings we treasure our old photos and home movies, pore over old maps, and browse the occasional book commemorating the park. The next morning we push through the turnstiles, have a great day, and savor hope for tomorrow. And hope abounds, as we shall see next.

Boat Rides
US

Hawaiian Punch Village.
(color films, food, soft drinks)
Miniature Band
CONTINUOUS

Skyride Terminal

Shamu, Killer Whale
SEE SCHEDULE

D

Chicken of the Sea Show
SEE SCHEDULE

Murata
Kabu

oth
DULES)
ale

D

Fresh Water dolphin poo

Main Entrance

Chapter Twelve

REDEMPTION

The line of humanity seemed endless, stretching nearly to the front gate. The Holy Grail lay clear on the other side of the park, but these poor souls wouldn't see it for at least five hours, sweltering in the Orlando heat and humidity. What possesses people to put up with such nonsense when they get irate if stuck more than three deep at the Target checkout?

June 18, 2010. Opening day for the Wizarding World of Harry Potter, a brand new land at Universal's Islands of Adventure.[1] But this wasn't just a land. Universal had changed the game, introducing a whole new rule book. Potter fans who for years queued up for the latest release at their local Barnes and Noble could finally realize what had until now existed only in their imaginations—you could actually step into Harry's world and walk in his footsteps, claim your wand at *Ollivanders,* and have a butterbeer at the *Three Broomsticks.* This was no mere collection of cleverly themed architecture and attractions. This *was* Hogsmeade—exactly like we all soaked in from the movies. The arched entryway cinematically revealed a vista rich with off-kilter buildings and Hogwarts castle rising majestically up on the hill. Thanks to an extraordinarily close collaboration between Universal

Creative and art directors from the movie franchise, including an almost manic control from J.K. Rowling, every last detail had been authentically reproduced.[2] It took Universal's "Ride the Movies" mantra to a completely different level.

THE FALL AND RISE OF DISNEY PARKS

To be sure, there had been outstanding attractions introduced over the preceding decades, rich with theme and backstory. The *Indiana Jones Adventure* at Disneyland, Frontierland at Disneyland Paris, and Disney's Animal Kingdom park immersed guests into extremely well-crafted environments. But a suddenly budget-conscience Disney, Universal randomly plopping attractions anywhere regardless of thematic impact, and a complete stripping of story or theme from the corporatized regionals took us further from the original concept of what a theme park was supposed to be. The entertainment business, like any other, is full of ups and downs. Parks thrive for awhile, then economic and other forces intervene, plunging the industry into a period of uncertainty.

Disney's most recent bleak period was triggered by the rough financial performance of the Disneyland Paris resort which opened in 1992. The company had been on a roll, defiantly declaring the 90s to be the "Disney Decade," full of optimism, expansion, and growth. The Paris property was beautifully designed and implemented, but due to a variety of factors such as regional economic uncertainty, over-exuberance in their hotel plans, and initial resistance from fiercely French patriots, performance stumbled. Eisner blinked and began pulling back the reins, rethinking the company's priorities and strategies for growth. Media acquisition continued unabated with the addition of Capital Cities/ABC and ESPN to their portfolio. The parks division, however, hit the brakes. The new rule of thumb: no more fully built-out parks that cost a fortune. More conservative properties was the new plan, manifested in such questionable outcomes as Hong Kong Disneyland, Disney's California Adventure, and especially the Walt Disney Studios park in Paris. Ever smaller and easily replicated location-based entertainment venues such as Disney Quest were planned for multiple locations around the country.[3]

Hong Kong's issue wasn't that it was a poorly designed park, but that it was small and gave the appearance as a "cheap" version of Disney's traditional castle parks. California Adventure, despite the valiant efforts of Imagineers who did what they could with very little, simply couldn't live up to what everybody expected from Disney. Especially since it was located literally in front of Walt's original playground—you know, the one that revolutionized the entire industry. Walt Disney Studios, suffering from the same lack of corporate support and under a contractual time constraint, was an under-capitalized question mark with cheap designs, lack of attractions, and little sense of that special Disney magic—the details that set their parks so far above everybody else.[4]

But this chapter is all about redemption, and hope abounds. New management realized something had to give, and so Bob Iger's first move after taking charge of the company was to bring Pixar into the fold.[5] The company needed popular, current intellectual property to provide a quick transfusion into the parks (and to the company's bottom line). Older attractions began to see overlays with new themes, such as Epcot's *The Living Seas* transformed into *The Seas with Nemo & Friends* and the original submarine attraction at Disneyland, long shuttered by previous management, brought back to life with another Nemo storyline. Somebody finally remembered that you have to spend money to make it, and so a massive reimagining of California Adventure took a lackluster entry area and transported it back to Walt's 1920s Los Angeles. Cars Land was by far the most Disney had done in a long time to build a movie property you could literally walk into and feel like you were there. They spent over a billion dollars on the park makeover,[6] and guess what—people loved it. The magic was back, Cars Land was an overwhelming success, and the proven formula was reinforced. Build something wonderful with a meaningful storyline and cohesive theme and people will come. In droves.

CHALLENGES FOR THE REGIONALS

The regional parks, as we have seen, faced even greater challenges. Disney and, to a somewhat lesser extent, Universal, were spared the constant corporate ownership swings that besieged the regionals. Fickle management, societal changes, and external fiscal issues affect everyone, but overall they could remain fairly true to their original mission and design premise. All the others have continuously wavered between being a *theme* or *amusement* park. An amusement park is a collection of stuff that allows people to have fun. This does not mean it can't be any good; on the contrary, parks such as Cedar Point have remained steadfastly wonderful amusement destinations. There might be glimmers of theme here and there, but it wasn't designed as a theme park and has never really pretended to be one. Many of the others that we have explored earlier in the book, though, were intended from the ground up to be a local Disneyland-lite. They were theme parks, representing local history, lore, and memories. Design principles from Disneyland were adapted and scaled for much smaller budgets and attendance expectations. So from the get-go these properties could never quite live up to their idol, losing some amount of attention to detail and the ability to completely immerse guests in effective spatial storytelling. But the designers worked to employ thematic overlays typically related to regional history—stories and legends that meant something to locals.

Lest we wax overly nostalgic, however, about those original designs and how wonderful they were, the fact is those historical themes came about largely because of something very pragmatic—they were free. Movie IP requires license fees; most of those parks didn't own any themselves, and this just wasn't in the budget. And we shouldn't go away believing that movie themes only came about because Paramount entered the picture, so to speak, wanting to capitalize on their properties, because the notion of movie IP in the parks goes back to the big enchilada itself, Disneyland. The Taft/Kings Entertainment parks were also infused with their popular Hanna-

Barbera franchise long before Paramount showed up. Duell's chief designer Ira West puts it very simply—there are a hundred good themes you can choose from, but not a hundred good plans.[7] You've got to design the layout and structure of a park to maximize the visitor's experience. This means determining how many and what kinds of rides, shows, food, merchandise, and restrooms. Figure out where all of this goes and how guests will get there. Then you pick a theme and design the overlay. Of course the park's owners already had some idea of the overall thematic concept, typically an homage to their particular region of the country. But once the designers got the nuts and bolts nailed down, they could take that overall storyline and come up with the specifics of how to apply it over everything.

Much, if not most, of this was lost over the decades, essentially morphing these regionally-relevant parks into a gaggle of generic amusement playgrounds. But as we keep reassuring ourselves, hope springs eternal, and there have been many signs of revival in the industry. And not just from Disney or Universal. Let's take a look at a few examples that give us hope while lifting our spirits out of the doldrums.

THE LOVE IS BACK

Cedar Fair bought the Paramount chain of parks in 2006.[8] A decade later, particularly with the appointment of Matt Ouimet as CEO in 2011, the fruits of that acquisition were in full swing with significant capital investment. The most visible aspect of this, of course, was bigger and better rides, but a core tenant of these upgrades has involved a return to the parks' original bones and stories. Take Carowinds, for example. The original lands in the park represented aspects of North and South Carolina from various time periods. It wasn't merely architecture, landscaping, and attraction names, but iconic structures such as the plantation house entry. In 2016 the water park was reinvigorated with a major expansion. Moving away from a long string of generic names such as Ocean Island, Riptide Reef,

WaterWorks, and Boomerang Bay, it was re-themed as Carolina Harbor. Attractions took on local, if somewhat cute, names such as *Blackbeard's Revenge, Pirate's Landing,* and *Kiddy Hawk Cove,* paying homage to the nearby coastal regions.[9] 2017 saw the original pirate island section in the upper-right corner of the park transformed into County Fair, complete with classic flat rides and other details paying tribute to the role of local fairs across the states.[10] The latest reimagining in the park, completed for the 2019 season, helped "activate" a back corner of the park that died when *Thunder Road* was removed (it was surely on life support even before then). This seven acre area is now Blue Ridge Junction, and it's a beautifully designed tribute to the mountain regions. As the park's general manager described, the immersive area is "...inspired by the majestic beauty and easy-going culture of the Blue Ridge Mountain region of the Carolinas."[11] *Copperhead Strike* is the signature attraction here, paying homage to such classic Carolina attributes as copperhead snakes, moonshine, and grumpy grannies. But it's the architecture that's the real feature, with the magnificent coaster station, extensive farm-themed queue, large stone outdoor fireplace with rocking chairs, and trees.

Although Cedar Point was never designed as a theme park, there are well-designed thematic sections sprinkled here and there. Frontier Town, which was later expanded into Frontier Trail, has for years been the destination of pleasant strolls through history with a combination of historically-themed structures as well as a healthy sprinkling of actual old buildings. The currently named *Trail Tavern* is a refurbished historic old log barn, while *Fort Sandusky* is a recreation of a 1761 British fort. *Addington Mill* originally came from North Carolina where it was built in 1861, and various other structures hail from other times and places. But then there's the *Panda Express* restaurant and the *Coca Cola Marketplace* overlay of the former *Cedar Junction Train Station*. Oh well.[12]

In 2018 Cedar Fair doubled-down on this area of the park by

transforming *Mean Streak* into *Steel Vengeance*. Along with this major coaster came a beautifully designed extension of Frontier Town centered around an actual storyline. Featuring "Maverick" Beauregard Chamberlain, "Digger" Wyatt Dempsey, "Wild One" Chess Watkins, and "Blackjack" Jackson Chamberlain, the area finally tells the full backstory of the drama between these characters and Frontier Town's development after the arrival of the "iron horse." Once a quiet, backwoods sort of place, Maverick's arrival in town triggered prosperity, prospectors, and upheaval. He quickly rose to prominence with his newly-found wealth and land ownership, and that didn't always sit well with the townspeople. Blackjack's got his number, though, and after threatening to blow the whistle, accepts a wagon full of treasure on the promise to leave town. That he does, but then returns with Chess and Digger to wreak *Steel Vengeance* on the shady character.[13]

With this major reimagining of one of the early areas of the park, Cedar Point has restored, rejuvenated, and modernized it in a way harmonious with the original thematic environment.

Knott's Berry Farm slowly morphed from a roadside attraction into a major theme park. But as with any large-scale development, this comes with its ups and downs. The old Knott's *felt* like a theme park, focused on western history with its original, relocated ghost town structures, steam train, the *Calico Mine Ride*, and *Timber Mountain Log Ride*. But then came the coaster wars that pushed most parks toward modern rides. The authentic streetscapes of Ghost Town became overshadowed by brightly-colored steel tracks piercing the skyline. Ever-taller and ever-faster doesn't play well with spatial storytelling environments.[14] Recently, however, Cedar Fair has recognized the rich heritage Knott's played in the industry and has invested heavily in bringing back some of that original goodness. 2013 saw the renovation of the 1969-vintage log ride, followed the next year by a complete restoration of the 1960 mine ride.[15] This was no mere fresh paint job; all-new animatronics and show scenes brought these classics to life better than ever. Most recently, the park's water rapids ride was re-themed as *Calico River Rapids*, complete with animatronics and show scenes along the twisting, churning journey.[16] At a time when many parks have ripped out their decades-old rapids, Knott's saw an opportunity to create a special, fun environment that brings new energy to an otherwise also-ran attraction.

July 4, 1966. 75-year-old Walter Knott oversaw the dedication of one of his most personal projects. A deeply patriotic man who loved politics, he had decided some time back that he wanted to build a replica of Independence Hall in Philadelphia. So he did, brick by brick, precisely down to the square inch. Bud Hurlbut rose to the challenge yet again, measuring everything and taking extensive notes, including forging a near-exact copy of the Liberty Bell.[17] When Cedar Fair bought the park, the building was thirty years old and showing it. Instead of selling it off or tearing it down, they chose to refurbish the grand structure. It's not a money-maker; there's no admission charge. It's just there for folks to go visit. But it's another example of doing the right thing in honor of the park's founders.[18]

Kudos to Cedar Fair for going the extra mile, making a statement about what's important, and resurrecting a bit of magic too many of us aren't able to enjoy in our own neck of the woods.

For 2019 Canada's Wonderland, another Cedar Fair property, finally fulfilled their original contractual obligation to the local government. In exchange for getting approval to build the park, then-owner Taft was required to make it distinctly Canadian.[19] That didn't quite happen, but 38 years later they returned to their roots by adding Frontier Canada and dusting off original nomenclature from other areas of the park. You can once again visit the Grande World Exposition of 1890 and Medieval Faire while enjoying such historically-named attractions as *Dragon Fyre, Viking's Rage, Wilde Knight Mares* and *Wilde Beast*. The *Canterbury Theatre* has also returned, and so at least we get a nod to the park's past.[20]

Even little steps make a difference. For 2020, California's Great America re-themed its water park as South Bay Shores, reflecting local interest in Northern California's beaches and the South Bay region.[21] Six Flags St. Louis introduced a smart new logo that capitalizes on the famous arch, featuring the tag line "Gateway to Thrills."[22] It's exciting to see a trend toward recognizing regional history, interest, and even dusting off ideas from the parks' early histories.

SeaWorld, looking for a way out from the 2013 Blackfish scandal, began transforming their image from a live animal show park to more themed experiences that paid homage to the sea, educating guests on its wonders. Attractions and rides such as *Antarctica: Empire of the Penguin* and *Mako* go far beyond your standard plywood signage and building facade. *Antarctica* takes you directly into the penguin's frigid home environment, a completely immersive experience that not only teaches you anything you'd want to know about the wee waddlers, but gets you up close and personal with their fun, quirky personalities. While nobody would mistake *Mako* for authentic spatial storytelling, it offers much more than is typical for amusement rides with its thematic station, queue, signage, and surrounding environment.

In 2019 SeaWorld Orlando stepped into the world of thematic placemaking by opening Sesame Street to several generations of folks who previously knew Big Bird and Oscar only from afternoon television. Now you could walk down the Street, check out *Big Bird's Nest* and *Hooper's Store*, and play with a variety of interactive elements scattered around the land. Potter-lite? Sure, but this is the sort of thing that will continue moving the needle in ever-better directions.[23]

TAKING IT TO THE NEXT LEVEL

Backstories and authentic placemaking have certainly been an exciting trend, but a few years back Disney upped the game again by experimenting with immersive role-playing adventures with guests inside the park. For 2014, Disneyland debuted *Legends of Frontierland: Gold Rush!* Park guests could take on the role of town citizen or one of those rowdy Rainbow Ridge ruffians, joining the struggle for land... land that just might be hiding untold riches in gold. Stop off first at the *Trading Post* for the latest happenings, then send an urgent message to a fellow citizen from the *Telegraph Station*. Rainbow Ridge types have their own *Hideout* for conspiracy conspiring. Get the inside scoop from the various characters you run into while earning "bits" that can be spent buying plots of land. The more you engage, the deeper the storyline and experience.[24] It was something totally new for park guests, requiring a great deal of thought and iterative design as the Imagineers worked to help participants learn the ropes and enjoy the game. It's also expensive, requiring much more in the way of entertainment staff. Clearly this was a test of concept, perhaps looking forward to the upcoming Stars Wars: Galaxy's Edge; it only ran the one season, but just down the road others were watching with a keen eye...

Ken Parks, who had worked on the *Legends* idea with fellow Imagineers Asa Kalama and Cory Rouse, had moved over to Knott's, leading the charge for developing a similar concept. *Ghost Town Alive!* literally brings the old west to life with you right smack dab in the middle of everything. Live actors roam the town, each day bringing a particular story and set of events. It's Founders Day in Calico, so grab a copy of the *Calico Gazette* to see the latest news and happenings for the day. As you wander around, various citizens will ask favors or try to get you involved in some intrigue. These interactions bring up all kinds of side stories that enrich the overall experience. Stop for a spell at the

Calico Saloon, then follow the map to discover clues to various puzzles and mysteries.[25]

Ghost Town Alive! is spatial storytelling at its finest, set in an authentic old west environment. The actors are fantastic and bring an entirely new level of energy and engagement to the park. It turns out guests are hungry for the opportunity to not just watch, but to step into the story and be part of it. To play a role and make a difference in the overall event. We see this in many other ways with the rising popularity of cosplay. Yes, it's costly to run, but the results speak for themselves. Repeat attendance is driven by ever-changing storylines, and many season pass holders come specifically for the experience. Revenue is up from food and merchandise sales.[26] Again, just like Walt said: build something great and people will come.

The success of *Ghost Town Alive!* prompted Cedar Fair to try the same formula at the Point. *Forbidden Frontier on Adventure Island* is an experiential attraction where you explore the park's water-bound, mysterious realm. Word has it there's locals livin' back there, but after a brutal ruckus some time ago the local cavalry from Frontier Town locked the place down, forbidding outsiders to enter for five years. Time's finally up, and so we have to find a way across the swamp, where we follow the trails and run into a variety of characters. First is Officer Etta Fox, cavalry, who warns you about the two warring clans, the Wapis and Cayugas. Today is Truce Day, but behind all this things are a bit more unsettled than they seem. As you follow the map, join up with one of these factions and see what you can find out about some sort of treasure. Meantime, you just might blunder into a robbery or something. Immerse yourself as much or as little as you want, but *Forbidden Frontier* is a bold change of direction for a park that's world famous for its iron rides.[27]

Hot on the heels of transforming the island itself, Cedar Point expanded the backstory with *Snake River Expedition*. Hearty souls set off on rustic explorer boats with one of Trapper John's pilots navigating the dangerous waters and enlisting your help to complete a secret mission. *Snake River* is full of actors, special effects, and surprises along the journey, again pulling guests into the story and engaging them in a way rarely seen in recent years.[28]

HAS SIX FLAGS RETURNED?

Let's face it, Six Flags gets a bad rap. And in some ways deservedly so, to be brutally honest, in part due to the company's business model; they're clearly an *amusement* park chain now with different budgetary priorities. Facades and theming, if present at all, are usually some form of painted plywood and fiberglas, often without much thought as to how they fit into the surroundings. Areas that do have some fragment of backstory or theme, such as Gotham City, are plastered with advertising banners. There really is no longer an "Over Texas" and "Over Georgia"; they're all McDonald's with the same everything. The original parks have meandered way off course from the original Angus Wynne/Randall Duell jewels. But then on August 28, 2014 came a surprise announcement: Six Flags was teaming up with Sally Corporation (the fabulous dark ride folks) to introduce *Justice League: Battle for Metropolis*. After an age where regional parks had been either removing their classic dark rides or converting them into relatively simple shooter attractions, this seemed to bring a touch of Disney-level magic. Here was a regional park operator investing in a completely reimagined attraction with motion-based vehicles from Oceaneering and advanced animatronics from Sally.[29] Does this bring back "Over Texas"? No way, but at least it's a step up for a regional park attempting to bring more story and immersion into the place.

Justice League is a younger, smaller cousin to *The Amazing Adventures of Spider-Man* attraction at Islands of Adventure. After getting instructions from the animatronic Cyborg, guests roar off in their wildly swaying vehicle, nearly getting blasted from an animatronic Joker, avoiding all other sorts of mayhem, all while desperately trying to save Metropolis. *Justice* is an example of how advances in technology, with its concurrent reduction in cost over time, bring capabilities to the regionals that were once exclusively the domain of the Big Two. Disney's *Soarin'* is another one, where you can now find similar, high quality flyover attractions all over the country. There is less excuse these days for creating amazing attractions with rich, engaging stories.

OIL TYCOON BUDGET NOT REQUIRED TO MAKE A DIFFERENCE

Less excuse, perhaps, but in spite of this technology and economic trend, one of the hangups for building deeply immersive attractions remains their significant cost. It still takes a lot of money, something the regional parks in the U.S. don't possess in unlimited supplies. This isn't the case in places like Saudi Arabia where Six Flags is currently building their largest, most fully-themed park ever. Six Flags Qiddiya is but a tiny part of a massive development plan that includes sports, entertainment, and the arts in zones known as the Resort Core, City Centre, Motion Zone, Eco Zone, & Golf Community. The Resort Core area includes a 79-acre park featuring six lands: City of Thrills, Discovery Springs, Steam Town, Twilight Gardens, Valley of Fortune, and Grand Exposition. Guests enter the park and find themselves at The Citadel, a hub with food, shops, and gateways to each of the lands. Concept art reveals greatly detailed, highly themed attractions, buildings, and so on that far exceeds anything the company has done (well, since maybe the original in 1961).[30]

The difference here, of course, is budget, but at least we're seeing progress in our own parks as we better understand guests' interests, take advantage of new techniques and technology, and remember our roots in spatial storytelling. After decades of belt tightening through the elimination of live entertainment and expensive, maintenance-intensive attractions, it's a breath of fresh air to see some vitality and energy again. Spending the extra money for actors, animatronics, rich experiences, and live performers requires that owners understand such things do indeed make a difference and encourage repeat visits.

FOND MEMORIES & FUTURE HOPE

So what's in store for us? We're not here to gaze into a crystal ball, but current trends include more of the examples we just looked at with rich backstories, increasingly sophisticated technology-based experiences, and personal interactivity/role play by guests. The days of floating people past semi-static displays are mostly over; we now have far more sophisticated ways of telling stories as well as engaging guests into those narratives. Smaller parks and attractions have more opportunity than ever to get into the game, offering immersive experiences limited more by imagination than by budgets. Parks will continue innovating ways to incorporate mobile technology into attractions. And the distinction between a theme park and themed experiences elsewhere, such as at the mall, museum, restaurant, or even train station, will become ever more blurred. Perhaps this trend will be a temporary one, lasting only until the next generation of management comes along without a creative mindset or willingness to open their wallets a bit wider. Or there will be an explosion of new ideas for spatial storytelling made possible by advances we can only dream about. We'll see.

If we were completely honest with ourselves, we'd have to admit much of our emotional connection with the parks we grew up with is just that—an emotional connection. Just like our favorite songs or movies we enjoyed during our formative years, whatever the parks happened to be at the time is what we fondly remember. Yes, locally-relevant themes and overlays made it even more personal, which is why we've devoted so much attention to the subject. But there are generations who came along during the Paramount times who don't know any different—that's the norm for them. Or those pesky Star Wars prequels. So it's mostly in the eye, and heart, of the beholder. Each of us has different priorities as to what's important and what we want to see in the parks. The original, regional parks weren't on the level of a Disneyland, but they were, for the most part, quite beautiful and well-designed. Much of that original love has been lost over the decades of change. But our hope is that firstly the parks will continue to survive, and secondly that owners will continue investing love, attention, and resources to making them the very best that can reasonably be accomplished. Finally, we owe a great debt of gratitude to those bigger-than-life entrepreneurs who, against the odds, applied sheer will of force to get these parks—our parks—built. To Angus Wynne, Judge Hofheinz, Irving Waugh, Gary Wachs, E. Pat Hall, Lamar Hunt, Warner LeRoy, George Millay, Grover Robbins, the Herschends, Busches, and Marriotts, Randall Duell, and yes, even C.V. —thank you for making our lives just a bit brighter each day.

DUELL DESIGN 101

Mel McGowan, Co-Founder & Chief Creative Officer, Storyland Studios

While touring former Disney Imagineers, executives, and theme park designers through our Storyland Studios "magic factory" in Southern California, we hear time and again that the experience reminded them of the magical alchemy of WED Enterprises while Walt Disney was still alive. Our good friend Tony Baxter, Disney Legend who learned the trade first-hand as a second-generation Imagineer, was particularly struck by the similarities. During this "golden age" at the precursor to today's Walt Disney Imagineering, the atmosphere was more intimate and close-knit. Designers gathered around the water cooler and solved problems without going through layers of committees, management, and red tape. Ideas flowed among professionals from different disciplines and backgrounds, the objective being to grab hold of Walt's vision and get it done. I must confess that the resemblance in our shop is not a coincidence. We find ongoing inspiration in that first generation of "spatial storytellers" and Imagineers.

However, one of the more memorable compliments came from my friend and industry veteran Rick Bastrup, who said that he was reminded of being in the midst of R. Duell & Associates as they were hitting their stride in the 1970s. Rick—who essentially served as their contracted Creative Director for themed attraction development—

was in a position to accurately assess the resemblance. From a pure productivity perspective, there has been no other team in history that was able to master plan, design, and produce the number of theme parks than this underrated and under-recognized "dream team" led by former MGM Art Director Randall Duell, Ira West, and Academy Award winners John DeCuir and Paul Groesse. The 1975 edition of Encyclopedia Americana states "Since Disney's death, Randall Duell... has become the number one force in theme park architecture."[1]

Graduating from University of Southern California's School of Architecture in 1925, lack of opportunity during the Great Depression eventually led Duell into the movie industry, ultimately serving as art director for over sixty films including *The White Cliffs of Dover* and *Singing in the Rain.* 1958 saw him retiring from the movie business and reverting to architecture, joining up with C.V. Wood at Marco Engineering to begin work on Pleasure Island, Magic Mountain (CO), and Freedomland. There he learned the ropes of park design from Wade Rubottom, who had worked on Disneyland's Main Street. Other architectural work sprinkled in over the years included commercial buildings such as the Avalon Casino on Catalina Island and Googie/Jetsons styled car dealerships.

With an extremely lean team of architects, artists, and art directors, Duell and his team completed designs at the prodigious rate of at least one park a year on average, peaking in the 1976 opening of three separate parks. Marriott's Great America parks in California and Illinois, as well as Libertyland in Tennessee, were each themed and timed to capitalize on America's Bicentennial celebration. This isn't even counting a third Marriott park intended for the Washington, DC metro area that failed to move into construction!

Having come from the aerospace industry and Stanford Research Institute (the firm that provided pre-development consulting on Disneyland), C.V. Wood undoubtedly taught Duell more about the "rollercoaster math," industrial engineering, and business economics of the industry than he could ever have coached him on architecture and art direction. The complimentary left and right brain mentoring by C.V. and Wade would prove invaluable to Duell's clients, where he served as a "sherpa" and overall real estate development guide to intrepid local businessmen, entrepreneurs, and non-entertainment corporations who knew nothing about the business. Clients learned to trust Duell and his designers on what the parks should look like and offer guests. While they were technically an architectural firm, they were essentially designing the business plan for the owner. If it failed, you're stuck. You can't do anything else with it—it's a park. You can't convert it into a mall, hotel, or housing without tearing everything down and starting over. And so most developers, while sometimes having opinions on what they wanted, mostly just wrote the check and let the experts take care of everything.

It all starts with the numbers. Any proposed park or attraction has to be financially feasible, so an economic study is performed to determine what kind of park, if any, would be suitable for the location. Harrison "Buzz" Price worked for Stanford Research Institute when Walt and Roy came looking for guidance on Disneyland. They needed a recommendation for where to put Walt's grand experiment, and so Buzz gradually narrowed it down to Anaheim. Seems like no big deal, but at the time Anaheim was only a brief mention on the Jack Benny show with nothing to show for itself. It was in the middle of nowhere, but the numbers revealed that the Los Angeles area was poised for great expansion, with a planned freeway stretching right through the sleepy town. He nailed it, moving on to found his own company and revolutionize this aspect of the park industry. Economics Research Associates was involved in nearly every park project for decades, providing rock solid advice to developers. Mostly they listened. Sometimes they didn't.

So what's a feasibility study? In order to get an idea of what might fly in a certain market, a long list of questions must be answered. Analysis must be conducted for potential sites, market size and predicted attendance, seasonality, ride and attraction capacity, per capita expenditures, and so on. Environmental impact, acoustic issues, traffic, and much more need to be examined. These can be determined from government and other sources, logic, and a bit of intuition. It's a relatively straightforward process, not that the results always make the client giddy with happiness. Harcourt Brace Jovanovich, owner of SeaWorld at the time, was looking to build their next park in the San Antonio area. ERA predicted between 1.2 and 1.5 million annual visitors, but Mr. J. wouldn't hear of it, defiantly determined to build for 3–5 million. Once overly aggressive promotion and discounts wore out, attendance settled right into the 1.422 million range. The park was over-built and barely managed to hang on until it found its footing. Numbers don't lie; the feasibility study essentially lays out your business plan and scope, so pay attention to it.

A regional park was generally considered to reach a primary market within roughly 50 miles, about an hour's drive to the park and back home the same day. The secondary market ranged 100–150 miles. This is very different from a Disney or Universal property, which draws nationally and is considered a resort destination with its hotels and multi-day experiences. Although many of the regionals incorporated plans for hotels and such, they still generally drew from a limited geographic range. Major population centers and easy access to freeways were essential, and you'll notice they generally settled on sites close to Interstates or other major roadways near big cities.

And after making such a definitive case for numbers, there are indeed those rare situations that seem to defy gravity. Holiday World is an independently owned theme park in Santa Claus, Indiana. The middle of nowhere. Way out from any major population center. And yet it boasts well over one million in annual attendance. Wherever those people come from, it reminds us again that if you build something fantastic, people will make the trip.

Initial design of a park is more of a planning problem than it is an artistic exercise. How many people do we need to entertain over the course of a season? How many are coming on a peak day? You're throwing a big party and need to service everybody's needs while they're there including parking, ticketing, food, merchandise, restrooms, rides, and shows. Once you have a budget and expected attendance, designers determine the overall size of the park and number of entertainment units—capacity from attractions, shows, and restaurants—required to meet what is known as "design day." The definition of design day varies a bit, but essentially it is the average of the fifteen–twenty most anticipated crowded days of the season, say around 2pm in the afternoon after everyone's arrived and before guests begin to leave for home. You can't build a park sized for the most crowded days; it'll sit fairly empty most of the time. It's the same concept as building a church for Easter Sunday. Design day tends to represent the 90th percentile, where roughly 10% of your operational days will be somewhat overcrowded.

Ideally you need at least 1.5 entertainment units per guest in order to minimize long lines; people standing in line are unhappy and not spending money. Two units per guest is better, but costs more to build and might be difficult to recoup. This also depends on the type of park; if it features longer-duration attractions, such as in a Disney or Universal park, you can aim a bit shorter. This then dictates an overall number of attractions which are divided into the various themed lands. Each of these areas is essentially a mini-park, featuring an assortment of rides, shows, food, merchandise, and restrooms. Not all lands offer a complete mix, but there must be a sufficient balance of these elements scattered throughout the entire park.

Ira West, who joined Duell's firm in 1965, makes the point that their primary job was to figure how to lay things out so as to accommodate guests: people flow, sidewalks, building and attraction locations, and so on. "And we learned as we went along; we never repeated our mistakes."[2] Restrooms became more efficient with people coming in one door and out the other. Women's restrooms had to be twice as large because they took longer. Large, attention-grabbing attractions such as major coasters were located toward the back of the park. This increases people flow by enticing them to keep moving around the pathways. Major restaurants were often placed there as well; people generally got hungry a couple hours after they arrived, and by that time they would have worked their way farther back.

How exactly do you lay out the pathways for a park? How do guests get from the main gate to everything else? Attractions need to be easy to find with a minimum of walking. There is no one-size-fits-all ideal park layout—it's a combination of preference and situation. Walt's original thinking behind the hub and spoke design was so guests wouldn't get "museum feet." That aspect didn't work out so well, since when you wander down a spoke to explore a themed area, you still have to walk back the way you came in order to try a different land. Over time the Disney parks opened pathways directly between lands to alleviate this. Several approaches have been developed over the years, and it depends on the particular type and size park. A wildly meandering path can be adventurous, but difficult for guests to understand where to find things. Too many branches from the main pathway leave people confused and frustrated. Duell and his team came up with a simple solution where a single main pathway loops around the entire park. Six Flags asked them to make sure everybody saw everything they had in the park, so the easiest way was to position it all along what became known as the *Duell loop*. We can see the evolution of the loop from Six Flags Over Texas to the Marriott parks; it's the same essential concept, but the Great America layouts are larger, meander creatively without confusing guests, and feature well-designed transitions between lands, including covered bridges, themed portals, and man-made waterways.

The loop concept works well, up to a point, in that you can't get lost. It's obvious which way to go to see everything. The downside is that you have to walk around the entire loop to experience the park. That's not so bad with a small to medium size park, but as you get bigger it becomes too cumbersome, time-consuming, and just plain fatiguing. Epcot is the obvious example, where it's a 1.2 mile walk just to circumnavigate the World Showcase lagoon. Universal has adopted this approach in all of their parks outside of Hollywood.

Central lakes and lagoons make for beautiful vistas, light displays, and river boat rides. They're also a maintenance nightmare due to the fact that utilities are usually designed to branch out from the center into each area of the park. This way if there's a problem in one section it doesn't bring down the entire park, be it electricity, water, or communications. So the center of the park serves as the hub, and if there's a problem, the lake must be drained, the water seal broken, and then put back together after repairs are completed. It's also a park's most valuable real estate; the center is where everything connects in terms of visuals and path layout. If there's a lake there, you can't put anything for people to do. Duell's team realized that if you placed major water features over to the side, they are still beautiful and can serve as an effective draw, freeing up prime land for more participatory uses. The Marriott parks are the ultimate result of this thinking, featuring lots of water scattered around the park in ways that do not inhibit utility maintenance and other needs. In fact, their ingenius solution for maintenance, utilities, and servicing of restaurants and retail was to incorporate a backstage pathway right down the middle of the park. This service spine is out of sight of park guests and provides complete access to the back doors of these facilities.

They planned for expansion, reserving plots of land around the perimeter of the park for future rides and even entire areas. In fact, today it's difficult to recognize original boundaries. Growth is necessary in order to generate repeat business; the industry learned that while there is always a core demographic that comes year after year, you can't stay in business without adding new things that will entice everybody else. Unfortunately, that almost always meant finding the latest big thing, usually a coaster or thrill ride. None of these fit into the original thematic surroundings, and so from the get-go we started to lose design coherence. What they also had to keep an eye on was balance; after adding a few thrill rides, the demographic at the park shifted toward teens. And so they'd add family attractions in order to maintain a healthy mix among age groups. It's a tricky equation, and in the urgency of hitting budgetary attendance numbers, story and theme were often after-thoughts, if they were thought about at all.

Notice we haven't mentioned theme yet. Surprisingly, Duell's design staff wasn't too concerned about theming in the early stages of a park's design. "There are a hundred good themes; there aren't a hundred good plans."[3] Get the practical issues figured out, then overlay your storyline. Theming a land or section of the park is known in the industry as *placemaking*. If an area is to be styled after the Wild West, then everything seen and experienced in that area needs to be straight out of that time period. Architecture, materials, technology (or lack thereof), employee costuming, paint colors, and so on are selected to be authentic to that time and place. An early Disneyland photographer learned all about authenticity after parking his car "onstage" within sight of the guests in Frontierland. He barely had the door open when he felt a finger in his chest. "What's this car doing in the 1800s?" Walt angrily demanded. It destroyed the illusion of being in that time period, referred to as the suspension of disbelief. The goal is to preserve this as much as possible, but it's expensive and takes a great deal of effort, which is why most parks only go so far (or don't try at all).

Theming in those days generally centered around regional culture and major time periods in American history. It fit the bill for giving each park its own regional identity; it was also free, unlike typical movie and character properties. The Wild West was not only popular in those days, but also relevant to the histories of many of these parks, and so they invariably included a frontier-style section with rustic architecture, forts, and rivers to explore. A few land concepts, like Astroworld's Mod Ville and Opryland's Music of Today, came from popular culture across the country at the time. While not as detailed and completely immersive as Disneyland, they were able to apply their background as movie art directors and designers in order to foster a sense of make-believe for guests that served the purpose.

In retrospect, one of the reasons for both the success and failure of Duell's designs was his inherent "minimalism" as an architect. Like many Disney Imagineers with similar backgrounds, such as Richard Irvine, Marvin Davis, and Bill Martin, he learned to adapt architectural design to the constrained needs of movie sets. Theatrical design for stage or film has always been, out of necessity, about visually suggesting a setting with the minimal possible effort in terms of construction, detailing, and permanence. Because of constrained production budgets, short duration of use, and the need for flexibility in backlot facades, two or three exterior walls were sufficient to infer a building rather than the normal four. A generic "European village" grouping of facades could represent war-time France in one film, a medieval English village in another, or Transylvania the following month, simply by changing paint colors, signage, graphics, vehicles, props, and entourage. It's a fascinating world, and for years film-makers and storytellers such as Walt Disney and Steven Spielberg (and even myself) could not resist the allure of sneaking onto a studio backlot and wandering around the empty street sets and exotic locales.

Following the Golden Age of Hollywood, many of the great studio backlots fell into disrepair, were either redeveloped, or sold off. Due to increased sophistication of global audiences, high-definition, and green screen filming, exterior location shooting has become the norm in feature films. However, if one were to compare the 20th Century Fox Western facades with those of Six Flags Over Texas, you would find strikingly familiar levels of detailing and scale. Both employ similar height to street width ratios, meandering street alignments, and forced perspective (in which upper floors are built to reduced scale to save costs and insinuate greater height). Streets were often aligned so as to close off terminating vistas in order to hide the chap-arral covered hillsides behind them. Duell believed that visitors should never look down an open street. There should always be another attraction around the corner to draw people forward while creating a sense of discovery and anticipation. Eventually Duell and his designers learned to smooth out the serpentine curves of their earliest parks in order to accommodate crowd flow, fire access, parade routes, and themed transportation. But the "backlot" level of facade finish and scale remained buildable by local contractors and affordable to regional park developers.

Dressing the sets also carried much of the heavy lifting in terms of spatial storytelling for the regional parks. Signs, props, vehicles, and costumed "extras" (employees) carried the day (or at least the hour or so) that a guest would spend in each land. Restaurants and retail outlets were not only easy to integrate behind the themed facades, but actually allowed guests to step deeper into the "rabbit hole" of make-believe where they would encounter appropriately themed food, merchandise, interior design, and costumed cast members.

Many trained architects are either uncomfortable or allergic to color, believing that unadorned building materials make for a more "honest" structure in which form follows function. At MGM, Randall learned that form can also follow fiction and that color is a powerful emotional scripting tool. "I don't think the public is aware that when we have a theme area, we color code it. I'll take a small scale plan and a palette of colors so that it looks like the colors found in New England, or the Southwest, and we'll pick six or eight of them that go together and give it to our design people and say, 'Here's your palette, use it throughout the whole area.'"[4] Over time this carefully considered, often historical-based color design would be forgotten, violating the most basic of John Hench's principles of visual chaos and contradiction.

Most major rides of the regional parks were clearly cut and pasted from Disneyland's charming, but rather low-tech opening day playbook: a narrow gauge railroad, trolleys, river cruises, stagecoaches, small scale dark rides, miniature cars, and usually a can can show. Each of these rides, shows, and attractions had been chosen by Walt Disney to enhance the *show* being presented to guests in that park. So for the regionals, rather than directly copy Disney's "African Queen" inspired *Jungle Cruise*, one could sail with Georgia's French explorer Jean Ribault or Texas' La Salle on regionally-inspired rivers. Instead of riding a mine cart with Snow White and the Seven Dwarfs in Fantasyland, you could explore the *Tales of the Okefenokee* with Brer Rabbit or sail with Huck Finn into *Injun Joe's Cave* in Missouri. Rather than adopt Disney's medieval fantasy fair setting as an appropriate home for carousels, flat rides, and kiddie rides, these off-the-shelf attractions were either placed in a turn-of-the-century Victorian amusement park or county fair type setting (such as Candy Apple Grove at Kings Dominion) or, more frequently, dispersed throughout the park. They would be discreetly placed behind a themed portal, queue building, landscaping, or other park structures and given predictably "punny" names. Thus the same Enterprise-type centrifugal force flat ride would be known as the *Apple Turnover* on the midway at Candy Apple Grove and the *Orleans Orbit* behind a grand French Quarter archway in Orleans Place at Marriott's Great America. "We take a manufacturer's ride—the shell of it or just the mechanics. We will control the color and design of the vehicles, other things that go into it. More than that, we'll come out front, where the public is, and we'll give it a marquee that's a pleasant thing to look at. Maybe we'll use hanging baskets of flowers, some trees, and maybe in back of that is all the honky-tonk fun you want. But even there we take off all the junk we can get off it."[5]

Simple affordability and constructability of dressing up pre-engineered soundstages with themed facades was a strength in getting these pioneering parks built. But over time the thinness of this place-making approach contributed toward the gradual loss of original design intent, with random paint, IP, and redevelopment often leaving these cherished places nearly unrecognizable. However, one of the many unrealized strengths of Duell's designs was the fact that his paradigm was less of a Hollywood backlot filled with rides, but rather that of throwing a garden party for 10,000 friends. Duell rose above his architectural training and art director background to truly become a master planner and site designer. He recognized that theme parks were in fact *parks* and descendants of the grand tradition of Frederick Law Olmstead, Tivoli Gardens, and royal pleasure grounds from Versailles to Hadrian's Villa.

Rather than Walt Disney's predilection for a flat *tabula rasa* site, Duell was known for selecting park sites with interesting geological features such as hills, water, and lots of trees, and then working around and incorporating these features. Randall helped select the location and designed the first layout for Busch Gardens in Williamsburg, a staggeringly beautiful park due to its natural setting. It has been consistently voted the "World's Most Beautiful Park" by the National Amusement Park Historical Association. A portion of Opryland was built in an existing forest, so they transplanted thousands of trees while keeping as many as possible in place, routing pathways and situating structures around natural features. Magic Mountain in California is located where it is precisely because of the mountain; while making everything more difficult and expensive, it was too good to pass up in terms of the creative possibilities. One of the most restful retreats at Six Flags Over Texas remains below the main circulation route, on a quiet boardwalk beside Johnson Creek, a natural waterway running through the park. Natural setting and landscaping is a common thread that elevates certain parks above the rest, a major feature clearly evident in all of Duell's projects.

Where did some of his ideas come from? Interestingly, Randall shared the fact that he would spend hours in bookstores looking at children's books. "If we can find things the kids are interested in and put it in three dimensions, we've accomplished something."[6] His designs were always premised on what the people wanted and needed; get to know your end-clientele and the project becomes much more personal and effective. And his conclusions about what makes a project work? As we have seen time and again with the dominant, driven individuals behind many of the parks he designed, "Behind each successful park you'll find one man who's totally involved. He has to live it, breathe it, walk it—and pick up the paper cups."[7]

Rare is it for a single individual to transform any particular industry. Walt Disney, benefitting from a long lineage of park development, added his own visionary genius to essentially create a brand new concept in outdoor amusement. Randall Duell, architect of car dealerships and Hollywood movie art director, came along at the right time to help define an off-shoot of this, ushering in the wave of regional parks across the country that we all have come to love over the decades. Today's themed designers, whether they realize it or not, call upon his design thinking and approach time and again as they hunch over their desks searching for that perfect, magical solution.[8]

LEARNING FROM LEGENDS: A PERSONAL RETROSPECTIVE

Rick Bastrup, President and Head Designer, R & R Creative Amusement Designs Inc.

When I first formed my design company in the early 80s with my business partner, Richard Ferrin, we were in a unique period of time in the amusement industry. This was well before the internet, computer aided design, and email resumes. We simply built architectural design models of our theme concepts and cold-called parks, design companies, and ride manufacturers to show them what we could do.

We were fortunate enough to meet with people such as Bud Hurlbut at Knott's Berry Farm, Jim Blacke and Jim Seay at Magic Mountain, Larry Cochran at Six Flags, Ira West at R. Duell & Associates, and Dave Bradley at Bradley and Kaye. We were soon working on design projects with all of them, each of whom appreciated our enthusiasm and youthful energy. What an opportunity to learn from the best!

Dave Bradley had a shop in Long Beach where he built carousels and such rides as the *Red Baron* and *The Barnstormer*. We became close friends, producing models and presentations for his company; in turn we contracted him to build animated props and characters for some of our early projects. Along the way we discovered Dave wasn't just another ride guy. He had actually worked with Walt Disney, eventually helping him with the creation of Disneyland. Realizing a story-to-be-told that was too good to pass up, in the early 80s I interviewed Dave for an article I was writing for *Amusement Park Journal*. I was fortunate to get a first-hand account and some little known facts about the genesis of Disneyland.

One of the sparks that started the serious thought of actually building a very special three-dimensional entertainment enterprise was Walt watching his daughters playing and having fun in a couple of local, small amusement parks. One of them was Beverly Park, and the experiences Walt had with the park's owner, Dave Bradley, helped guide Walt's vision. Bradley told me he first became interested in amusement parks in the late 1930s and early 40s when he traveled across the country as the road manager for big bands such as Freddy Martin. During that time he booked bands into many parks, including Elitch Gardens in Denver.

In 1945 the opportunity came for Dave to lease a small lot at the corner of Beverly and La Cienega in Los Angeles. He and a business partner, Don Kaye, acquired the property along with a small carnival that had been stranded there—the Bradley & Kaye Company had been born. Although Bradley bought out Kaye in 1946, the company retained the original name through the years. The carnival's inventory included a dodgem, carousel, Ferris wheel, and various kiddie rides. Bradley immediately restored the rides and opened Beverly Park in 1946. Billed as "The Friendly Park," it was conceived by Bradley as a family entertainment area. As more rides and attractions were added, including the *Tilt-A-Whirl* and a dark ride, the park remained geared toward kids and their parents.

The park included six themed picnic areas and hosted elaborate birthday parties and promotional events, many for Hollywood stars. Amazingly, the park was never larger than three quarters of an acre and consisted of up to twelve rides; they were ingeniously built around each other to best utilize the space. Bradley strove to make even the smallest attraction an adventure with the addition of themes, animated characters, and scenery. All employees wore uniforms. The park abounded in flowers and had a clean appearance at all times.

As Beverly grew and developed, Bradley continued to add and refine rides that would be adventures for his guests. In 1947 he designed and built the first portable children's coaster, *The Little Dipper* (Allan Herschell would eventually take over production). The ride was such a success that he was soon in the business of producing the coaster for other parks while also creating and designing attractions such as the children's helicopter ride, a circular boat ride, and the *Old 99* miniature train. This led to the creation of the Bradley & Kaye Amusement Company. Bradley also bought and restored old carousels for sale to other parks; at times he would have as many as three of these carousels running at Beverly Park.

In the late 40s Bradley's wife was the head of story research at the Walt Disney Studios. When she quit to assist Dave at the park, Disney came out to see what would make her leave. Walt and Dave became friends, and soon Walt was spending his Saturday afternoons at the park with his two daughters studying the operation and discussing how it could be improved. Although Walt always spoke fondly of sitting on a bench watching his daughters ride on one of Dave's carousels, he spent much of his time perched on a stool next to Dave while he ran the dark ride, or at the maintenance building drawing concepts and discussing ideas.

In 1950 Walt asked Dave to come to the studio so he could show him a new project in development. Revealing the original plans for Disneyland, the two were soon discussing and rendering their ideas for the ultimate park. Dave was hired as a consultant to Walt's personal design company, WED, and between 1950 and 1955 he worked with Disney creating ideas for the new park. The two of them remained good friends through the years; though Disney was always the creative genius and master planner, he was wise enough to utilize the talents and experience of people like Dave Bradley to bring his visionary concepts to life.

In 1973 Dave Bradley opened the Bradley & Kaye manufacturing plant in Long Beach, California, and soon began building custom ride vehicles, children's rides, and carousel horses. But by the early 1970s Beverly Park had become nearly surrounded by a growing oil company complex. As the area continued to deteriorate, Bradley found less time to devote to the park and closed it for good in 1974; it is now the site of the Beverly Center. For 29 years Dave Bradley had shown with this amazing small park that quality and imagination are much more important than size.

Meanwhile, the Bradley & Kaye Amusement Company continued to prosper with ride systems functioning in most major parks throughout the United States. In 1983 Disneyland, during the major renovation and redesign of Fantasyland, brought Dave back to oversee the rehab, rebuild, and relocation of one of Disneyland's most endearing icons, the *King Arthur Carousel.* Dave Bradley passed away in 1988 shortly after selling his patents, molds, and ride systems to Chance Industries, Inc. of Wichita, Kansas. In 1991 the International Association of Amusement Parks and Attractions Hall of Fame recognized him, not for his personal success alone, but for his significant contributions to the entire industry, his community, and the world. We were fortunate to have known him and learned a great deal through the knowledge he imparted and the support he showed us.

I first met Bud Hurlbut in the late 70s while working in Security and Operations at Knott's Berry Farm. He had a two-story shop in the parking lot north of the park where he built custom miniature train rides. Most people assume that everything at Knott's was owned by the family, but Bud was actually the designer and builder, along with construction chief Ed Cooper, of the Knott's *Timber Mountain Log Ride, Calico Mine Ride,* and Fiesta Village. He ran those attractions as concessions to the park, eventually selling them to Knott's in the 70s.

All of Bud's creations were finely themed and detailed, such as the use of actual mining and logging equipment and machinery in his western themed rides. I would often go over to talk to Bud at his shop and study the scale models he had built of the *Log* and *Mine* rides, along with looking at the trains under construction. We would later use one of those trains when R & R designed Adventure City children's park in nearby Anaheim.

After leaving Knott's, Bud designed and built Castle Park in Riverside, CA in 1976. The park included a castle arcade building, a ride area with two of his trains, a miniature car ride, and a huge mini golf course. Every ride, building, and attraction was incredibly detailed and ornate. The trains have etched glass details and finely painted designs, and all the wrought iron fencing was beautiful and themed to the areas. The miniature golf course was a work of art with each theme taken to a level where every hole was an adventure of detail.

We began working with Bud on renovations and new attractions in the 80s. He actually had a second-story apartment in the middle of the ride park, similar to what Walt Disney had built at Disneyland. Bud was a gracious and generous man, and we spent many hours hearing stories of the early days at Knott's, including how Disney would visit him and tour his attractions after Disneyland had opened. He said Walt was particularly impressed at how the *Calico Mine Ride* queue was designed to weave through the exterior of the ride, hiding many of the waiting guests while providing an entertaining introduction to the ride and the theme. Of course this is a common design today.

After Bud sold Castle Park to Palace Entertainment with the intention to semi-retire, he would call me up to discuss building a new and better park. Castle Park was his baby, and he regretted selling it. I would tell him that we needed to get busy and get it built, but he passed away in 2011 and alas, that never was to be.

What I learned from Bud was respect for our audience and attention to details. Each prop, set, or detail should be authentic and designed to convey the story we are telling. Even though our guests may not see or notice every detail that we provide, the total experience should be a feeling that someone put in the effort to make it a great attraction. I always studied and was inspired by his work; Bud Hurlbut was truly a class act.

In the late 70s I had the opportunity to visit Arrow Dynamics and see parts of the prototype suspended coaster and bobsled rides. I would later meet Ron Toomer, Arrow's president, at the IAAPA shows and was fortunate to work with him and Arrow designing the theme and show on Magic Mountain's *Ninja* and their last coaster, *Adventure Express* at Kings Island. Ron was an engineer developing early innovations such as the looping *Corkscrew* at Knott's. He would bend and twist thin metal rods to simulate some of the new coaster track concepts he was working on. Ron's rides are legendary in the amusement business with multiple inversions and records, including the first 200 foot high coaster, *Magnum XL-200* at Cedar Point, Ohio.

Ron was a soft-spoken guy, not prone to bragging, but he was one of the ground-breaking innovators of the complex coaster attractions we see today. He told me that even though he suffered from motion sickness, he would ride his creations once or twice to review the experience. That was enough for him to get on to the next coaster breakthrough.

Another great legend we worked with extensively was Ira West, President of R. Duell & Associates. We again brazenly set up a meeting at their office and were thrilled to find we were in the heart of the creators of many of the Six Flags, Marriott, and other theme parks which we had traveled around to visit and study. We soon became affiliates and worked on many projects together, providing thematic and show design for such parks as Bonfante Gardens in Gilroy, California; Everland in Seoul, South Korea; and the MGM Grand Adventures in Las Vegas.

Randall Duell and his team literally created the modern regional theme park and were innovators of much of what we take for granted today. The loop layout, attraction placement, ride mix, and many other design principles were created by Randall, Ira, and the other creative staff at the company. By the 1990s the United States was largely saturated with theme parks (most designed by Duell), and much of the major work was in other countries. Though we worked on several international projects with Duell in China, South Korea, and India, they found it harder to compete with the mega international design companies, eventually deciding to close the business.

Ira West was a fountain of information about the design and function of theme parks. We spent many hours discussing past projects and how attractions had to be designed and built on a solid foundation of reality, budget, function, and operations. The thematic shows, rides, and details we designed were the frosting on top which brought the park to life. I spent many hours pouring through Duell's library of plans, concepts, and artwork studying projects such as Freedomland in New York and Opryland in Tennessee. Unfortunately, all of these historical documents were lost to history when the firm closed and all their records were destroyed.

I learned a lot about designing for different cultures on the projects we worked together on in China and South Korea. At Everland, a massive multi-attraction theme park in Seoul, we spent a couple of days with Ira studying the park and riding the attractions we were tasked to renovate and re-theme. One of the more memorable situations was a ride-thru safari with live animals. The ride vehicle was a large bus with seats facing sideways looking out through large windows. As Ira, Richard, and I were finding our seats, we saw employees scrambling around doing something on top of the bus, but didn't pay much attention. At some point the bus stopped where several lions were lounging on platforms close to the road. Suddenly, with a roar they all lunged at the bus, smashing against the windows and tearing at meat appearing from nowhere! This, of course, was startling and somewhat disturbing, but quite a show. We later learned that the employees had been on ladders, hanging the meat on hooks out of our sight over the windows. A lesson learned was that different areas or cultures could have very diverse thoughts of what they find acceptable or entertaining.

Another major project that we teamed up on with Ira and Randall was the MGM theme park in Las Vegas. As we had designed or created themed rides for several waterparks and water-related rides such as *Jaws* at Universal Studios Orlando, we were known as the "Water Guys" and were asked to design the two major themed rides in the park, *The Backlot River Tour* and *Grand Canyon Rapids*. The *River Tour* was a narrated boat ride through a number of fictional movie sets, including the grand finale where we raised a 43-foot Bell Huey helicopter nineteen feet next to the boat amidst water explosions and machine gun fire. The boats were from the original *Jaws* attraction at Universal, available for us to purchase after they decided to re-engineer the ride. Ira and project manager Carl Sawyer worked closely with us to design and produce these two large attractions.

It just so happened that Francis Ford Coppola was a friend to some of the MGM management team, and they came up with the idea to do a recreation of "Apocalypse Now." So Ira, Richard, and I met with Mr. Coppola at his house a few times to discuss the idea; he was very gracious, and we worked on how we might recreate the crashed B-52 bomber scene and other highlights from the movie. What we had a hard time figuring out, though, was how to incorporate this powerful and disturbing film into a family amusement park. We started working on scripts, with kind of a "making of the movie" theme, then got word that the deal had fallen through. This was actually somewhat of a relief to us, but we stuck with the idea of incorporated our own helicopter attack concept, calling the ride scene "Jungle Storm." This is just one example of countless "might have been" rides or themes no one has heard of. Unfortunately, the MGM park only lasted a short while due to the lack of interest by some of the owners and the desire to move away from a family atmosphere.

Ira West passed away in 2017 after a battle with brain cancer. For many years, and even after Duell's company had disbanded, I would often call Ira for information such as how wide a walkway or queue line should be. Likewise, he would often call me to discuss theme and show concepts for a project he was working on. He was a generous and supportive gentleman and one of my best friends. Ira West, like Dave Bradley, Randall Duell, and Bud Hurlbut, was a pioneer in our industry. Though their names are not as well known as some other more publicized members of our business, they were all truly innovators and helped to create the amusement park industry we all enjoy today. I was blessed to have known and worked with so many of them.

FINAL COMMENTS

WHERE'S MY PARK?

For those of you who tore open the package, ripped the book out, and started thumbing through to find your park…in vain…I'm really sorry. I had to draw a rather fuzzy line, and there's no way I could cover every park that was based on some sort of thematic topic, such as scores of Christmas parks, Wild West parks, and so on. But Tweetsie and Rebel Railroad, for example, are crucial because if it wasn't for Grover Robbins there'd be no Dollywood as we know it. Magic Mountain in California is included even though it's not really a theme park, the rationale being it was a continuation of George Millay's story. And there are a few curious omissions, such as Cedar Point. The book is focused on the major regional *theme* parks. The early Duell parks met this criteria, but many, such as Valleyfair and Cedar Point, are truly *amusement* parks. There is no shame in this; the Point, for example, is fabulous. But they're not theme parks and were never intended to be. And yes, it's a loose definition which really doesn't beg a decisive answer, but there it is. I hope you'll still invite me over for Thanksgiving dinner.

YOU KNOW, YOU MISSED...

And you'd be absolutely right, mostly. You'd be surprised, though, how much stuff out there is plain wrong. I tried to find multiple sources to confirm what I could, but it's pretty sparse with lots of contradictions. And for sure I missed some details, so please do send me corrections or other tidbits that I can post on the website.

SOURCES

It drives me crazy to read a book and not be able to see where they got their information. Facts on these parks are especially troublesome to pin down because most sources end up quoting the same material without having any idea whether the first source actually knew what they were talking about. It becomes a circular argument, and so I tried to drill down to original references as much as possible. I found quite a bit...a sixty-some page list of items sitting in my Dropbox. Even though most readers don't care so much about this, I'd rather err on the side of "here's a whole bunch of stuff you might not care about" rather than "don't you have more in there somewhere?"

I'm fortunate to have access to academic research databases, and even more fortunate to have a terrific research librarian at my institution. So, thank you Donna Miller. You're free now to go hiking for two months in the Sierras. Other than books, most sources come from news publications of various types, but I was particularly interested in any scholarly works on the subject due to their much higher standards for publication (spoiler alert...there aren't many). Having said that, even the academic sources don't always agree. The challenge for the Evolution chapter was making sense of all the corporate changes—who bought whom and when, and it's a highly tangled financial picture that I've tried to summarize as accurately as possible without boring everyone. There are certainly discrepancies throughout the history of the parks, but for the most part it's not really that crucial in the grand scheme of things.

My book collection grew a wee bit with titles covering the

industry as well as individual parks. There aren't many, though, which speaks to the dearth of attention spent on anything other than Disney. Of course there is Arcadia's fairly comprehensive *Images of America* series, precious few biographies, and even fewer books on (or even from) a particular park.

Finally, a number of enthusiastic park historians were kind enough to review the sections on their home park, clarifying any details I missed. See the *Thanks to...* section below to pay appropriate tribute and peruse their sites.

WHAT? NO PICTURES?

Yeah, I know, but there are already great sources for these such as the *Images of America* series and enthusiast Facebook groups. Thankfully you can pretty much find enough photos on your favorite park to keep you happy for hours. On the other hand, the actual stories behind these parks are few and far between, so that's the gap I wanted to fill. It would also make the book too long. Sorry. Go draw your own.

VINTAGE PARK MAPS

Along the way I acquired a small collection of original park maps, mostly opening season. These are awesome because, first of all, who doesn't think old park maps are cool? The art design on most of them is quite beautiful, and they are full of fun details to discover. They helped greatly in determining original park layouts and attractions, and one of my early ideas was to include excerpts to accompany the walk-through descriptions. There are complications with this, however, including making the book too long. So instead I'm posting many of them on the book's website, so you can follow along as you read.

DID YOU RECOGNIZE THE PARK IMAGES FOR EACH CHAPTER?

Don't cheat...here they are in order:

1. Chicago World's Columbian Exposition of 1893
2. Coney Island, NY (1920)
3. Freedomland USA *(© 1960 Freedomland, Inc.)*
4. Six Flags Over Georgia *(© 1969 Great Southwest Corp)*
5. Astroworld *(© 1969 Astroworld)*
6. Kings Dominion *(© 1975 Kings Dominion)*
7. Marriott's Great America California *(1976 Marriott Corp)*
8. Busch Gardens Williamsburg *(© 1975 Anheuser-Busch)*
9. Hersheypark *(1973 Hersheypark)*
10. Hard Rock Park *(© 2008 Hard Rock Park)*
11. Magic Mountain *(© 1971 Magic Mountain)*
12. SeaWorld *(© 1966 Marine Park Corp)*

ENDURING FANS

There's clearly a lot of love for the regional park. The quantity of fan sites and Facebook groups, some numbering thousands of members, is a testament to how enduring these experiences are for local populations. It's especially true for those who lost their park along the way. As the early generations move on it's important to pass along the rich heritage and story behind these regionals. I guess that means take your kids and talk about the good old days. And buy them copies of this book.

And for those of you still searching for the chapters on Disney and Universal, keep going...you're almost there...

WANT MORE PARK GOODNESS?

While researching the book I uncovered all kinds of fantastic extras along the way, especially newspaper articles that featured early park advertisements, photos, and concept art. These help fill out the story while taking us back to a different time. They're too good to just sit in a Dropbox folder, so I'm posting them in dribs and drabs at www.rivershorecreative.com.

THANKS TO...

Ok, you really oughta read these, even though you're awfully tempted to go eat dinner about now. But these people are important, so here goes. Rob Decker, awesome creative dude who while at Cedar Fair helped bring the love back to the regionals; his foreword for the book helps connect the story to what real-life professionals do for the industry every day. Rick Bastrup, long-time industry veteran who worked closely with Ira and Randall's company; thank you for giving them some love and attention they richly deserve. My creative partners and friends at Themed Attraction: Mel McGowan (who contributed his thoughts on Duell's design approach), Freddy Martin, and Nathan Naversen.

Mark Eades, theme park writer/producer and former Imagineer (and a super nice guy), read over the final draft just to make sure it made sense. Tim Hollis, travel destination author extraordinaire, provided advice and information on Six Flags Over Georgia and other aspects. Author and history fanatic Bob McLaughlin probably knows more about the C.V. Wood parks than anyone else on Earth—thanks for the goodies, Bob. Harry Michelson of AmusementParkives.com pulled out his extensive database on Hersheypark and corrected a couple early-year details which even the company itself had missed for years. The amazing Donna Miller, research librarian at Lebanon Valley College. And even more: Brad Thomas and his super nice colleagues at Silver Dollar City and Dollywood. Dennis Speigel, who was there at the beginning for KI and KD. Eddie Sotto, who provided background to the Herbie Ryman "bad taste" quote. Michael Parham at Opryland Memories Facebook group, John Stevenson at Coaster101.com & RememberLibertyland.com, Jennifer Lovesee-Mast at worldsoffun.org, Michael Hicks at SFOT Current Happenings Facebook group, Harry Applegate at greatadventurehistory.com, and Mike Virgintino of *Freedomland USA: The Definitive History*. The awesome concept art from Magic Mountain in Colorado, originally produced by artists Wade Rubottom and Dick Kelsey, was provided by the Gardner Family Collection. Thanks Rick!

My wife Shelley, who puts up with my obsession, my keen-eyed daughter Jenna, who formatted every jot and tittle for the zillions of sources. And my son Jon, who has shared my love of parks and coasters for many years—thank you for the trips, discussions, encouragement, and memories.

PARK OPENING TIMELINE

- 1897 Steeplechase Park
- 1903 Luna Park
- 1904 Dreamland
- 1946 Santa Claus Land (Holiday World)
- 1955 Disneyland
- 1957 Tweetsie Railroad
- 1958 Pacific Ocean Park
- 1958 Magic Mountain (CO)
- 1959 Pleasure Island (MA)
- 1959 Busch Gardens Tampa
- 1960 Freedomland USA
- 1960 Silver Dollar City (officially opened as a theme park)
- 1961 Six Flags Over Texas
- 1961 Rebel Railroad
- 1964 SeaWorld San Diego
- 1966 Busch Gardens Los Angeles
- 1967 Six Flags Over Georgia
- 1968 Dogpatch USA
- 1968 Astroworld
- 1968 Knott's Berry Farm (redesigned as a gated theme park)

- 1970 SeaWorld Ohio
- 1970 Land of Oz
- 1971 Six Flags Over Mid-America
- 1971 Magic Mountain (CA)
- 1971 Busch Gardens Houston
- 1972 Opryland
- 1972 Kings Island
- 1973 Carowinds
- 1973 Worlds of Fun
- 1973 Hersheypark (redesigned as a gated theme park)
- 1973 SeaWorld Orlando
- 1974 Great Adventure
- 1975 Kings Dominion
- 1975 Busch Gardens Williamsburg
- 1976 Marriott's Great America (CA)
- 1976 Marriott's Great America (IL)
- 1976 Libertyland
- 1981 Canada's Wonderland
- 1984 Holiday World (redesigned as a multi-land theme park)
- 1985 Australia's Wonderland
- 1986 Dollywood (formerly Silver Dollar City, TN)
- 1988 SeaWorld San Antonio
- 1992 Fiesta Texas
- 1993 MGM Grand Adventures
- 2008 Hard Rock Park

SELECTED BIBLIOGRAPHY

40 Years of Fun: The Story of Busch Gardens Williamsburg. SeaWorld Parks & Entertainment, Inc, 2015. DVD.

A Blast From the Past: The History of Tweetsie Railroad. Tweetsie Railroad, no date (park publication).

Adams, Judith A. *The American Amusement Park Industry: A History of Technology and Thrills.* Twayne Publishers, 1991.

Applegate, Harry, and Thomas Benton. *Images of Modern America: Six Flags Great Adventure.* Arcadia Publishing, 2016.

Barnes, Doug. "#243: The Jon Binkowski Interview 8/29/13." *The Season Pass: Your Ticket to Ride.* Podcast. August 29, 2013. www.seasonpasspodcast.com.

Barnes, Doug. "#339: The Ira West Interview 1/24/17." *The Season Pass: Your Ticket to Ride.* Podcast. January 24, 2017. www.seasonpasspodcast.com.

Barrier, Michael. *The Animated Man: A Life of Walt Disney.* University of California Press, 2007.

Bolotin, Norman, and Christine Laing. *The World's*

Columbian Exposition: The Chicago World's Fair of 1893. University of Illinois Press, 2002.

Bright, Randy. *Disneyland: Inside Story*. Harry N. Abrams, 1987.

Broggie, Michael. *Walt Disney's Railroad Story: The Small-Scale Fascination That Led to a Full-Scale Kingdom*. The Donning Company Publishers, 2006.

Bruno, Lee. *Panorama: Tales from San Francisco's 1915 Pan-Pacific International Exposition*. Cameron Books, 2014.

Burns, Ric, dir. *Coney Island*. Steeplechase Films, 1991. DVD.

Clave, S. Anton. *The Global Theme Park Industry*. CABI, 2007.

Davis, Robert S. Jr., *Requiem for a Lost City: Sarah Clayton's Memories of Civil War Atlanta*. Mercer University Press, 1999.

Environmental Impact Statement for Frontier Worlds Plan. February 20, 1973.

France, Van Arsdale. *Window on Main Street: 35 Years of Creating Happiness at Disneyland Park*. Theme Park Press, 2015.

Freedomland U.S.A.: The World's Largest Entertainment Center, Complete Official Guide with Maps. 1960 opening year guidebook.

Gennawey, Sam. *The Disneyland Story*. Keen Communications, 2014.

Havighurst, Craig. *Air Castle of the South: WSM and the Making of Music City*. University of Illinois Press, 2011.

Hench, John, and Peggy Van Pelt. *Designing Disney: Imagineering and the Art of the Show*. Disney Editions, 2008.

Hollis, Tim. *Images of America: Six Flags Over Georgia*. Arcadia Publishing, 2006.

Hollis, Tim. *Images of Modern America: The Land of Oz*. Arcadia Publishing, 2016.

Jacques, Charles J., Jr. *Cincinnati's Coney Island*. Amusement Park Journal, 2002.

Jacques, Charles J., Jr. *Hersheypark: Sweetness of Success*. Amusement Park Journal, 1997.

Koch, Pat, and Jane Ammeson. *Images of America: Holiday World*. Arcadia Publishing, 2006.

Kyriazi, Gary. *The Great American Amusement Parks: A Pictorial History*. Castle Books, 1976.

Lipsky, William. *San Francisco's Panama-Pacific International Exposition*. Arcadia, 2005.

MacCambridge, Michael. *Lamar Hunt: A Life in Sports*. Andrews McMeel Publishing, 2012.

Manby, Joel K. *Love Works*. Zondervan Books, 2020.

Mangels, Bob, dir. *Freedomland U.S.A.: America's Theme Park*. A Tootsie Production, 2008. DVD.

Marling, Karal Ann, ed. *Designing Disney's Theme Parks: The Architecture of Reassurance*. Flammarion, 1997.

McCown, Davis G. *Six Flags Over Texas: The First Fifty Years*. Lavaca Publications and Media, 2016.

McLaughlin, Robert, and Frank R. Adamo. *Images of America: Freedomland*. Arcadia Publishing, 2010.

McLaughlin, Robert. *Images of America: Pleasure Island*. Arcadia Publishing, 2009.

McLaughlin, Robert. *Images of Modern America: Freedomland 1960–1964*. Arcadia Publishing, 2015.

McLaughlin, Robert. *Images of Modern America: Magic Mountain*. Arcadia Publishing, 2016.

McLaughlin, Robert. *Images of Modern America: Pleasure Island 1959–1969*. Arcadia Publishing, 2014.

McMorrow-Hernandez, Joshua. *Images of Modern America: Busch Gardens Tampa Bay*. Arcadia Publishing, 2017.

Memories of Opryland: A Thrill Ride of Great Memories! Nashville Public Television, 2008. DVD.

Merritt, Christopher, and Domenic Priore. *Pacific Ocean Park: The Rise and Fall of Los Angeles' Space-Age Nautical Pleasure Pier*. Process, 2014.

Merritt, Christopher, and J. Eric Lynxwiler. *Knott's Preserved: From Boysenberry to Theme Park, the History of Knott's Berry Farm*. Rev. ed. Angel City Press, 2015.

O'Brien, Tim. *The Wave Maker: The Story of Theme Park Pioneer George Millay and the Creation of Sea World, Magic Mountain, and Wet'n Wild*. Ripley Entertainment Inc, 2005.

Onosko, Tim. *Fun Land USA: The Complete Guidebook to 100 Major Amusement and Theme Parks All Across the Country*. Ballantine Books, 1978.

Payton, Crystal. *The Story of Silver Dollar City: A Pictorial History of Branson's Famous Ozark Mountain Theme Park*. A Lens & Pen Production, 1997.

Peri, Don. *Working with Walt: Interviews with Disney Artists*. University Press of Mississippi, 2008.

Phillips, Cedar Imboden. *Images of America: Early Pasadena*. Arcadia Publishing, 2008.

Phillips, Stephen W. *Images of Modern America: Opryland USA*. Arcadia Publishing, 2016.

Pierce, Todd James. *Three Years in Wonderland: The Disney Brothers, C.V. Wood, and the Making of the Great American Theme Park*. University Press of Mississippi, 2016.

Pirtle, Caleb, III. *The Grandest Day: A Journey Through Opryland U.S.A., The Home of American Music*. Opryland U.S.A., 1979.

Price, Harrison "Buzz." *Walt's Revolution! By the Numbers*. Ripley Entertainment, 2004.

Ray, Edgar W. *The Grand Huckster: Houston's Judge Roy*

Hofheinz, Genius of the Astrodome. Memphis State University Press, 1979.

Register, Woody. *The Kid of Coney Island: Fred Thompson and the Rise of American Amusements*. Oxford University Press, 2001.

Reynolds, Robert. *Roller Coasters, Flumes and Flying Saucers: The Story of Ed Morgan & Karl Bacon, Ride Inventors of the Modern Amusement Park*. Northern Lights Publishing, 1999.

Riding History to the Limits. CET Documentaries. PBS, 2009. www.pbs.org/video/cet-documentaries-riding-history-limits/.

Rutherford, Scott N. *Images of Modern America: Kings Dominion*. Arcadia Publishing, 2015.

Rutherford, Scott. *Images of America: Carowinds*. Arcadia Publishing, 2013.

SeaWorld: Mission Bay Park / San Diego. Souvenir book, 1966.

Smith, Dave, comp. *The Quotable Walt Disney*. Disney Editions, 2001.

Stevenson, John R. *Images of Modern America: Libertyland*. Arcadia, 2017.

Suess, Jeff. *Lost Cincinnati*. History Press Library Editions, 2015.

TEA/AECOM 2018 Theme Index and Museum Index: The Global Attractions Attendance Report. Themed Entertainment Association (TEA).

The Park That Rock Built. Hard Rock Park, 2008.

Themed Attraction. "#14: TA Podcast E14: Rick Bastrup." *The Themed Attraction Podcast*. August 1, 2019. www.themedattraction.com.

Thomas, Bob. *Walt Disney: An American Original*. Hyperion, 1976.

Virgintino, Michael. *Freedomland U.S.A.: The Definitive History*. Theme Park Press, 2019.

Whitenack, Pamela Cassidy. *Images of America: Hersheypark*. Arcadia Publishing, 2006.

Wilson, Steven W. *Images of Modern America: California's Great America*. Arcadia Publishing, 2014.

Wilson, Steven W. *Images of Modern America: Six Flags Great America*. Arcadia Publishing, 2017.

NOTES

1. BEFORE DISNEYLAND

1. Walt Disney, interview by Fletcher Markle, *Telescope* (CBC), 25 Sept, 1963; Michael Barrier, *The Animated Man: A Life of Walt Disney* (University of California Press, 2007), Ch 6, Kindle.
2. Karal Ann Marling, ed, *Designing Disney's Theme Parks: The Architecture of Reassurance* (Flammarion, 1997), 81.
3. Marling, *Designing Disney's Theme Parks*, 39.
4. Sam Gennawey, *The Disneyland Story* (Keen Communications, 2014), 16; Marling, *Designing Disney's Theme Parks*, 52.
5. Barrier, *The Animated Man*, Ch 8, Kindle.
6. "Electric Park Was Midtown's Coney's Island," Midtown KC Post, July 7, 2014; Gennawey, *Disneyland Story*, 5-6.
7. Marling, *Designing Disney's Theme Parks*, 20.
8. Marling, *Designing Disney's Theme Parks*, 20-21.
9. Marling, *Designing Disney's Theme Parks*, 21.
10. Norman Bolotin and Christine Laing, *The World's Columbian Exposition: The Chicago World's Fair of 1893* (University of Illinois Press, 2002), 15; Judith A. Adams, *The American Amusement Park Industry: A History of Technology and Thrills* (Twayne Publishers, 1991), 28-29.
11. Marling, *Designing Disney's Theme Parks*, 21.
12. "Sky Ride: 1933 Chicago's World Fair," The Gondola Project, http://gondolaproject.com/category/installations/1934-chicago-worlds-fair.
13. Lee Bruno, *Panorama: Tales from San Francisco's 1915 Pan-Pacific International Exposition* (Cameron Books, 2014), 100-101.
14. Adams, *American Amusement Park Industry*, 31.
15. "Lifesaver's Candy Parachute Jump," 1939 New York World's Fair, https://www.1939nyworldsfair.com/worlds_fair/wf_tour/zone-7/parachutte_jump.htm.
16. William Lipsky, *San Francisco's Panama-Pacific International Exposition* (Arcadia, 2005), 86-89.
17. Woody Register, *The Kid of Coney Island: Fred Thompson and the Rise of American Amusements* (Oxford University Press, 2001), 69-71; "A Trip to the Moon: Crowning Feature of the Pan-American Midway," Springville (NY) Journal, August 29, 1901; "Half Rate Excursions to the Moon Via the 'Luna.'" The Buffalo Enquirer, October 16, 1901; Ron Miller, "In 1901, You Could Pay 50 Cents to Ride an Airship to the Moon," Gizmodo, May 31, 2012, https://io9.gizmodo.com/in-1901-you-could-pay-50-cents-to-ride-an-airship-to-t-5914655.
18. Lipsky, *San Francisco's Panama-Pacific*, 83-91.
19. Marling, *Designing Disney's Theme Parks*, 22.
20. Register, *The Kid of Coney Island*, 66-67.

21. Adams, *American Amusement Park Industry*, 57-60; Marling, *Designing Disney's Theme Parks*, 22.
22. Adams, *American Amusement Park Industry*, 66-67.
23. Marling, *Designing Disney's Theme Parks*, 21; Adams, *American Amusement Park Industry*, 43.
24. Adams, *American Amusement Park Industry*, 31-32.
25. Jeffrey Stanton, "Coney Island - First Steeplechase Park (1897 - 1907)," Coney Island History Site, April 1, 1998, https://www.westland.net/coneyisland/articles/steeplechase1.htm.
26. Adams, *American Amusement Park Industry*, 43; Robert C. Ford and Andy Milman, "George C. Tilyou: Developer of the Contemporary Amusement Park," The Cornell Hotel & Restaurant Administration Quarterly 41, no. 4 (August 2000): 62; "Coney Island History: The Story of Captain Paul Boyton and Sea Lion Park," Heart of Coney Island, 2015, https://www.heartofconeyisland.com/sea-lion-park-coney-island.html.
27. Adams, *American Amusement Park Industry*, 43-46; "Steeplechase Park Open: Famous Coney Island Amusement Place Begins the Season of 1902," The Brooklyn Citizen, June 24, 1902; "Rockaway's New Attractions: Seashore Resort Will Offer Many New Novelties This Season," The Brooklyn Daily Eagle, April 7, 1901; "La Marcus Edna Thompson," Coney Island History Project, https://www.coneyislandhistory.org/hall-of-fame/la-marcus-edna-thompson.
28. Adams, *American Amusement Park Industry*, 46-52; Register, *The Kid of Coney Island*, 91-93; "Luna Park First Night," The New York Times, May 17, 1903; "Coney Island History: The Story of Thompson & Dundy's Luna Park," Heart of Coney Island, 2015, https://www.heartofconeyisland.com/luna-park-coney-island.html.
29. Adams, *American Amusement Park Industry*, 52-53; "Coney Island History: The Story of William Reynolds and Dreamland," Heart of Coney Island, 2015, https://www.heartofconeyisland.com/dreamland-coney-island.html.
30. Adams, *American Amusement Park Industry*, 49.
31. Adams, *American Amusement Park Industry*, 52.
32. Todd James Pierce, *Three Years in Wonderland: The Disney Brothers, C.V. Wood, and the Making of the Great American Theme Park* (University Press of Mississippi, 2016), 32.
33. Marling, *Designing Disney's Theme Parks*, 26-27.
34. Marling, *Designing Disney's Theme Parks*, 39.
35. Michael Broggie, *Walt Disney's Railroad Story: The Small-Scale Fascination That Led to a Full-Scale Kingdom* (The Donning Company Publishers, 2006), 52-58.
36. Marling, *Designing Disney's Theme Parks*, 43-45; Broggie, *Walt Disney's Railroad Story*, 73-82.
37. Marling, *Designing Disney's Theme Parks*, 45; Broggie, *Walt Disney's Railroad Story*, 85-87.
38. Barrier, *The Animated Man*, Ch 9.
39. Randy Bright, *Disneyland: Inside Story* (Harry N. Abrams, 1987), 39-41; Marling, *Designing Disney's Theme Parks*, 47-52.
40. Pierce, *Three Years in Wonderland*, 34-38; Barrier, *The Animated Man*, Ch 8.
41. Don Peri, *Working with Walt: Interviews with Disney Artists* (University Press of Mississippi, 2008), Ch 13, Kindle.
42. Marling, *Designing Disney's Theme Parks*, 52.
43. Broggie, *Walt Disney's Railroad Story*, 88-91.

44. Marling, *Designing Disney's Theme Parks*, 52.
45. Marling, *Designing Disney's Theme Parks*, 39.
46. Pierce, *Three Years in Wonderland*, 42-44.

2. WALT SETS A NEW STANDARD

1. Barrier, *The Animated Man*, Ch 8; Marling, *Designing Disney's Theme Parks*, 81.
2. John Hench and Peggy Van Pelt, *Designing Disney: Imagineering and the Art of the Show* (Disney Editions, 2008), 2.
3. Pierce, *Three Years in Wonderland*, 36-37.
4. Marling, *Designing Disney's Theme Parks*, 58; Bright, *Disneyland: Inside Story*, 45.
5. Hench, *Designing Disney*, 67-77.
6. Marling, *Designing Disney's Theme Parks*, 86-90.
7. Hench, *Designing Disney*, 37-42.
8. Hench, *Designing Disney*, 50-54.
9. Marling, *Designing Disney's Theme Parks*, 83.
10. Hench, *Designing Disney*, 50-54.
11. Hench, *Designing Disney*, 69-78.
12. Hench, *Designing Disney*, 79.
13. Hench, *Designing Disney*, 78.
14. Marling, *Designing Disney's Theme Parks*, 81.
15. Van Arsdale France, *Window on Main Street: 35 Years of Creating Happiness at Disneyland Park* (Theme Park Press, 2015), Ch 11, Kindle; Hench, *Designing Disney*, 29.
16. Hench, *Designing Disney*, 20-22; Barrier, *The Animated Man*, Ch 8.
17. Harrison "Buzz" Price, *Walt's Revolution! By the Numbers* (Ripley Entertainment, 2004), 35.
18. Hench, *Designing Disney*, 32.
19. Dave Smith, comp, *The Quotable Walt Disney* (Disney Edition, 2001), 58.
20. Pierce, *Three Years in Wonderland*, 249-250.
21. Bright, *Disneyland: Inside Story*, 29.

3. DUPLICATING DISNEYLAND IS HARDER THAN YOU THINK

1. Pierce, *Three Years in Wonderland*, 3, 5-6; Price, *Walt's Revolution*, 129-131.
2. France, *Window on Main Street*, 10; Price, *Walt's Revolution*, 132.
3. Pierce, *Three Years in Wonderland*, 11-17, 104, 109; Price, *Walt's Revolution*, 132.
4. Pierce, *Three Years in Wonderland*, 92, 126-127; Price, *Walt's Revolution*, 133; France, *Window on Main Street*, 4-5.
5. Pierce, *Three Years in Wonderland*, 49, 101-102.
6. Pierce, *Three Years in Wonderland*, 146; Price, *Walt's Revolution*, 137.
7. Pierce, *Three Years in Wonderland*, 140-145; Price, *Walt's Revolution*, 137; France, *Window on Main Street*, 58.
8. Pierce, *Three Years in Wonderland*, 93, 109-110, 147-148, 246, 248; France, *Window on Main Street*, 22.
9. Pierce, *Three Years in Wonderland*, 3-4; France, *Window on Main Street*, 90.

10. Michael Virgintino, *Freedomland U.S.A.: The Definitive History* (Theme Park Press, 2019), Ch 4, Kindle.
11. Robert McLaughlin, *Images of Modern America: Magic Mountain* (Arcadia Publishing, 2016), Introduction, Kindle.
12. McLaughlin, *Magic Mountain*, Ch 1.
13. "Genesis & Exodus: Magic Mountain," Golden Landmarks Association, http://goldenlandmarks.com/genesis-exodus.
14. Park description: McLaughlin, *Magic Mountain*; "Genesis & Exodus: Magic Mountain"; "Magic Mountain: One of the 1st," Gardner History & Preservation, http://gardnerhistory.com/magicmountain/themepark.htm.
15. "Magic Mountain Investors Asked for More Money," Colorado Springs Gazette-Telegraph, May 22, 1960; "Securities Commission Hits Lefferdink with Complaint," The Daily Sentinel (Grand Junction, Colorado), October 23, 1959; "A Very Real Problem on Magic Mountain," The Daily Sentinel (Grand Junction, Colorado), December 18, 1960; "Lefferdink Enterprise Lists More Liabilities," The Daily Sentinel (Grand Junction, Colorado), November 21, 1959; "Judge Requests Report on Magic Mountain Woes," Amusement Business, 1962.
16. McLaughlin, *Magic Mountain*, Ch 2-4; "Genesis & Exodus"; "Magic Mountain: One of the 1st."
17. McLaughlin, *Magic Mountain*, Ch 5.
18. Elizabeth Hernandez, "'An iconic moment': Auction of Heritage Square's Rides Signals Final Farewell For Beloved Colorado Amusement Park," The Denver Post, October 26, 2018.
19. Robert McLaughlin, *Images of Modern America: Pleasure Island 1959–1969* (Arcadia Publishing, 2014), Ch 1, Kindle; "Moby Dick to Swim in Wakefield Soon: Pleasure Island Opens in June," The Boston Globe, March 27, 1959; "Pleasure Island Shunpike: The Old West Moves East—to Wakefield," The Boston Globe, June 14, 1959; "Pleasure Island: A Man's Dream Come True!" The Boston Globe, August 10, 1959; "East Meets West at Pleasure Island," The Boston Globe, August 18, 1959; "Big Construction Job at 80-Acre Pleasure Island Nears Completion," The Boston Globe, June 14, 1959; "Pleasure Island Opening," The Boston Globe, April 24, 1966; "Site Preparation Now Under Way at Pleasure Island," The Boston Globe, November 2, 1958; "Wal, Blow Us Down—Landlubbers Got Moby Dick's Spout Too Far Aft, Matey," The Boston Globe, July 16, 1959; "1,200,000 to Visit Pleasure Island," The Boston Globe, April 9, 1959.
20. McLaughlin, *Modern America: Pleasure Island*, Ch 2.
21. Park description: McLaughlin, *Modern America: Pleasure Island*; Robert McLaughlin, *Images of America: Pleasure Island* (Arcadia Publishing, 2009); Park map.
22. McLaughlin, *Modern America: Pleasure Island*, Ch 3; France, *Window on Main Street*, 95.
23. McLaughlin, *Modern America: Pleasure Island*, Ch 3.
24. "Korda Plans to Make Offer to Pleasure Island Creditors," The Boston Globe, January 8, 1960.
25. McLaughlin, *Modern America: Pleasure Island*, Ch 4.
26. McLaughlin, *America: Pleasure Island*, 105; "Pleasure Island Bought by Three Businessmen: To Reopen in June," The Boston Globe, May 4, 1960; "Pleasure Island Sold for $1.7M," The Boston Globe, April 22, 1969.

27. "Apartments to Replace Pleasure Island," The Boston Globe, February 3, 1970; McLaughlin, *Modern America: Pleasure Island*, Ch 5.
28. "Pleasure Island Stories and Memories," Friends of Pleasure Island, http://friendsofpleasureisland.org/stories.
29. Virgintino, *Freedomland U.S.A.*, Ch 2; "Huge Play Project Planned in Bronx," The New York Times, May 1, 1959; "Exhibit Park Planned in Bronx," The New York Times, May 26, 1959.
30. *Freedomland U.S.A.: The World's Largest Entertainment Center, Complete Official Guide with Maps*, 1960 guidebook.
31. Robert McLaughlin, *Images of Modern America: Freedomland 1960–1964* (Arcadia Publishing, 2015), 83; Virgintino, *Freedomland U.S.A.*, Ch 4, 26; "Bronx Amusement Park Stock is Offered to the Public Today," The New York Times, June 21, 1959; "Firm Sells $16 Million of Common to Finance Disneyland-Type Park," The New York Times, July 21, 1959; "Webb & Knapp Plans to Sell 3 More Hotel Leases, Boost Holdings in Freedomland," Wall Street Journal, September 20, 1960; "Webb & Knapp Would Control Freedomland Under Financing Plan," The Wall Street Journal, May 25, 1961.
32. Virgintino, *Freedomland U.S.A.*, Ch 1, 4.
33. *Freedomland* guidebook.
34. Park description: *Freedomland* guidebook; McLaughlin, *Modern America: Freedomland*; Robert McLaughlin and Frank R. Adamo, *Images of America: Freedomland* (Arcadia Publishing, 2010); Virgintino, *Freedomland U.S.A.; "Chicago is Saved Every 20 Minutes From the "Great Fire,"* The New York Times, June 19, 1960; "Freedomland -- A "Nation" on Wheels!" The New York Times, June 19, 1960; "Today the Gates to the World's Largest Showplace Swing Open!" The New York Times, June 19, 1960; "25,000 See Freedomland Dedicated in the Bronx," The New York Times, June 19, 1960; "Freedomland in the Bronx: Biggest Disneyland-Type Playground of Them About to Start Entertaining 35,000 Visitors at One Time," The New York Times, June 12, 1960; "Animated History in East Bronx's Freedomland is Revealed in a Preview," The New York Times, April 29, 1960; "Freedomland, U.S.A.: By the Travel Guide," The Bridgeport Post, October 18, 1959; "Freedomland Facts and Figures," The New York Times, June 19, 1960.
35. McLaughlin, *Modern America: Freedomland*, 83.
36. France, *Window on Main Street*, 97.
37. "Webb & Knapp Adds Hotel Site to Items It Plans to Auction," Wall Street Journal, June 20, 1963; Virgintino, *Freedomland U.S.A.*, Ch 4.
38. Virgintino, *Freedomland U.S.A.*, Ch 28.
39. Virgintino, *Freedomland U.S.A.*, Ch 15.
40. McLaughlin, *Modern America: Freedomland*, 83; Virgintino, *Freedomland U.S.A.*, Ch 25.
41. "Freedomland is Sued for 'Changing Character,'" The New York Times, September 5, 1962; Vernon Griffin, "Amusement Parks Put More Stress on Rides Instead of Pageantry," Wall Street Journal, October 4, 1963.
42. Virgintino, *Freedomland U.S.A.*, Ch 25.
43. "Trouble in Freedomland," Time, September 26, 1960.
44. McLaughlin, *Modern America: Freedomland*, 83; Virgintino, *Freedomland U.S.A.*, Ch 27; "Freedomland Park Seeks Court Protection From Creditors, Cites World's Fair as Rival," Wall Street Journal, September 16, 1964.

45. "New York Slates Huge Mid-Income Housing Project: State, City to Help," Wall Street Journal, February 10, 1965; "15,500 Apartment Co-op to Rise in Bronx," The New York Times, February 10, 1965.
46. Virgintino, *Freedomland U.S.A.*, Ch 27.
47. McLaughlin, *Modern America: Freedomland*, 83.
48. "Disneyland Frills May Decorate Aquarium," Kings Courier (Brooklyn, NY), January 24, 1959.
49. "$7 Million Circusland Scheduled," Orlando Evening Star, April 18, 1959; "Circusland Project Set for Florida," The Miami Herald, April 19, 1959.
50. "Gotham Playland," Public Opinion (Chambersburg, PA), September 28, 1959.
51. "$5 Million Plan to Start Soon at Jungleland," Press-Courier (Oxnard, CA), February 11, 1958.
52. "Disneyland Type Gold Rush Center at Rocklin to be Started in Spring," The Placer Herald (Rocklin, California), December 17, 1959.
53. "Park Planned," The Austin American, June 1, 1961.
54. "Fair Board Asks State to Take Over Its Woes," The Courier-Journal (Louisville), December 17, 1959.
55. "Resort Expects to Spend Six Million: Confirm 'Disney' Project," The Sandusky Register, March 28, 1960.
56. "Disney-Type Park Value Revealed Here," San Antonio Express, May 6, 1958.
57. Pierce, *Three Years in Wonderland*, 5; Price, *Walt's Revolution*, 130.

4. ANGUS WYNNE GETS IT DONE

1. "Tom J. Vandergriff," Arlington, www.arlingtontx.gov/residents/about_arlington/history_of_arlington/hall_of_mayors/tom_j_vandergriff; "Former Arlington Mayor Tom Vandergriff dies at 84," The Dallas Morning News, December 30, 2010, www.dallasnews.com/news/2010/12/30/former-arlington-mayor-tom-vandergriff-dies-at-84.
2. Price, *Walt's Revolution*, 108; Davis G. McCown, *Six Flags Over Texas: The First Fifty Years* (Lavaca Publications and Media, 2016), 3-4; "'Great Southwest' Has 5,800 Acres," Grand Prairie Daily News, April 20, 1963; "Fort Worth, Dallas Get Together in Cow Pasture," Abilene (TX) Reporter-News, July 20, 1959; "6 Flags Continue 'Wynne Streak,'" The Daily News-Texan (Grand Prairie, TX), August 6, 1961.
3. McCown, *Six Flags Over Texas*, 5-6; "Former Arlington Mayor..."
4. McCown, *Six Flags Over Texas*, 7; Tim Onosko, *Fun Land USA: The Complete Guidebook to 100 Major Amusement and Theme Parks All Across the Country* (Ballantine Books, 1978), 61-62.
5. Price, *Walt's Revolution*, 109.
6. Onosko, *Fun Land USA*, 61-62; Doug Barnes, "#339: The Ira West Interview 1/24/17," The Season Pass: Your Ticket to Ride (blog), January 24, 2017, www.seasonpasspodcast.com.
7. McCown, *Six Flags Over Texas*, 15; "Under Nothin," Time, August 18, 1961.
8. Pierce, *Three Years in Wonderland*, 37.
9. Price, *Walt's Revolution*, 110.
10. Ira West Interview.
11. Hench, *Designing Disney*, 79.

12. Onosko, *Fun Land USA*, 65; Ira West Interview.
13. Park description: McCown, *Six Flags Over Texas*; "Six Flags: Rides and Attractions," Special Collections UT-Arlington, https://www.flickr.com/photos/spcouta/sets/72157629884434077; "Six Flags Over Texas," University of Texas Arlington, https://library.uta.edu/exhibits/six-flags-over-texas; "Six Flags Over Texas, At 'Entertainment Center': No Disneyland," Clarion-Ledger (Jackson, MS), August 20, 1961; "Six Flags Over Texas Plays to 400,000 in Two Months," Hobbs (NM) Daily News-Sun, October 17, 1961; "Six Flags Over Texas Fabulous: Opens to Public August 5," The Gilmer (TX) Mirror, June 29, 1961; "'Six Flags' Center Slates August Opening in Texas," Victoria (TX) Advocate, December 18, 1960; Park maps (1961, 1962).
14. Onosko, *Fun Land USA*, 64.
15. Robert Reynolds, *Roller Coasters, Flumes and Flying Saucers: The Story of Ed Morgan & Karl Bacon, Ride Inventors of the Modern Amusement Park* (Northern Lights Publishing, 1999).
16. McCown, *Six Flags Over Texas*, 23-24.
17. Christopher T. Baer, "PRR Chronology," Pennsylvania Technical and Historical Society, January 20, 2013, http://www.prrths.com/newprr_files/Hagley/PRR_hagley_intro.htm.
18. Glenn Fowler, "News of Realty: Big Suffolk Deal," The New York Times, August 18, 1965; Tim Hollis, *Images of America: Six Flags Over Georgia* (Arcadia Publishing, 2006), Introduction, Kindle; "Six Flags' Profit Hits $4 Million," The Atlanta Constitution, November 18, 1966; "$7 Million Amusement Park Here May Be Georgia's Top Attraction," The Atlanta Constitution, August 18, 1965.
19. "6 Flags Boss to Discuss Effect Here," The Atlanta Constitution, April 13, 1967.
20. Hollis, *Six Flags Over Georgia*, Introduction.
21. "Amusement Center Shaping," The Atlanta Constitution, July 13, 1966.
22. Hollis, *Six Flags Over Georgia*, Ch 1; "Georgia, GSW To Construct 'Six Flags Over Georgia,'" Grand Prairie Daily News, July 28, 1966.
23. Hollis, *Six Flags Over Georgia*, Ch 1; Mark Johnson, "Georgia Joy," Travel, April 1968, 37.
24. Robert S. Davis Jr., *Requiem for a Lost City: Sarah Clayton's Memories of Civil War Atlanta* (Mercer University Press, 1999), 41.
25. Park description: Hollis, *Six Flags Over Georgia*; "Seen 6 Six Flags Yet? Well, You Oughta," The Atlanta Constitution, September 21, 1967; "Topp Brass in Latin Style Play in British Section," The Atlanta Constitution, October 21, 1967; "Krofft Circus is Smothers Act," The Atlanta Constitution, March 25, 1967; Park maps (1967, 1969, concept art); Tim Hollis, email messages to author, June 7-11, 2018.
26. "Southwest County Looks Forward to Prospect of Six Flags Park," St. Louis Post-Dispatch, July 25, 1969; "Eureka, A Quiet Town Faces Future Hubbub," St. Louis Post-Dispatch, April 14, 1971; "Eureka, Six Flags Study Joint Water, Sewer Plan," St. Louis Post-Dispatch, October 16, 1969; "To Build 'Six Flags Over Mid-America' at St. Louis," The Chillicothe (MO) Constitution-Tribune, July 16, 1969; "Penn Central Unit Plans New Amusement Park," Wall Street Journal, July 18, 1969.
27. "Some Endorse, Some Oppose Amusement Park Near Eureka," St. Louis Post-Dispatch, April 16, 1969.
28. "Towns Jockeying for Dates on Six Flags Annexation," St. Louis Post-Dispatch, April 15, 1971; "The Fight to Claim Missouri's Six Flags," Business Week, April 24,

1971; "Six Flags Will Contest Proposals for Annexation," St. Louis Post-Dispatch, April 18, 1971; "Pacific Voters Down Six Flags Annexation," Springfield (MO) Leader and Press, May 13, 1971; "Eureka to Meet Tonight to Decide Six Flags Policy," St. Louis Post-Dispatch, April 14, 1971.

29. "60 Six Flags Buildings Rise Year After Decision to Build," St. Louis Post-Dispatch, April 23, 1970.
30. "He Rides Herd on Construction of $22,000,000 in Make-Believe," St. Louis Post-Dispatch, December 8, 1969.
31. "Southwest County Looks Forward..."
32. "Without Reservations," Springfield (MO) Leader and Press, March 7, 1971; "He Rides Herd on Construction..."
33. Price, *Walt's Revolution*, 110; Ira West Interview.
34. Park description: "Six Flags Over Mid-America Offers Lots of Family Fun," St. Joseph (MO) News-Press/Gazette, September 9, 1971; "Six Flags Over Mid-America Exceeding All Expectations," Springfield (MO) Leader and Press, September 9, 1971; "Six Flags Over Mid America: Then and Now," Living the Small Town Life on a Full Time Basis, April 11, 2017, https://fuzzy64.livejournal.com/227783.html; Valerie Schremp Hahn, "Jet Scream, MoMo the Monster, Mule-Go-Round and More: Six Flags Attractions of Yore," St. Louis Post-Dispatch, August 1, 2019; Park map (1971).
35. Ira West Interview.
36. "Wynne to Build for World's Fair: Texan in Yankeeland," The Daily News-Texan (Grand Prairie, TX), December 1, 1962; "Beneficence," The Tyler (TX) Courier-Times, April 28, 1963; Price, *Walt's Revolution*, 110-111.
37. Al Harting, "Remember Seven Seas?" D Magazine, February 1980, https://www.dmagazine.com/publications/d-magazine/1980/february/remember-seven-seas; "Arlington Okays Big Bond Issue," The Bonham Daily Favorite (Bonham, Texas) May 13, 1970; McCown, *Six Flags Over Texas*, 127-129.

5. ENTREPRENEURS, VISIONARIES, & MAVERICKS

1. Edgar W. Ray, *The Grand Huckster: Houston's Judge Roy Hofheinz, Genius of the Astrodome* (Memphis State University Press, 1979); Jill S. Seeber, "Hofheinz, Roy Mark," Handbook of Texas Online, June 15, 2010, https://tshaonline.org/handbook/online/articles/fho87.
2. Ray, *The Grand Huckster*; Gary Cartwright, "A Barnum Named Hofheinz: A Big Top Called Astrodome," The New York Times, July 21, 1968; J. Michael Kennedy, "7 Floors Decorated in 'Early Farouk': Hofheinz's Gaudy Suite in Astrodome Being Razed," Los Angeles Times, March 18, 1988, www.latimes.com/archives/la-xpm-1988-03-18-mn-1682-story.html.
3. "Here Comes the Judge—Again," Newsweek, May 27, 1968.
4. "Hofheinz Unveils Astroworld Plans," The Kilgore (TX) News Herald, September 17, 1967; "Astroworld Will Be Amusement," The Corpus Christi Caller-Times, October 22, 1967; "Astroworld—Truly a Family Affair," The Baytown (TX) Sun, September 24, 1967.
5. Ray, *The Grand Huckster*, 366.

6. Ray, *The Grand Huckster*, 365; Karen Guenther, "Judge Roy's Playground: A History of Astroworld," East Texas Historical Journal 36, no. 2 (October 1998).
7. Park description: "Show Biz is Big Biz at Houston's Astroworld," Del Rio (TX) News Herald, August 22, 1971; "AstroWorld Opening Day (1968)," Texas Archive of the Moving Image, www.texasarchive.org/library/index.php?title=2018_00425; "The Lost World Adventure River Ride at Astroworld," Astroworld Memorial Page, www.astroworld-houston.com/lost-world-adventure-river-boat-astroworld.htm; "The Alpine Sleighs," Dark Attraction and Funhouse Enthusiasts, 2020, www.dafe.org/articles/darkrides/alpineSleighs.html; "Amazing Vintage Photos of Astroworld," Houston Press, September 16, 2015, www.houstonpress.com/slideshow/amazing-vintage-photos-of-astroworld-7766913; Park map (1969).
8. "Astroworld Will Be Amusement."
9. Ira West Interview.
10. "AstroWorld Theme Park in Houston to Close at Year's End," The Associated Press, September 12, 2005; "What's Next for Astroworld Lot?" Click2Houston.com, December 15, 2009, https://web.archive.org/web/20100721052727/http://www.click2houston.com/newsarchive/21962931/detail.html#story; Craig Hlavaty, "This Week in 2005 Houston's Playground AstroWorld Closed its Gates for Good," Houston Chronicle, November 1, 2017, www.chron.com/news/houston-texas/houston/article/This-week-in-2005-AstroWorld-closed-its-gates-10307466.php; Jennifer Dawson, "Local Developer to Acquire Former Astroworld Site," Houston Business Journal, May 11, 2006, www.bizjournals.com/houston/stories/2006/05/08/daily27.html.
11. Ray, *The Grand Huckster*, 407-414.
12. "Texas-Size Troubles in the Astrodomain," Business Week, November 17, 1975.
13. Craig Hlavaty, "Judge Roy Hofheinz's Custom Railroad Car Surfaces in a Houston Warehouse," New Haven Register, April 5, 2018, www.nhregister.com/news/houston-texas/houston/article/Judge-Roy-Hofheinz-s-custom-railroad-car-surfaces-12802711.php; Cory McCord and Ryan Korsgard, "The History Behind Judge Hofheinz's Astrodome-AstroWorld Railroad Car," Click2Houston.com, April 10, 2018, www.click2houston.com/news/the-history-of-judge-hofheinzs-infamous-astrodome-astroworld-railroad-car.
14. Caleb Pirtle, III, *The Grandest Day: A Journey Through Opryland U.S.A., The Home of American Music* (Opryland U.S.A., 1979), 17-19; Craig Havighurst, *Air Castle of the South: WSM and the Making of Music City* (University of Illinois Press, 2011), 227.
15. Pirtle, *The Grandest Day*, 21; Havighurst, *Air Castle of the South*, 227-229.
16. Pirtle, *The Grandest Day*, 21.
17. Pirtle, *The Grandest Day*, 22; Havighurst, *Air Castle of the South*, 227.
18. "WSM Plan: Big 'Opryland': Survey favors $16 Million Center," The Tennessean (Nashville), September 28, 1969.
19. Havighurst, *Air Castle of the South*, 227-229; Pirtle, *The Grandest Day*, 17-23.
20. Stephen W. Phillips, *Images of Modern America: Opryland USA* (Arcadia Publishing, 2016), 8; "Opryland USA Moves into Final Stages," Sullivan County News (Blountville, TN), November 24, 1971; "Opryland, U.S.A. to Offer Facilities 'Like No Other,'" The Tennessean (Nashville), October 14, 1969; "Opryland USA: Blend of Authenticity and Showmanship," Johnson City Press-Chronicle (Johnson City, Tennessee), January 29, 1972.

21. Chas Sisk and Ryan Underwood, "Hotel-Convention Site's Size Could Nearly Double," The Tennessean (Nashville), December 2, 2006.
22. "LA Firm to Design 'Opryland,'" The Tennessean (Nashville), November 19, 1969.
23. Pirtle, *The Grandest Day*, 28.
24. Pirtle, *The Grandest Day*, 27.
25. "No Animated Gadgetry for Opryland," The Tennessean (Nashville), May 20, 1971; "Opryland USA: blend..."; "Opryland 'Skeleton' Growing," The Tennessean (Nashville), October 10, 1971; "Coming at Nashville: Opryland, U.S.A.," The Jackson (TN), August 27, 1971.
26. "Circular Switchbacks," Dingles Fairground Heritage Centre, 2020, www.fairground-heritage.org.uk/learning/swings-and-roundabouts/circular-switchbacks.
27. Park description: Phillips, *Opryland USA*; Pirtle, *The Grandest Day*; Park map (1972); *Memories of Opryland: A Thrill Ride of Great Memories!* DVD, Nashville Public Television, 2008; "Old Time Skills Shown at Opryland," The Tennessean (Nashville, Tennessee), May 21, 1972; Michael Parham, email messages to author, May 8-18, 2020.
28. Joe Edwards, "Opry Sold to Gaylord Broadcasting Co. of Dallas," The Associated Press, July 1, 1983.
29. Will Pinkston, "The New Gaylord: New Leadership, Strategies Changing Face Of Company," The Tennessean (Nashville), April 12, 1998; Phillips, *Opryland USA*, 9.
30. "Fiesta Texas Park Under Development," The Kilgore (TX) News Herald, September 30, 1990; "New Fiesta Texas Theme Park Set for San Antonio," Longview (TX) News-Journal, June 23, 1991; Phillips, *Opryland USA*, 9.
31. "Could Upscale Shops, Restaurants, Theaters Be Opryland's Future?" The Tennessean (Nashville), October 5, 1997; Jane DuBose, "Mall Expected to Draw More Than Opryland," The Atlanta Journal and Constitution, December 18, 1997; "Park to Give Way to Entertainment-Retail Center," Johnson City (TN) Press, November 5, 1997; "Gaylord to Shut Down Its Opryland Park, Resulting in Charge," Wall Street Journal, November 5, 1997; "Retail Makeover Planned for Opryland as Visits Drop," The Daily News-Journal (Murfreesboro, TN), November 4, 1997; "Opryland Theme Park's Demise Due to Economics," The Tennessean (Nashville), October 30, 1997.
32. Vicki Brown, "Opryland to Give Way to a Big Mall: A Few of the Theme Park's Rides Will Stay," The Philadelphia Inquirer, November 9, 1997; "Changes May Partially Close Opryland Theme Park," The Tennessean (Nashville), September 25, 1997; "Opryland May Give New Theme to Park," The Tennessean (Nashville), September 24, 1997.
33. "Sun Sets on Opryland Park," The Tennessean (Nashville), January 1, 1998; Joe Edwards, "Opryland U.S.A Closed After 26 Years," The Associated Press, March 28, 1998.
34. "13 Opryland Rides Sold," The Tennessean (Nashville), November 21, 1997; "Gaylord Entertainment Sells 13 Opryland Theme Park Rides to Premier Parks," In Business Wire [database online], Business Wire, November 20, 1997.
35. "More Shopping Not Answer for Opryland Theme Park," The Leaf-Chronicle (Clarksville, TN), November 20, 1997; Amber Austin, "Grand Opening Raises Questions on Necessity of New Mega Malls," The Associated Press State and Local Wire, May 11, 2000; Amber Austin, "Opry Mills Shoppers Question Neces-

sity of New Mega Mall," The Associated Press State and Local Wire, May 12, 2000.

36. Havighurst, *Air Castle of the South*, 244-245.
37. Havighurst, *Air Castle of the South*, 244-245; Jim Patterson, "Gaylord Net Income Falls; Closing of Opryland Theme Park Cited," The Associated Press, July 30, 1998; "Summer of '98 Painful for Music City Tourism," The Tennessean (Nashville), August 23, 1998; "Is Something Wrong at Opryland Hotel?" The Tennessean (Nashville), September 20, 1998; "Opryland Officials Insist All Is Well," The Tennessean (Nashville), September 20, 1998; Jason Moon Wilkins, "Curious Nashville: Why Did Opryland USA Go Away?" Nashville Public Radio, January 5, 2018, www.nashvillepublicradio.org/post/curious-nashville-why-did-opryland-usa-go-away#stream.
38. "Don't Be Quick to Criticize Opry Mills," The Tennessean (Nashville), November 4, 1997.
39. Sisk, "Hotel-Convention Site's…"; Phillips, *Opryland USA*, 10.
40. Gaylord Entertainment 2011 Annual Report; "Gaylord, Dolly Parton Announce Plans For Theme Park," NewsChannel5.com, January 19, 2012; "Dollywood Drops Nashville Water Park Plans," knoxnews.com, September 28, 2012, www.knoxnews.com/news/2012/sep/28/dollywood-drops-nashville-water-park-plans; Phillips, *Opryland USA*, 10.
41. "Mills Joins Opryland Complex," Chain Store Age, May 2000; Amber Austin, "After One Year, Opry Mills Shopping Mall Appears Successful," The Associated Press State and Local Wire, May 13, 2001; "Nashville Entertainment Mall Outdraws Opryland," The Times Colonist (Victoria, British Columbia), October 21, 2000; Tim O'Brien, "Opryland Successor Big Draw," Amusement Business, May 28, 2001.
42. "Pat Hall, Carowinds Developer, Dies at 57," The Charlotte (NC) Observer, November 10, 1978; "Huge Amusement Park Near Charlotte Near Completion," The Greenville News (Greenville, South Carolina), December 24, 1972.
43. "Pat Hall Made Millions with Textile Machinery," The Daily Times-News (Burlington, North Carolina), January 1, 1973; "Pat Hall, Carowinds Developer, Dies…"
44. "Carowinds Sale Hinted," Statesville (NC) Record and Landmark, November 27, 1974; "Broadcasting Firm Eyes Purchase of Carowinds," The Robesonian (Lumberton, NC), November 28, 1974; "Agreement Reached on Carowinds Sale," Statesville (NC) Record and Landmark, December 18, 1974.
45. "Hall, Carowinds Head for the Top," The Gastonia (NC) Gazette, March 17, 1973.
46. "Luxury Hotel Complex is Planned for 'Carowinds,'" The Robesonian (Lumberton, NC), August 9, 1973; "Carowinds Theme Park Scheduled to Begin Operations On March 31," The Daily Times-News (Burlington, NC), January 1, 1973; "Resort Community Plans Are Announced," The High Point (NC) Enterprise, October 10, 1969; "'Disneyland' Planned for Charlotte," The Daily Times-News (Burlington, NC), October 11, 1969.
47. "6,000 Open Carowinds in Downpour," Asheville (NC) Citizen-Times, April 1, 1973.
48. "Carowinds Has Successful First Season," The Robesonian (Lumberton, NC), December 3, 1973.
49. Park description: Scott Rutherford, *Images of America: Carowinds* (Arcadia Publishing, 2013); Park map (1973); "Planned for Carowinds: Heritage Show to Open," Statesville (NC) Record and Landmark, February 3, 1973; "Early Visitors Praise

Park: Carowinds Complex Taking Shape," Statesville (NC) Record And Landmark, December 14, 1972; "Strip Marks State Line at Entrance to Carowinds," Statesville Record And Landmark (Statesville, North Carolina), July 25, 1972; "Carowinds," The Robesonian (Lumberton, North Carolina), March 27, 1973; www.carowindsearlyyears.com.

50. "Huge Amusement Park..."
51. "Pat Hall, Carowinds Developer..."
52. "Pat Hall, Carowinds Developer..."; Cindy Tyson and Kensy Lamm, "Benvenue Elementary School Faculty Visits Charlotte," Rocky Mount Telegram (Rocky Mount, North Carolina), January 20, 1973.
53. "Hall May Run For Governor," The Daily Times-News (Burlington, NC), November 21, 1974.
54. "Pat Hall, Carowinds Developer..."
55. "Gift From Beyond," Asheville (NC) Citizen-Times, December 15, 1978; "Gifts are Sent After Man Dies," Rocky Mount Telegram (Rocky Mount, North Carolina), December 20, 1978.
56. "Pat Hall, Carowinds Developer..."
57. "Pat Hall, Carowinds Developer..."
58. "Baseball Franchises a Gyp at $13 Million, Says Hunt," The Miami News, February 16, 1970; "Neatly Attired Lamar Hunt Earthy Sorta Guy Despite His Millions," Great Bend (KS) Tribune, June 7, 1970; Michael MacCambridge, *Lamar Hunt: A Life in Sports* (Andrews McMeel Publishing, 2012), Prologue, Ch 10, Kindle.
59. "Lamar Hunt's Problem: He's Too Busy," The Miami News, January 9, 1973; MacCambridge, *Lamar Hunt*, Ch 10.
60. "Lamar Hunt's Problem..."; "Sweat Tycoon," The San Francisco Examiner, November 18, 1970.
61. "Neatly Attired Lamar..."; "Baseball Franchises a Gyp..."; "Sweat Tycoon..."; MacCambridge, *Lamar Hunt*, Prologue.
62. MacCambridge, *Lamar Hunt*, Ch 8.
63. MacCambridge, *Lamar Hunt*, Ch 9, 12.
64. MacCambridge, *Lamar Hunt*, Ch 13; "Company Timeline," Hunt Midwest, 2009, http://huntmidwest.com/pdfs/timeline_short_092509.pdf; Subtropolis, HuntMidwest, https://huntmidwest.com/industrial-space-for-lease/what-is-subtropolis.
65. "Fun Park for Kansas City," Springfield (MO) Leader and Press, August 15, 1971; "Announce New 'World's of Fun' Park at Kansas City," The Chillicothe (MO) Constitution-Tribune, August 4, 1971; "Set May 26 for Opening of KC's Fantasy Worlds," The Atchison (KS) Daily Globe, April 23, 1973; "International Playground to Open in KC," The Salina (KS) Journal, May 20, 1973.
66. "Football, Mortgages Do Mix," Hartford (CT) Courant, December 19, 1971.
67. "Ground Broken for Fun Park," The Parsons (KS) Sun, November 11, 1971.
68. "Worlds Of Fun Grand Opening 1973: 10 Fun Facts," Worlds of Fun, May 25, 2018, https://www.worldsoffun.com/blog/2018/worlds-of-fun-history-grand-opening.
69. "Announce New 'World's..."
70. "Judy's Slippers Dance for $15,000 at Auction," Arizona Republic (Phoenix), May 20, 1970.
71. "Judy's Slippers Dance..."
72. Park description: James Nirider, "Arrowhead Stadium," The Emporia Gazette (Emporia, Kansas), September 23, 1972; "Set May 26 for Opening..."; "Fun Park for

Kansas City…"; "KC's Worlds of Fun Lives Up to Its Name," The Hutchinson (KS) News, June 10, 1973; "Indian Carvings Attract," The Atchison Daily Globe (Atchison, Kansas), March 1, 1973; Park map (1973); Jennifer Lovesee-Mast, email messages to author, April 25-28, 2020.

73. "Cedar Fair Completes Purchase," The Wall Street Journal, July 31, 1995.
74. "Worlds of Fun Gone But Not Forgotten: The Defunct Rides & Attractions," worldsoffun.org, www.worldsoffun.org/history/defunctattractions.html; Jennifer Lovesee-Mast, email messages…"
75. "They Call Him P.T. Hunt," The Palm Beach Post (West Palm Beach, FL), March 26, 1971; "Hall of Fame Nod to Hunt," The Iola Register (Iola, Kansas), February 9, 1972.
76. Ric Asimov, "Warner LeRoy, Restaurant Impresario, Is Dead at 65," The New York Times, February 24, 2001, www.nytimes.com/2001/02/24/nyregion/warner-leroy-restaurant-impresario-is-dead-at-65.html; Rebecca Bricker, "Warner LeRoy's Restaurants Make Him the Wizard of Odd," People, November 2, 1982.
77. "The Prince of Flash," Vogue, December 1976.
78. "'No Clogging on Route 537' Anticipated When Park Opens," Asbury Park (NJ) Press, March 31, 1974; "Safari Park to Have Job Openings," Asbury Park (NJ) Press, October 31, 1973; www.greatadventurehistory.org.
79. "Happy Financial Ending for a Near Disaster," Business Week, July 12, 1976; "Great Adventure Restraint Sought," Asbury Park (NJ) Press, November 30, 1973; "Work Restraint on Park Job Is Challenged," Asbury Park (NJ) Press, January 4, 1974; "Zebras Subject of Suit, Search," Asbury Park (NJ) Press, September 13, 1973; "Plans Needed for Approval of Park Idea," Asbury Park (NJ) Press, September 25, 1973; "Site Plan Passes for Safari Park," Asbury Park (NJ) Press, November 13, 1973.
80. Park description: "'Great Adventure' Has Carnival Style," The Ridgewood (NJ) News, July 31, 1974; "Great Adventure Wraps Up Pre-Opening Details," Asbury Park (NJ) Press, June 30, 1974; "'Great Adventure' in Ocean County: Disney-Style Center to Open July 1," The Daily Journal (Vineland, NJ), June 24, 1974; "New Concepts of Design Displayed at New Jersey's 'Great Adventure,'" The Millville (NJ) Daily, July 3, 1974; Park map (1974); www.greatadventurehistory.org.
81. "Fabulous Great Adventure Park Opens for '75 Season," The Millville (NJ) Daily, May 8, 1975.
82. "Safari Park to Have Job…"; "'Great Adventure' Has Carnival…"
83. Ira West Interview.
84. www.greatadventurehistory.org.
85. "Great Adventure Has Great Drawbacks Too," The Herald-News (Passaic, NJ), August 10, 1974; "Great Adventure Work Completed," Asbury Park (NJ) Press, July 21, 1974.
86. "Great Adventure, Jackson Interweave Fates," Asbury Park (NJ) Press, February 6, 1977; "Fabulous Great Adventure…"
87. www.greatadventurehistory.org.
88. Gary Rothbart, "Great Adventure Getting 3rd Operator in 4 Years," Asbury Park (NJ) Press, December 11, 1977; "Six Flags New Operator of Great Adventure Park," Asbury Park (NJ) Press, October 15, 1977.
89. Eric Asimov, "Warner LeRoy, Restaurant…"

90. Tim O'Brien, *The Wave Maker: The Story of Theme Park Pioneer George Millay and the Creation of Sea World, Magic Mountain, and Wet'n Wild* (Ripley Entertainment Inc, 2005), 25-33.
91. O'Brien, *The Wave Maker*, 36.
92. O'Brien, *The Wave Maker*, 36-38.
93. O'Brien, *The Wave Maker*, 38-40; Conor Friedersdorf, "The Fantastical Vision for the Original SeaWorld," The Atlantic, March 21, 2014, www.theatlantic.com/business/archive/2014/03/the-fantastical-vision-for-the-original-seaworld/284561.
94. O'Brien, *The Wave Maker*, 47; "Mission Bay Sea World: New Dimension in Human Knowledge," The Los Angeles Times, May 26, 1963.
95. O'Brien, *The Wave Maker*, 42, 45.
96. Park description: O'Brien, *The Wave Maker*; Sea World: Mission Bay Park/San Diego, souvenir book (1966); Friedersdorf, "The Fantastical Vision..."; "$4.5 Million Marine Showplace: L.B. Group Building San Diego 'Sea World,'" Independent Press-Telegram (Long Beach, CA), November 17, 1963.
97. Friedersdorf, "The Fantastical Vision..."
98. O'Brien, *The Wave Maker*, 127-128.
99. "Magic Mountain: Pleasure Park Due in Valencia," The San Bernardino County Sun (San Bernardino, California), March 18, 1971.
100. O'Brien, *The Wave Maker*, 132.
101. Mary B. Murphy, "Opening Day Jitters at Magic Mountain," The Los Angeles Times (Los Angeles, California), May 25, 1971; Leonard Metz, "Magic Mountain's Preview Reviewed," The San Bernardino County Sun (San Bernardino, California), May 24, 1971.
102. O'Brien, *The Wave Maker*, 134-136.
103. Mike Goodman, "Magic Mountain Hope for Magic," The Los Angeles Times (Los Angeles, California), October 15, 1972; "Magic Mountain Grows," The Desert Sun (Palm Springs, California), September 29, 1972; "One Pay Gate in Valencia: Magic Mountain Reopens Today," Santa Maria Times (Santa Maria, California), May 27, 1972.
104. O'Brien, *The Wave Maker*, 128; Ira West Interview.
105. O'Brien, *The Wave Maker*, 129.
106. "Magic Mountain Brings New Dimensions in Entertainment and Recreation to Southern Californians," The Los Angeles Times (Los Angeles, California), June 13, 1971.
107. Gint Gudas, "Six Flags Over Magic Mountain," The Signal (Santa Clarita, California), June 8, 1979; Susan Starbird, "Magic Mountain May Be Sold For $53 Million," The Signal (Santa Clarita, California), May 4, 1979.
108. O'Brien, *The Wave Maker*, 174-218.

6. DAVY CROCKETT TANGLES WITH...YOGI BEAR?

1. Charles J. Jacques, Jr., *Cincinnati's Coney Island* (Amusement Park Journal, 2002); Jeff Suess, *Lost Cincinnati* (History Press Library Editions, 2015), 83-89; "Cincinnati's Coney Island: A History," http://retrospect.sid-hill.us/moments_in_time/coney_history/cincinnati_coney_island_history.htm.

2. Jacques, *Cincinnati's Coney Island,* 144; Suess, *Lost Cincinnati,* 86.
3. Jacques, *Cincinnati's Coney Island,* 188; "Riding History to the Limits," CET Documentaries, pbs.org, 2009, www.pbs.org/video/cet-documentaries-riding-history-limits.
4. Jacques, *Cincinnati's Coney Island,* 188-189; Hillary Delaney, "Frontier Worlds," Chronicles of Boone County, Boone County Public Library, July 17, 2018, www.bcpl.org/cbc/doku.php/frontier_worlds; Todd James Pierce, "Remembering Fess Parker and Frontier World," Jim Hill Media, March 19, 2010, http://jimhillmedia.com/contributors1/b/todd_james_pierce/archive/2010/03/19/the-fess-parker-theme-park.aspx; "Riding History…"
5. "It'll Cost $40 to $50 a Day to Enjoy Area's New Park," The Cincinnati Enquirer, May 31, 1969.
6. "Riding History…"
7. "Riding History…"
8. "Coney Island Purchase Completed By Taft Co," Dayton (OH) Daily News, July 22, 1969.
9. "Coney Buying Warren Home," The Journal Herald (Dayton, OH), April 3, 1969.
10. "Taft Firm in Deal to Buy Coney Island," The Cincinnati Enquirer, April 22, 1969; "Kings Island's Biggies Impress Sneak Peekers," Dayton (OH) Daily News, December 10, 1971.
11. "Riding History…"
12. "Ground Broken for 'New Coney,'" The Cincinnati Enquirer, June 16, 1970.
13. Dennis Speigel, email messages to author, February 18, 2020.
14. Mel McGowan, "Parkology: Disneylandia Debunked Myth #2 'Disneyland was a reaction against Coney Island and traditional amusement parks,'" Blooloop, June 5, 2012, https://blooloop.com/parkology-disneylandia-debunked-adh-myth-2-aodisneyland-was-a-reaction-against-coney-island-and-traditional-amusement-parksao; "A Disney Artist's Designs for a Hanna Barbera Land," imagineeringdisney.com, November 6, 2010, www.imagineeringdisney.com/blog/2010/11/6/a-disney-artists-designs-for-a-hanna-barbera-land.html; "Riding History…"
15. "Coney Island, Still Popular, Closes After 85 Years of Fun," News-Journal (Mansfield, OH), September 6, 1971.
16. "Riding History…"
17. "Kings Island's Biggies…"
18. Jacques, *Cincinnati's Coney Island,* 189-191; "Riding History…"
19. Jacques, *Cincinnati's Coney Island,* 176; "Riding History…"
20. Julie Sullivan, "Big Happy Land: Kings Island Offers a Feast of Fun," Cincinnati Magazine, July 1972.
21. "Kings Island a Winning Name," Dayton (OH) Daily News, August 26, 1970.
22. Sullivan, "Big Happy Land…"
23. John Keeter, "Remembering the Enchanted Voyage," Kings Island, January 9, 2018, www.visitkingsisland.com/blog/2018/january/remembering-the-enchanted-voyage.
24. "Gingkos Moved to Kings Island," Dayton (OH) Daily News, October 19, 1971.
25. "Riding History…"; Thomas Clark, "Free Wheelin': From Legoland To The Kentucky Derby Museum, Jack Rouse Keeps Cruising From One Major Design Project To The Next. And He's Having A Blast," Cincinnati Magazine, Nov 1998.

26. Park description: Sullivan, "Big Happy Land…"; "Kings Island: A Fantasy Land at Our Doorstep," Wilmington (OH) News-Journal, March 18, 1972; "Riding History…"; Park map (1972).
27. "Kings Island's Biggies…"; Sullivan, "Big Happy Land…"; Park map (1972).
28. "Riding History…"
29. Scott N. Rutherford, *Images of Modern America: Kings Dominion* (Arcadia Publishing, 2015), 6, 8; "Kings Dominion: Four Decades in the Making," KDGoldenYears, 2015, https://youtu.be/IbSzo54xmPY.
30. "Kings Dominion: Four Decades…"
31. "Taft TV Firm Starts Vast Amusement Park," The Evening Sun (Baltimore, MD), April 11, 1973.
32. "Lion Country Safari Is Planned," The News Leader (Staunton, VA), April 11, 1973; "The Pride of Kings Island," The Cincinnati Enquirer, June 16, 1974.
33. "Kings Dominion: Four Decades…"
34. "Kings Island Developers to Open Similar Park Near Richmond, VA," Dayton (OH) Daily News, April 6, 1975; "Kings Dominion: Four Decades…"
35. "Kings Dominion: Four Decades…"
36. Rutherford, *Kings Dominion*, 6; "Kings Dominion: Four Decades…"
37. "If You're Planning to Visit Kings Dominion This Weekend, Please Read This," Advertisement, Daily Press (Newport News, VA), May 17, 1975.
38. "Millions of Dollars Spent for Access Roads at Recreational, Industrial Sites," The Danville (VA) Register, August 31, 1975.
39. "Kings Island Developers…"
40. Dennis Speigel, email messages to author, February 18, 2020.
41. "Yogi's Cave is Happy Land at Kings Dominion," Daily Press (Newport News, VA), August 3, 1975; "Building an Illusion: 'Quite a Job,'" Daily Press (Newport News, VA), May 22, 1975.
42. Park description: Rutherford, *Kings Dominion*; "New Entertainment Mecca Debuts," The Times-Tribune (Scranton, Pennsylvania), May 4, 1975; Park map (1975).
43. "Business Booming at Theme Park," The Bee (Danville, VA), October 24, 1975; "Kings Dominion Parking Lot Filled to Capacity," The News Leader (Staunton, VA), May 11, 1975.
44. "Top Value, Taft Join in Amusement Venture," The Cincinnati Enquirer, May 2, 1972.
45. "$80 Million Theme Park is Planned Near Toronto," The Windsor Star (Windsor, ON, Canada), April 15, 1978; "'Canada's Wonderland': Firms Cooperate to Build $105 Million Amusement Park at Maple, North of Toronto," The Ottawa Citizen, April 3, 1979; "Big Amusement Parks in Canada?" National Post (Toronto), August 23, 1975.
46. "Whose Wonderland? Canada's? You've Got to Be Kidding," The Vancouver Sun, September 8, 1979.
47. Janice Bradbeer, "How Canada's Wonderland Got Built Despite Heated Debates," The Star, June 23, 2016, www.thestar.com/news/gta/2016/06/23/once-upon-a-city-its-a-wonder-it-got-built.html.
48. Jamie Bradburn, "Historicist: 'The Dream That is Canada's Wonderland,'" Torontoist, April 9, 2016, https://torontoist.com/2016/04/historicist-the-dream-that-is-canadas-wonderland.
49. Bradbeer, "How Canada's Wonderland…"

50. Bradburn, "Historicist: 'The Dream..."
51. Bradburn, "Historicist: 'The Dream..."; "Despite Objections, Park Approved," The Leader-Post (Regina, SK, Canada), September 11, 1979.
52. Bradbeer, "How Canada's Wonderland..."
53. Bradburn, "Historicist: 'The Dream..."
54. Bradburn, "Historicist: 'The Dream..."
55. TEA/AECOM 2018 Theme Index and Museum Index: The Global Attractions Attendance Report, Themed Entertainment Association (TEA).
56. Bradburn, "Historicist: 'The Dream..."
57. Park description: Joel Levy, "Canada's Wonderland Opening Year Vintage Photographs," Toronto Guardian, July 7, 2016, https://torontoguardian.com/2016/07/canadas-wonderland-opening-year; Park map (1981, 2019).
58. Richard Macey, "Park Brings 900 Jobs to West," The Sydney Morning Herald (Sydney, New South Wales, Australia), July 27, 1985.
59. Park description: Robin Hill, "Why Wonderland is Riding the J-Curve," The Sydney Morning Herald (Sydney, New South Wales, Australia), September 20, 1986; Park map (1985).
60. Hill, "Why Wonderland is..."
61. "The Lights Go Out at Wonderland, Where Millions Got Their Thrills," The Sydney Morning Herald, Feb 17, 2004, www.smh.com.au/national/the-lights-go-out-at-wonderland-where-millions-got-their-thrills-20040217-gdiddg.html.
62. Vanessa Brown, "Remnants of Wonderland Waste Away in Theme Park Graveyard," News.com.au, January 23, 2019, www.news.com.au/travel/australian-holidays/secret-spots/remnants-of-wonderland-waste-away-in-theme-park-graveyard/news-story/dbb36d4e771ec9c01eae0e5922abb900.
63. "Taft Drops Plan for Cedar Point," The Cincinnati Enquirer (Cincinnati, Ohio), June 6, 1973.
64. "Taft Corp. Claims Land," Dayton (OH) Daily News, May 21, 1973; "Taft Investigating Area As Amusement Complex Location," Cardunal Free Press (Carpentersville, Illinois), May 23, 1973.
65. "J.W.T. to Handle Kings World," Chicago Tribune, September 4, 1974.
66. "Two Big 'Theme' Amusement Parks May Be Built in Area," The Wheeling (IL) Herald, May 31, 1973.
67. "The Flintstones and Yogi Bear Are Planning to Move to Huntley!" The Herald (Crystal Lake, IL), June 26, 1973.
68. "Development Unit Reviews Huntley Amusement Center," The Daily Sentinel (Woodstock, IL), November 1, 1973.
69. "Citizen's Group Opposes Park: Company Restates Huntley Amusement Park Position," The Daily Sentinel (Woodstock, IL), February 12, 1974.
70. "Protest Disneyland Type Center: Residents Aren't Amused By Park," Chicago Tribune, January 17, 1974; "Kane County Group Claims Theme Park Could Deplete Water," The Herald (Crystal Lake, IL), June 30, 1975.

7. MASTERS OF THE FRANCHISE

1. "'Great America' Amusement Parks Open," The Clarksdale (MS) Press Register, May 12, 1976.
2. "Park Planned Near Capital," Tampa Bay Times (St. Petersburg, FL), January 27, 1972.
3. "Marriott's Hot Shop," Newsweek, May 22, 1972, vol. 79, pp. 84-85.
4. "Many Howard Countians Like Idea of Proposed Super-Playground," The Evening Sun (Baltimore, MD), January 27, 1972; "Park Planned Near..."
5. "A Reluctant Howard Nears 'Great America' Decision," The Baltimore Sun, June 12, 1972.
6. "Favorable Marriott Study Faulted," The Baltimore Sun, September 17, 1972.
7. "Many Howard Countians Like..."
8. "A Reluctant Howard Nears..."
9. "Planners Blast Marriott Plan," The Capital (Annapolis, MD), June 3, 1972.
10. "New 'Great America' Park Faces Problems in Virginia," The Evening Sun (Hanover, PA), April 21, 1973; "Great American Park Moving Ahead," The Evening Sun (Hanover, PA), June 25, 1973.
11. "Va. Rescinds Marriott Approval," The Baltimore Sun, January 18, 1974.
12. "Major Marriott Park Protest is Called Possible," The Baltimore Sun, March 11, 1977.
13. "Marriott Park Loses in Howard," The Baltimore Sun, October 4, 1977; "Marriott Weighs 3rd Try in Howard," The Baltimore Sun, October 20, 1977.
14. "Marriott Looks to Arundel for Park," The Baltimore Sun, January 25, 1978.
15. William H. Jones, "Marriott Drops Its Plans for Va. Amusement Park," The Washington Post, March 2, 1978; "Marriott Is In 'No Rush' to Seek New Site After Losing $2 Million," The Baltimore Sun, March 3, 1978.
16. "Environmental Impact Statement for Frontier Worlds Plan," February 20, 1973; Steven W. Wilson, *Images of Modern America: California's Great America* (Arcadia Publishing, 2014), 8-9; Todd James Pierce, "Remembering Fess Parker and Frontier World," Jim Hill Media, March 19, 2010, http://jimhillmedia.com/contributors1/b/todd_james_pierce/archive/2010/03/19/the-fess-parker-theme-park.aspx; Ira West Interview.
17. Eddie Sotto, "'Bad Taste Costs No More' – Hard Fun and the Value of Themed Design (and Good Research)," Blooloop, January 8, 2018, https://blooloop.com/theme-design-immersive-worlds-herbert-ryman.
18. Eddie Sotto, email messages to author, May 20, 2020.
19. Ira West Interview.
20. Ira West Interview.
21. Ira West Interview.
22. "MGA Attention to Detail, Service Access Road, Early Years," GreatAmericaParks.-com, May 23, 2008, www.greatamericaparks.com/forums/search.php?st=0&sk=t&sd=d&sr=posts&keywords=ambulance.
23. Steven W. Wilson, *Images of Modern America: Six Flags Great America* (Arcadia Publishing, 2017); Wilson, *California's Great America*; "Marriott's Great America Rising Out of Gurney Farms," Chicago Tribune, October 16, 1975; Park map (CA, 1976).

24. Martha M. Hamilton, "Land Values, Disappointing Profits Cited: Marriott Theme Park for Sale," The Washington Post, August 11, 1983; "Marriott Leaves Amusement Parks," Industry Week, May 14, 1984.
25. "Bally Mfg To Acquire Marriott Corp's Great America Theme Park Near Chicago," Business Wire, April 26, 1984; "Bally Paying $144.5 Million for Great America Theme Park," Associated Press, April 26, 1984.
26. Kent Pierce, "$100 Million Debt Sale Proceeds to Pay for Santa Clara Theme Park," The Bond Buyer, July 13, 1984.
27. No Headline In Original, United Press International, Sept 4, 1984 (Financing and legal issues with Santa Clara's plan to purchase the park).
28. Pierce, "$100 Million Debt..."; "Marriott Park Purchase Called Ride to Fiscal Folly," The San Diego Union-Tribune, February 2, 1984.
29. Sally Lehrman, "Reshaping Great America: New Team's Got Plenty of Plans," The San Francisco Examiner (San Francisco, California), July 15, 1985; Dennis Walters, "Santa Clara, Calif., to Redeem Certificates If Company Purchases Amusement Park," The Bond Buyer, March 31, 1988.
30. Michele Chandler, "Paramount to Sell Great America, Other Theme Parks," San Jose (CA) Mercury News, January 27, 2006; Michele Chandler, "Great America Sold in CBS Deal," San Jose (CA) Mercury News, May 23, 2006.
31. Howard Mintz and Lisa Fernandez, "49ers Owners Part Of The $70 Million Deal To Buy Great America Theme Park," mercurynews.com, September 19, 2011, https://www.mercurynews.com/2011/09/19/49ers-owners-part-of-the-70-million-deal-to-buy-great-america-theme-park.
32. Mike Rosenberg, "Great America Finally Agrees To 49Ers Stadium In Santa Clara, For A Big Price," mercurynews.com, January 6, 2012, https://www.mercurynews.com/2012/01/06/great-america-finally-agrees-to-49ers-stadium-in-santa-clara-for-a-big-price.
33. "Marriott Turns Table, Will Not Move Engine," The Baltimore Sun, November 3, 1978.

8. ADOLPHUS PLANTS A GARDEN

1. "Busch Gardens Now for Sale," The Los Angeles Times, June 18, 1919; Cedar Imboden Phillips, *Images of America: Early Pasadena* (Arcadia Publishing, 2008), 48.
2. "Busch to Open Gardens," The Los Angeles Times, May 23, 1909.
3. "Busch Gardens Now for Sale," The Los Angeles Times, June 18, 1919.
4. "Busch Gardens Now..."
5. "Busch Gardens Will Be Open Again Soon," Monrovia (CA) Daily News, April 30, 1920; "Busch Sunken Gardens Again Made Public," The Fresno (CA) Morning Republican, May 13, 1920.
6. Phillips, *Early Pasadena*, 49.
7. *This article exported without complete information which I did not discover until too late. Dated September 9, 1958, from a local California newspaper, it provided a historical review of the Gardens.*
8. Sandi Hemmerlein, "Top Ten Places to Trace the Remains of Pasadena's Busch Gardens," SoCal Wanderer, January 8, 2018, www.kcet.org/shows/socal-wanderer/top-ten-places-to-trace-the-remains-of-pasadenas-busch-gardens.

9. "Busch to Build $25 Million Plant in Tampa," The Tampa Bay Times (St. Petersburg, FL), July 26, 1957.
10. "Busch Gardens Dedicated," The Tampa (FL) Times, March 31, 1959.
11. "His Office Has Wheels and a TV Antenna," The Palm Beach Post (West Palm Beach, FL), November 20, 1960.
12. "Brewery Bows Tomorrow: Budweiser to Dedicate Busch Gardens," The Tampa (FL) Times, March 30, 1959; "New Busch Brewery Unveils Gardens," The Tampa Bay Times (St. Petersburg, FL), April 1, 1959.
13. "Busch Gardens Dedicated..."
14. "City to Study Busch Gardens Parking Jams," The Tampa (FL) Times, November 17, 1959.
15. "800,000 See Busch Gardens in 10 Months," The Tampa (FL) Tribune, May 28, 1960.
16. "How to Get There," The Tampa Bay Times (St. Petersburg, FL), June 26, 1959.
17. "New Busch Brewery Unveils..."
18. "The Ultimate in Audio for Anheuser-Busch," Advertisement, The Tampa (FL) Tribune, June 15, 1959.
19. Joshua McMorrow-Hernandez, *Images of Modern America: Busch Gardens Tampa Bay* (Arcadia Publishing, 2017), 15.
20. Park description: McMorrow-Hernandez, *Busch Gardens*; "New Busch Brewery Unveils..."; "Brewery Bows Tomorrow..."; "Gardens Dedicated: Great Grandson Unveils Adolphus Busch Marker," The Tampa (FL) Tribune, April 1, 1959; "Busch Gardens Are Previewed," News-Press (Fort Myers, FL), April 23, 1959; "Birds, Beauty, Beer: Tampa's Fabulous Busch Gardens," The Tampa Bay Times (St. Petersburg, FL), October 19, 1960; Park ticket/map (1964).
21. "Million Visit Gardens Site Since Opening in Spring '59," The Palm Beach Post (West Palm Beach, FL), October 2, 1960; "Schedule Changed at Busch Gardens," The Pittsburgh Press, July 24, 1960; "Brewer's Fla. Garden a Blooming Success," Daily News (New York, NY), March 1, 1970; "Busch Unveils Expansion: Cost Set at $12.6 Million," The Tampa (FL) Times, June 5, 1970; "Vast Busch Gardens Expansion Detailed," The Tampa (FL) Tribune, June 6, 1970; "Anheuser-Busch Plans to Expand Gardens in Diversification Bid: Facility at Tampa Plant Will Be Prototype, New Rides Plus Ad Admission Charge Slated," Wall Street Journal, June 8, 1970; "Busch to Add Amphitheater, African Railway Attraction," The Tampa (FL) Tribune, October 24, 1970; "Busch Gardens Unit in Florida Plans Expansion," The Van Nuys (CA) News, March 30, 1973.
22. "Busch 'Wonderland' Shapes Up: Gardens to Lure Two Million a Year," Valley Times (North Hollywood, CA), May 22, 1965.
23. "A New Look at Busch Gardens," The Signal (Santa Clarita, CA), June 30, 1976; "Busch Gardens Dream Ends," The Los Angeles Times, February 15, 1979.
24. "More Than Two Million Visitors Flock to Busch Gardens," The Van Nuys (CA) News, February 6, 1968.
25. "Busch Gardens Opening Set," The Signal (Santa Clarita, CA), May 12, 1966; "Busch Gardens Opens to Public May 26," The Los Angeles Times, May 15, 1966.
26. "34' Tour Boats From Busch Gardens," Sales advertisement, The Los Angeles Times (Los Angeles, California), December 8, 1979.
27. Park description: "Busch Gardens Opening Set..."; "Busch Gardens Opens to..."; "A Touch of the South Seas in Los Angeles," The San Bernardino (CA) County Sun,

October 19, 1969; "Busch Gardens 70% Ready," The Los Angeles Times, July 18, 1965; "Busch Gardens Add Tropical Splendor to Valley Scene: Brewery Puts Emphasis on Beautification in Building 17 1/2 Acre Industrial Plant," Valley News (Van Nuys, CA), February 7, 1967; "What's Brewing at Busch Gardens," The Los Angeles Times, September 1, 1972; Park map (1972).

28. "Vast Busch Gardens Expansion…"; "Busch Unveils Expansion…"
29. "What's Brewing at Busch…"; "Busch Gardens to Add Facilities, Charge Fees," The Los Angeles Times, June 10, 1970; "New Rides a Thrill at Busch Gardens," The Press Democrat (Santa Rosa, CA), February 25, 1973.
30. "East Meets West in New Gardens," Austin (TX) American-Statesman, September 29, 1971.
31. "Busch Amusement Park Dedicated in Houston," Valley News (Van Nuys, CA), June 1, 1971; "Houston Opens Busch Gardens," The Austin (TX) American, July 15, 1971. *Author's note: The park was 27 acres, parking another seven, plus miscellaneous facilities for a total of 40 acres.*
32. "Local Firms to Design Houston Busch Gardens," The Los Angeles Times, September 21, 1969; "New Busch Gardens Planned in Houston," Denton (CA) Record-Chronicle, September 26, 1969; "Trouble at Busch Gardens," Express and News (San Antonio, TX), December 23, 1972.
33. "East Meets West…"; "Busch Gardens Try to Give People a Happy Feeling," The Journal Times (Racine, WI), January 25, 1973; "Busch Gardens Give Houston New Type of Tourist Attraction," The Brazosport Facts (Freeport, TX), May 14, 1971.
34. Park description: "East Meets West…"; "Houston Opens Busch…"; "Busch Gardens Try to…"; "Oh, How the Busch Gardens Are Growing!" The Austin (TX) American, April 22, 1971; "Busch Gardens Houston Summer 1972," 2015, https://youtu.be/FWYk7t0f0Q4.
35. "Busch to Close Gardens in Texas, No Affect Here," Daily Press (Newport News, VA), December 27, 1972; "Trouble at Busch Gardens…"; "Oh, How the Busch Gardens…"
36. "Busch Gardens to Add Facilities…"; "New Rides a Thrill…"; "What's Brewing at…"
37. "$4.4 Million Expansion of Busch Gardens Announced," The Van Nuys (CA) News, April 22, 1973; "$4.4 Million Expansion Plan Scheduled at Busch Gardens," Daily News-Post (Monrovia, CA), July 6, 1973; "Busch Gardens Marks Highly Successful '72: Expansion, Improvement Scheduled," The Van Nuys (CA) News, February 6, 1973; "A New Look at Busch…"
38. "Busch Gardens Returns to Its Former Role," Progress Bulletin (Pomona, CA), February 26, 1977; "Busch Gardens to Change Format in Economy Move: Entry Fee, Rides to Go," The Los Angeles Times, December 23, 1976; "Amusement Shutdown Set at Busch Gardens," The San Bernardino (CA) County Sun, December 23, 1976; "Busch Gardens to Add Fun House, Bumper Cars," Santa Cruz (CA) Sentinel, December 26, 1976.
39. "Amusement Shutdown Set…"
40. "Old Country to Bring Changes," Daily Press (Newport News, VA), May 11, 1975; Editorial, Richmond Times-Dispatch, June 26, 1912.
41. "Anheuser-Busch Buys Virginia Tract for Plant, Residential Community," Wall Street Journal, September 17, 1969; "Beer Firm May Build $50 Million Plant Complex in James City County," Daily Press (Newport News, VA), August 29, 1969;

"Eventual $200 Million Investment by Busch Predicted: Humelsine Explains Land Sale," Daily Press (Newport News, VA), March 26, 1970.

42. "Eventual $200 Million…"; "Sale of Plantation, Other Land to Busch Completed," Daily Press (Newport News, VA), January 16, 1970; "CW Plan for Road Announced: To Link Plantation," Daily Press (Newport News, VA), January 22, 1970; "Carter's Grove Development Slated for '76 Completion," Daily Press (Newport News, VA), January 27, 1970; "Land Swap to Provide Canning Plant to Serve Anheuser-Busch Brewery," Daily Press (Newport News, VA), October 24, 1970.
43. "Anheuser-Busch Shows 'Interest' in Camp Wallace," Daily Press (Newport News, VA), September 24, 1969; "Land Swap to Provide…"
44. "Busch Gardens to Be 'Business,'" Daily Press (Newport News, VA), March 8, 1970; "Busch Gardens to Open in 1973," Daily Press (Newport News, VA), January 10, 1970.
45. "Busch Gardens Planning Starts: Team Introduced at Meeting," Daily Press (Newport News, VA), June 30, 1970.
46. "Busch Residential Community, Garden Plans Being Prepared," Daily Press (Newport News, VA), January 9, 1972.
47. "Announcement on Busch Gardens Plan to Come Soon?" Daily Press (Newport News, VA), April 1, 1973.
48. "Busch Gardens to Be…"
49. "Busch to Start Construction on Gardens Immediately," Daily Press (Newport News, VA), April 26, 1973.
50. "Announcement on Busch Gardens Plan to Come Soon?" Daily Press (Newport News, VA), April 1, 1973.
51. "Busch Site Yields Historic Find," Daily Press (Newport News, VA), August 19, 1974.
52. "Williamsburg Busch Gardens to Be Ready in 1975," Daily Press (Newport News, VA), May 31, 1973; "Busch Gardens to Feature Old World Villages," The Danville (VA) Register, May 31, 1973.
53. "$30 Million Busch Facility Develops 'Old Country' Theme," Daily Press (Newport News, VA), December 1, 1974.
54. *NO TITLE: Regulations over selling branded items in the park,* The Danville Register (Danville, Virginia), May 26, 1973.
55. Lynn Darling, "Bane or Blessing? Jury Still Out on Two Virginia Theme Parks: 2 Theme Parks Make Impact in Va., But Is It Good or Bad?" The Washington Post, August 27, 1978; "Busch Gardens Officials Decline Tax Comment," Daily Press (Newport News, VA), September 26, 1974.
56. "Busch Catches Up on Building Permits," Daily Press (Newport News, VA), May 1, 1975.
57. "'Old Country' Taking Shape at Busch Gardens," Daily Press (Newport News, VA), September 8, 1974.
58. "Busch Gardens Draws 15,000 on Opening Day," Daily Press (Newport News, VA), May 11, 1975.
59. Various sales ads in local newspapers.
60. Park brochure (1975).
61. "Williamsburg Site for Branch Bank," The News Leader (Staunton, VA), January 30, 1975.
62. Park visitor's guide (1975).

63. "Westinghouse Today...The Old Country Gets a 21st Century Transportation Idea," Advertisement, Wall Street Journal, August 6, 1975.
64. Park brochure (1975).
65. Park visitor's guide (1975).
66. "An 'England', 'France', and 'Germany' Are Being Re-Created in Williamsburg," The Danville (VA) Register, August 11, 1974.
67. *40 Years of Fun: The Story of Busch Gardens Williamsburg,* DVD (SeaWorld Parks & Entertainment, Inc, 2015).
68. Park description: "'Old Country' Taking Shape..."; "Busch Gardens 'Shining Jewel,'" Daily Press (Newport News, VA), May 24, 1975; "Busch Gardens' Old Country Ready for Saturday Opening," Daily Press (Newport News, VA), May 9, 1975; "Germany: It's Land of Boats, Bobsleds," Daily Press (Newport News, VA), May 24, 1975; Park brochure (1975); Park visitor's guide (1975); Park map (1975); *40 Years of Fun...*
69. "Tourists Flock to Busch Gardens," The News Leader (Staunton, VA), May 11, 1975; "Busch Gardens Draws 15,000..."; "Amusement Parks Draw Large Crowds," The Bee (Danville, VA), May 12, 1975; "Busch Gardens Closed Temporarily," Daily Press (Newport News, VA), July 9, 1975; "Busch Gardens Attract 416,900," Daily Press (Newport News, VA), July 11, 1975; "Crowds Close Busch Gates Again," Daily Press (Newport News, VA), August 21, 1975.
70. "Anheuser-Busch Slates $20 Million of Work at 2 Amusement Parks," Wall Street Journal, September 25, 1975.
71. Price, *Walt's Revolution*, 264-271.
72. "Busch Gardens for the Family" (letter to the editor), Daily Press (Newport News, Virginia), May 28, 1975.
73. Edwin Wilson, "Those Groans Are From Shakespeare," Wall Street Journal, August 8, 1975.
74. Darling, "Bane or Blessing..."
75. Darling, "Bane or Blessing..."
76. Darling, "Bane or Blessing..."
77. "Busch Gardens Dream Ends..."
78. Cecilia Rasmussen, "Somehow, You Always Knew It Would Be..." Los Angeles Times, March 7, 1994.
79. "Busch Relocates Birds," News-Pilot (San Pedro, CA), March 22, 1979.

9. MUNCHKINS, BERRIES & HERSHEY BARS

1. Pat Koch and Jane Ammeson, *Images of America: Holiday World* (Arcadia Publishing, 2006), Ch 1, Kindle.
2. Koch, *Holiday World*, Ch 2.
3. Ira West Interview.
4. Park history: Koch, *Holiday World*; Holiday World, "1960's 'Santa Claus Land' Film (Now Holiday World)," 2010, https://youtu.be/2u4WKeEVS6Q; "The Happiest Day of the Year Is Everyday at Santa Claus Land," The Cincinnati Enquirer, June 16, 1974; "America's Original Theme Park in Scenic Southern Indiana: Santa Claus Land," The Cincinnati Enquirer, June 16, 1974.

5. Gerry Dick, "Holiday World to Invest $5.5 Million," Inside Indiana Business, October 11, 2018, www.insideindianabusiness.com/story/39271473/holiday-world-to-invest-55-million.
6. Christopher Merritt and J. Eric Lynxwiler, *Knott's Preserved: From Boysenberry to Theme Park, the History of Knott's Berry Farm, Rev. ed.* (Angel City Press, 2015).
7. "Say Goodbye to Tweetsie—and to an Era Gone Except in Realm of Nostalgia," Johnson City Press-Chronicle (Johnson City, Tennessee) September 17, 1950; "Tweetsie Railroad Abandonment Granted," Johnson County News (Mountain City, TN), September 14, 1950; "'Tweetsie,' Hampton Bridge, Torn Down," Elizabethton (TN) Star, November 17, 1953; "Protest 'Tweetsie' Tax," The Knoxville (TN) News-Sentinel, September 28, 1951.
8. *A Blast From the Past: The History of Tweets Railroad* (Tweetsie Railroad, no date), 18-19.
9. "Robbins out on Limb to Hear Tweetsie Toot," The Charlotte (NC) News, August 12, 1957; "In the Cool Mountains," Asheville (NC) Citizen-Times, August 28, 1957; "Tweetsie's Staging a Comeback," Asheville (NC) Citizen-Times, May 14, 1957; "Pining for the Blue Ridge," Alabama Journal (Montgomery, AL), September 1, 1958; *A Blast From the Past*, 2-9.
10. "Tweetsie's Staging..."
11. "Tweetsie's Staging..."; "Charlotte Firm Awarded Citation," The Charlotte (NC) Observer, June 29, 1958; "Tweetsie Trip is Delayed," Asheville (NC) Citizen-Times, May 21, 1957; "Robbins out on Limb..."
12. *A Blast From the Past*, 10-13.
13. Park description: *A Blast From the Past*; Tweetsie Railroad, 2020, www.tweetsie.com; Park map (2020).
14. "Robbins out on Limb..."
15. "Robbins out on Limb..."
16. "May Add Engines," The Knoxville (TN) News-Sentinel, January 15, 1961.
17. *A Blast From the Past*, 20; Photo of #190 Yukon Queen unloaded from ship after trip from Alaska, Tweetsie Railroad Facebook Page, May 23, 2013; "White Pass & Yukon No. 192," Locomotive Wiki, https://locomotive.fandom.com/wiki/White_Pass_%26_Yukon_No._192.
18. "'Rebel Railroad' Opens in Smokies," Elizabethton (TN) Star, June 8, 1961; "Quiet Time at Rebeltown, Close Call for Rebels, Arms Are Issued, Gets His Man, Tense Lookout, Defending the Fort: Photographic feature," The Knoxville Journal (Knoxville, Tennessee), August 17, 1961; "A Travel Series on Tenn. Attractions: Rebel Railroad," The Greeneville (TN) September 6, 1962; "Rebel Railroad Train Ride 1962 Pre-Dollywood," 2018, https://youtu.be/kVt5Y2bsasU.
19. "Grover Robbins, 59, Resort Developer," The New York Times, March 6, 1970.
20. "Dollywood History," Dollywood, 2020, www.dollywood.com/About-Us/Dollywood-History; "Goldrush Junction Plans Earlier Opening Date," January 23, 1971; "Goldrush Junction: Beyond the Hill," August 5, 1971.
21. "Missouri Firm Buys Goldrush Junction," The Chillicothe (MO) Constitution-Tribune, April 6, 1976; "Dollywood History..."
22. "Dollywood History..."; Silver Dollar City, TN park map.
23. Crystal Payton, *The Story of Silver Dollar City: A Pictorial History of Branson's Famous Ozark Mountain Theme Park* (A Lens & Pen Production, 1997); "History of Silver

Dollar City (as told by Frisco Jack)" 2014, https://youtu.be/o_nrFGaGg9c; Brad Thomas, email messages to author, March 31, 2020.

24. "'Land of Oz' Is Newest Tourist Spot for State," Statesville (NC) Record And Landmark, June 20, 1970.
25. Heather Leah, "Hidden History: Exploring North Carolina's Land of Oz Theme Park," WTVD-TV Raleigh-Durham, June 11, 2018, https://abc11.com/hidden-history-exploring-north-carolinas-land-of-oz-theme-park/3578712.
26. "'Land of Oz' Is Newest..."; "Beech's 'Land of Oz' to Open on June 15," Asheville (NC) Citizen-Times, May 3, 1970; Tim Hollis, *Images of Modern America: The Land of Oz*, (Arcadia Publishing, 2016), 7.
27. "'Land of Oz' Is Newest..."; Hollis, *Land of Oz*, 9.
28. "'Land of Oz' Is Newest..."
29. "Beech's 'Land of Oz'..."; "Debbie Reynolds Coming for Land of Oz Debut," Asheville (NC) Citizen-Times, June 30, 1970.
30. "Land of Oz Attracting Many Visitors," Statesville (NC) Record And Landmark, July 8, 1972; "Here's Savings for Vacationists," Asheville (NC) Citizen-Times, June 23, 1974; Hollis, *Land of Oz*; Park map (1970).
31. "Grover Robbins, 59..."
32. "S.E.C. Suspends Trading in Stocks of 4 Concerns," The New York Times, November 15, 1974.
33. "'Dorothy's Dress' Stolen From 'Land of Oz' Park," Asheville (NC) Citizen-Times, December 30, 1975; Hollis, *Land of Oz*, 7.
34. "Land of Oz Won't Open in Summer," Asheville (NC) Citizen-Times, February 21, 1981; "Oz: Theme Park Was Leading N.C. Tourist Attraction Until It Closed," Asheville (NC) Citizen-Times, October 9, 2004; "Mountain Attraction Battles Bankruptcy," Statesville (NC) Record And Landmark, June 28, 1975.
35. "Land of Oz," Land of Oz Theme Park, 2020, www.landofoznc.com; Heather Leah, "Hidden History..."
36. Christopher Merritt and Domenic Priore, *Pacific Ocean Park: The Rise and Fall of Los Angeles' Space-Age Nautical Pleasure Pier*, (Process, 2014), 7.
37. Merritt, *Pacific Ocean Park*.
38. Gabe Bullard, "The Weird History of Hillbilly TV," The Bitter Southerner, 2020, https://bittersoutherner.com/the-weird-history-of-hillbilly-tv; Rodger Brown, "Dogpatch, USA: The Road to Hokum," The Journal of the Southern Regional Council 15, no. 3 (1993): 18-26.
39. "New Attraction Taking Shape," Baxter Bulletin (Mountain Home, AR), November 30, 1967; "Capp Enthused at the Kickoff of 'Dogpatch,'" Baxter Bulletin (Mountain Home, AR), October 5, 1967; "'Dogpatch' Is Coming to Area; Capp Involved," Baxter Bulletin (Mountain Home, AR), January 12, 1967; "Dogpatch, USA: New Settlement in Ozarks," The El Dorado (AR) Times, February 23, 1968; "Capp to Open Dogpatch," Baxter Bulletin (Mountain Home, AR), May 16, 1968; Brown, "Dogpatch, USA..."; Kaitlyn McConnell, "The Slow Demise (Or Rebirth?) of Dogpatch, U.S.A." Ozarks Alive, January 23, 2017, www.ozarksalive.com/the-slow-demise-or-rebirth-of-dogpatch-u-s-a/.
40. "Dogpatch, USA: New..."; "'Dogpatch' Is Coming..."; McConnell, "The Slow Demise..."

41. "Comic Strip Characters Come Alive at Dogpatch," Baxter Bulletin (Mountain Home, AR), June 5, 1975; "Dogpatch USA," Abandoned AR, November 2013, https://abandonedar.com/dogpatch-usa.
42. "Dogpatch USA: Abandoned Theme Park," The Art of Abandonment, January 26, 2015, www.artofabandonment.com/2015/01/dogpatch-u-s-a-abandoned-theme-park/; McConnell, "The Slow Demise..."
43. "Dogpatch USA," Abandoned AR...
44. "At Dogpatch: Developer Plans Snowskiing Attraction," Baxter Bulletin (Mountain Home, AR), June 29, 1972; Red Six Three, "Dogpatch USA - The Life and Death of a Theme Park," 2018, https://youtu.be/CB3qJd7LyHA.
45. Park history: McConnell, "The Slow Demise..."; Red Six Three, "Dogpatch USA..."
46. Red Six Three, "Dogpatch USA..."
47. Brown, "Dogpatch, USA: The Road..."; "Dogpatch USA," Abandoned AR...
48. Bullard, "The Weird History..."
49. "Dogpatch, USA Loses Appeal, Must Pay $1.4 Million," Baxter Bulletin (Mountain Home, AR), February 3, 1987.
50. "Dogpatch USA," Abandoned AR...; "Dogpatch USA," The Abandoned Carousel, https://theabandonedcarousel.com/dogpatch-usa/.
51. McConnell, "The Slow Demise..."
52. Bill Bowden, "Entertainment Company Plans Resort at Former Theme Park," The Washington Times, December 11, 2017, www.washingtontimes.com/news/2017/dec/11/entertainment-company-plans-resort-at-former-theme; Hicham Raache, "Dogpatch USA to Return With New Name & Attractions, but Classic Spirit," KNWA Fox24, March 28, 2018, www.nwahomepage.com/news/dogpatch-usa-to-return-with-new-name-attractions-but-classic-spirit/1086003521.
53. John R. Stevenson, *Images of Modern America: Libertyland*, (Arcadia, 2017), 8.
54. "Historic Memphis Fairgrounds...From 1897 to the Present," Historic-Memphis, https://historic-memphis.com/memphis-historic/fairgrounds/fairgrounds.html; Charlie Lambert, "Before Libertyland: Memories of the Old Fairgrounds Amusement Park," Storyboard Memphis, June 27, 2019, https://storyboardmemphis.com/memphis-heritage-keystone/before-libertyland-memories-of-the-old-fairgrounds-amusement-park.
55. NO TITLE (Original park proposal), The Jackson Sun (Jackson, Tennessee), May 5, 1971.
56. Stevenson, *Libertyland*, 8.
57. "Memphis May Expand Fair," The Clarksdale Press Register (Clarksdale, Mississippi), September 26, 1972.
58. "New Memphis Family Park Dispels 'Gloomies,'" The Jackson Sun (Jackson, Tennessee), July 25, 1976.
59. Stevenson, *Libertyland*, 8.
60. "New Memphis Family..."
61. Park description: Stevenson, *Libertyland*; "New Memphis Family..."; Park map; Planning concept map.
62. Ira West Interview.
63. Stevenson, *Libertyland*, 75.
64. Ben Popper, "Saving Libertyland," Memphis Flyer, March 3, 2006, www.memphisflyer.com/memphis/saving-libertyland.
65. Stevenson, *Libertyland*, 76.

66. Stevenson, *Libertyland*, 77.
67. Popper, "Saving Libertyland..."
68. Popper, "Saving Libertyland..."; Stevenson, *Libertyland*, 78.
69. Stevenson, *Libertyland*, 90-91.
70. "The Story of the Carousel," The Children's Museum of Memphis, October 2018, https://cmom.com/content/uploads/2018/10/Carousel-Story.pdf.
71. "Historic Memphis Fairgrounds..."; Stevenson, *Libertyland*, 87.
72. Amicia Ramsey, "New Proposal For Memphis Fairgrounds Includes Sports Complex, Shopping, Housing, & More," Fox 13 News, www.fox13memphis.com/top-stories/new-proposal-for-memphis-fairgrounds-includes-sports-complex-shopping-housing-more/998813720.
73. Millie Landis Coyle, "Milton Snavely Hershey," Hershey Derry Township Historical Society, 2016, http://hersheyhistory.org/component/content/article/52-library-archives/hershey/54-milton-snavely-hershey; Charles J. Jacques, Jr. *Hersheypark: Sweetness of Success* (Amusement Park Journal, 1997), 5-7.
74. "The Opening of Hershey Park," The Sun (Hummelstown), May 25, 1906.
75. Jacques, Jr. *Hersheypark*, 10.
76. Jacques, Jr. *Hersheypark*, 50.
77. Jacques, Jr. *Hersheypark*, 32-33.
78. Jacques, Jr. *Hersheypark*, 51-52.
79. Jacques, Jr. *Hersheypark*, 45.
80. Jacques, Jr. *Hersheypark*, 112-119.
81. Jacques, Jr. *Hersheypark*, 119-120.
82. Jacques, Jr. *Hersheypark*, 122-123.
83. Harry Michelson, "Hersheypark in 1971," The Amusement Parkives, April 6, 2017, https://amusementparkives.com/2017/04/06/hersheypark-in-1971.
84. Pamela Cassidy Whitenack, *Images of America: Hersheypark* (Arcadia Publishing, 2006), 36; Harry Michelson, email messages with author, April 16, 2020.
85. Jacques, Jr. *Hersheypark*, 122-129.
86. Jacques, Jr. *Hersheypark*, 132.
87. Park description: Jacques, Jr. *Hersheypark*; Whitenack, *Hersheypark*; Park maps (1972, 1973).
88. TEA/AECOM 2018 Theme Index and Museum Index: The Global Attractions Attendance Report, Themed Entertainment Association (TEA).

10. WHO SAYS WE CAN'T BUILD A THEME PARK NOW?

1. Havighurst, *Air Castle of the South*, 240-243.
2. "Theme Park Development Case Study - Fiesta Texas / Economics Research Associates," Raymond Braun, 1999, conference presentation, https://www.hotel-online.com/Trends/ERA/ERAStudyFiesta.html; "New Fiesta Texas Theme Park Set for San Antonio," Longview (TX) News-Journal, June 23, 1991.
3. "Theme Park Development Case Study..."; "Fiesta Texas Park Under Development," The Kilgore (TX) News Herald, September 30, 1990; "Fiesta Texas—Largest U.S. Theme Park Built in 20 Years—Offers Music, Rides, Attractions," PR Newswire, February 11, 1992.

4. Park description: "Theme Park Development Case Study..."; "Fiesta Texas Park Opens in San Antonio," Victoria (TX) Advocate, March 16, 1992; "Fiesta Texas—Largest..."; "Fiesta Texas Was Built, and Now They've Come," Austin (TX) American-Statesman, July 30, 1992; Sandi Davis, "San Antonio's New Theme Park Fun-Filled," Daily Oklahoman (Oklahoma City, OK), March 29, 1992; "Shane's Amusement Attic - 1992 Opening Year Souvenir Book and Brochure," Theme Park Review, www.themeparkreview.com/parks/photo.php?pageid=47&linkid=8869&pageno=1; Park map (1994).
5. "Theme Park Development Case Study..."; "Fiesta Texas Park Opening Called Success," Tyler (TX) Morning Telegraph, March 16, 1992.
6. "Fiesta Texas—Largest..."
7. "Theme Park Development Case Study..."
8. "Six Flags Partnership Wins Bid to Manage Theme Park in Texas," Wall Street Journal, November 26, 1997.
9. "History Timeline," SFFT Source, 2020, www.sfftsource.com/history-timeline.
10. Doug Barnes, "#243: The Jon Binkowski Interview 8/29/13," The Season Pass: Your Ticket to Ride (blog), August 29, 2013, www.seasonpasspodcast.com; *The Park That Rock Built* (Hard Rock Park, 2008), 6-8.
11. Park description: *The Park That Rock Built*; Jon Binkowski Interview; Josh Young, "Hard Rock Park 1: The Birth of The World's First Rock N Roll Theme Park," Theme Park University, 2013, https://themeparkuniversity.com/category/extinct-attractions/hard-rock-park-extinct-attractions; Park map (2008).
12. Jon Binkowski Interview; Themed Entertainment Association, "2017 TEA Summit Day 1 — The Rise and Fall of Hard Rock Park," YouTube, 2017, https://youtu.be/Kv7Xqz0Xo5Q; Price, *Walt's Revolution*, 114.
13. "Why Projects Fail: Hard Rock Park," International Theme Park Services, http://www.interthemepark.com/parksfail.html; Theme Park University, 2013...
14. "MGM Grand: World's Largest Hotel-Casino Opens Saturday," Reno Gazette-Journal, December 13, 1993; "World's Largest Hotel-Casino Opens Today: Las Vegas Evolving—Gaming Capital Becoming Family Resort Destination," Reno Gazette-Journal, December 18, 1993.
15. "It's Not Kids' Town Yet, but Vegas Trying," Reno Gazette-Journal, January 17, 1994; "Upgrading in Vegas," Elko (NV) Daily Free Press, June 3, 1994; "World's Largest Hotel-Casino..."; "Las Vegas," Reno Gazette-Journal, November 14, 1993; "Las Vegas: Will Crowds, Kids Come?" Reno Gazette-Journal, January 10, 1994.
16. Ira West Interview.
17. Themed Attraction, "#14: TA Podcast E14: Rick Bastrup," ThemedAttraction.com (blog), August 1, 2019, www.themedattraction.com.
18. Josh Young, "MGM Grand Adventures," ThemeParkUniversity.com, August 17, 2013, https://themeparkuniversity.com/tag/mgm-grand-adventures; "From The Vault: MGM Grand Adventures 1993," NewsPlusNotes.com, October 7, 2012, http://newsplusnotes.blogspot.com/2012/10/from-vault-mgm-grand-adventures-1993.html; TimeTravelMemories, "MGM Grand Adventures Theme Park 1997," (Parts 1-5), YouTube, 2018, https://youtu.be/ELZp8NC9itU; TA Podcast E14: Rick Bastrup; Park map; Rick Bastrup, email messages with author, July 2019–April 2020.

19. "MGM to Spend $250 Million to Upgrade Las Vegas Resort," Elko (NV) Daily Free Press, May 11, 1996; "MGM to Lay off 770 Workers, Lease out Three Restaurants," Reno Gazette-Journal, August 2, 1995.
20. David Strow, "MGM converts theme park to group-rental operation," Las Vegas Sun, February 7, 2001; Rebecca Clifford-Cruz, "Sun's list of shuttered family-friendly Vegas attractions," Las Vegas Sun, February 23, 2012, https://lasvegassun.com/news/2012/feb/23/shuttered-child-friendly-atractionsmultiplier.
21. "It's Not Kids' Town..."; "Las Vegas: Will Crowds..."; JakeOrl, "MGM Grand Adventures REMNANTS! Closed Theme Park - History Hunters," YouTube, 2018, https://youtu.be/Di2_vEwJddU.
22. Ira West Interview.
23. "It's Not Kids' Town..."; NO TITLE (disappointment with park), Reno Gazette-Journal (Reno, Nevada), December 11, 1995.
24. JakeOrl, "MGM Grand..."

11. EVOLUTION

1. Carowinds Gas Information Center, The High Point Enterprise (High Point, North Carolina), April 7, 1974.
2. "Taft Broadcasting Co., Kroger Venture to Buy an Amusement Park," Wall Street Journal, December 18, 1974; "Family Leisure Signs Pact to Buy Amusement Park," Wall Street Journal, January 16, 1975; Rutherford, *Carowinds*, 54; "Pat Hall, Carowinds Developer..."
3. "Texas-Size Troubles..."; "Great Southwest Unit Is Assuming Operation of Texas' Astroworld," Wall Street Journal, May 20, 1975.
4. Price, *Walt's Revolution*, 112, 114.
5. Price, *Walt's Revolution*, 96, 113; Ira West Interview; "Renovation for Magic Mountain," The Signal (Santa Clarita, California), January 5, 1972.
6. Jon Binkowski Interview; "2017 TEA Summit Day 1..."; "Why Projects Fail..."; Theme Park University, 2013...
7. Christopher T. Baer, "PRR Chronology..."
8. "Great Adventure, Jackson Interweave Fates..."; "Fabulous Great Adventure..."; Gary Rothbart, "Great Adventure Getting 3rd Operator in 4 Years," Asbury Park (NJ) Press, December 11, 1977; "Six Flags New Operator of Great Adventure Park," Asbury Park (NJ) Press, October 15, 1977; Price, *Walt's Revolution*, 114.
9. Mark D. Frank, "Theme Park Boom Slows; Parks Ease off Thrill Ride Image; Key Attractions More to Families," United Press International, June 7, 1981; Graeme K. Deans, Fritz Kroeger, and Stefan Zeisel, "The Consolidation Curve," Harvard Business Review, December 2002; Will Kenton, "Defining a Mature Industry," Investopedia.com, June 26, 2019, www.investopedia.com/terms/m/matureindustry.asp; Will Kenton, "Consolidation Phase," Investopedia.com, March 19, 2018, www.investopedia.com/terms/c/consolidationphase.asp.
10. Price, *Walt's Revolution*, 312-325; Ira West Interview.
11. Ira West Interview.
12. S. Anton Clave, *The Global Theme Park Industry*, (CABI, 2007), 124; Martha M. Hamilton, "Land Values, Disappointing Profits Cited..."; "Marriott Leaves Amuse-

ment Parks..."; "Taft to Unload Parks," The Ottawa Citizen, December 22, 1983; Adams, *The American Amusement Park Industry*, 122.

13. McLaughlin, *Modern America: Freedomland*, 83; "AstroWorld Theme Park in Houston to Close..."; "Could Upscale Shops, Restaurants..."; Jane DuBose, "Mall Expected..."; "Park to Give Way..."; "Gaylord to Shut Down..."; "Retail Makeover Planned..."; "Opryland Theme Park's Demise..."
14. "Six Flags, Inc. Mid-Quarter Conference Call," FD (Fair Disclosure) Wire, June 22, 2006; Roger Vincent, "Magic Mountain Owner Seeks Package Sale," Los Angeles Times, August 19, 2006.
15. "What's Next for Astroworld Lot..."; Havighurst, *Air Castle of the South*, 244-245; Jim Patterson, "Gaylord Net Income..."; "Summer of '98 Painful..."; "Is Something Wrong at Opryland..."; "Opryland Officials Insist..."; Jason Moon Wilkins, "Curious Nashville..."
16. Memories of Opryland: A Thrill Ride...
17. No Headline In Original, United Press International, Sept 4, 1984 (Financing and legal issues with Santa Clara's plan to purchase the park); Pierce, "$100 Million Debt..."; "Marriott Park Purchase Called..."; Ira West Interview.
18. Kelly T. Kaak, "Theme Park Development Costs: Initial Investment Cost per First Year Attendee – A Historic Benchmarking Study," (no date). Author's note: Some reports say as high as $52M for Mid-America; a Penn Central report indicated an additional $34M allocation to their Great Southwest division after the park opened to pay construction loans, so it's unclear exactly how much this park cost.
19. Adams, *The American Amusement Park Industry*, 118.
20. Adams, *The American Amusement Park Industry*, 114.
21. Kaak, "Theme Park Development Costs..."; Ira West Interview; Price, *Walt's Revolution*, 114.
22. Christopher T. Baer, "PRR Chronology..."; "Six Flags, Inc. Company Profile, Information, Business Description, History, Background Information on Six Flags, Inc," Reference for Business, 2020, www.referenceforbusiness.com/history2/80/Six-Flags-Inc.html.
23. "Great Southwest Unit Is Assuming Operation of Texas' Astroworld," Wall Street Journal, May 20, 1975.
24. "Six Flags New Operator of Great Adventure Park," Asbury Park (NJ) Press, October 15, 1977; "Great Adventure to Expand," Asbury Park (NJ) Press, December 8, 1977; Gary Rothbart, "Great Adventure Getting 3rd Operator in 4 Years," Asbury Park (NJ) Press, December 11, 1977.
25. Gint Gudas, "Six Flags Over Magic Mountain," The Signal (Santa Clarita, CA), June 8, 1979; "Magic Mountain's New Owners to Expand Live Entertainment," Five Cities Times Press Recorder (Arroyo Grande, CA), July 11, 1979.
26. Adams, *The American Amusement Park Industry*, 120; "Bally to Purchase Six Flags Corp," Asbury Park Press (Asbury Park, NJ), December 1, 1981; "Six Flags, Inc. Company Profile..."
27. Adams, *The American Amusement Park Industry*, 120; "Six Flags, Inc. Company Profile..."
28. Adams, *The American Amusement Park Industry*, 121; "Bally Manufacturing Sells Six Flags to Wesray Capital Affiliate," PR Newswire, April 21, 1987; Chris Scott, "Sale of Six Flags to Cut Bally Debt," Crain's Chicago Business, April 27, 1987; "Six Flags, Inc. Company Profile..."

29. Kevin Goldman, "Time Warner Buys 19.5% of Six Flags for $19.5 Million," Wall Street Journal, April 23, 1990; Eben Shapiro, "Time Warner Seeking to Sell 51% of Six Flags: Head of Theme Parks," Wall Street Journal, April 13, 1995; "Six Flags, Inc. Company Profile..."
30. Shapiro, "Time Warner Seeking..."; "Time Warner Sells Six Flags: Firm Cuts a $1 Billion Deal," The Californian (Salinas, CA), April 18, 1995; "Six Flags, Inc. Company Profile..."
31. "Six Flags, Inc. Company Profile..."
32. Tim O'Brien, "Pittman: Six Flags to Continue Backing Big Promises with Major Investments," Amusement Business, April 17, 1995; "Six Flags, Inc. Company Profile..."
33. Clave, *The Global Theme Park Industry*, 107; "Six Flags, Inc. History," Funding Universe, http://www.fundinguniverse.com/company-histories/six-flags-inc-history; "Premier Parks, Inc. - Company Profile, Information, Business Description, History, Background Information on Premier Parks, Inc.," Reference for Business, www.referenceforbusiness.com/history2/31/Premier-Parks-Inc.html; "Time Warner Completes Sale of Stake in Six Flags for $440 Million in Cash," Warner Media, April 1, 1998, www.timewarner.com/newsroom/press-releases/1998/04/01/time-warner-completes-sale-of-stake-in-six-flags-for-440-million; Tim O'Brien, "Industry Stunned, Excited About Premier Move," Amusement Business, February 16, 1998; Tim O'Brien, "Six Flags Acquisition a 'Premier' Purchase," Amusement Business, February 16, 1998.
34. "Six Flags, Inc. Company Profile..."; Kate Laughlin, "High-Yield Bonds: Six Flags Bonds Falter On Shortfall Prediction," Investment Dealers Digest, July 3, 2006; "Six Flags, Inc. Mid-Quarter Conference Call - Final," FD (Fair Disclosure) Wire, June 22, 2006; "Six Flags Spares Magic Mountain From Sell-off," The Hollywood Reporter, January 12, 2007; Jeffrey McCracken, "No Fun for Six Flags As Parks Face Slump," The Wall Street Journal, August 5, 2008.
35. Adams, *The American Amusement Park Industry*, 113; Lawrence H. Rogers, II, *History of U.S. Television: A Personal Reminiscence* (1st Book Library, 2000); "Hanna-Barbera Acquired By Taft Broadcasting Co.," The New York Times, December 29, 1966; "Taft Broadcasting," Wikipedia, https://en.wikipedia.org/wiki/Taft_Broadcasting.
36. "Riding History..."
37. "Top Value, Taft Join in Amusement Venture," The Cincinnati Enquirer, May 2, 1972.
38. "Taft Broadcasting Co., Kroger Venture to Buy an Amusement Park," Wall Street Journal, December 18, 1974; "Family Leisure Signs Pact to Buy Amusement Park," Wall Street Journal, January 16, 1975.
39. Adams, *The American Amusement Park Industry*, 114; "Taft Broadcasting Co. and the Kroger Co. Announced Tuesday They Are Ending Their Nine-Year Joint Venture Into the Amusement Park Business," UPI, February 10, 1981, www.upi.com/Archives/1981/02/10/Taft-Broadcasting-Co-and-the-Kroger-Co-announced-Tuesday/4175350629200/.
40. Adams, *The American Amusement Park Industry*, 114-115; "Kings Entertainment Co." The Cincinnati Enquirer, September 29, 1985.
41. Clave, *The Global Theme Park Industry*, 121; Julian Gill, "What It Looked Like To Vacation In Houston As A Kid In The 1970s And 80s," Chron.com, January 3, 2019,

https://www.chron.com/news/houston-texas/houston/article/What-it-looked-like-to-vacation-in-Houston-as-a-13506749.php.

42. Chris Woodyard, "More Studios Open Theme Park Attractions That Tie Into Their Movies: Entertainment: Mca, Paramount, Walt Disney And Time Warner Now Control 13 Of The Top 20 Most Popular Parks In The U.S. And Canada," Los Angeles Times, August 23, 1992; Clave, *The Global Theme Park Industry*, 121–124; Dennis K. Berman, "Cedar Fair to Buy CBS's Parks Unit For $1.24 Billion, " The Wall Street Journal, May 23, 2006; "Cedar Fair Buys Amusement Parks from CBS," May 22, 2006, NBCNews.com, www.nbcnews.com/id/12915414/ns/business-us_business/t/cedar-fair-buys-amusement-parks-cbs/#.XtGFoi2z2uU.
43. "Cedar Fair, LP History," Funding Universe, www.fundinguniverse.com/company-histories/cedar-fair-l-p-history; Adams, *The American Amusement Park Industry*, 128; Clave, *The Global Theme Park Industry*, 110, 121–124; Tim O'Brien, "Cedar Fair Buys Worlds of Fun, Oceans of Fun," Amusement Business, June 26, 1995; Mary Vanac, "Theme Park Owner Cedar Fair L.P. to Buy Knott's Berry Farm in California," Akron Beacon Journal, October 22, 1997.
44. O'Brien, *The Wave Maker*, 127–128, 137–138; "Magic Mountain: Pleasure Park Due in Valencia," The San Bernardino County Sun (San Bernardino, California), March 18, 1971.
45. O'Brien, *The Wave Maker*, 150–158; Adams, *The American Amusement Park Industry*, 122–123; Price, *Walt's Revolution*, 100–103; Clave, *The Global Theme Park Industry*, 126.
46. O'Brien, *The Wave Maker*, 159–161; Adams, *The American Amusement Park Industry*, 122–123; Price, *Walt's Revolution*, 104; "Harcourt Brace To Sell Its Six Theme Parks," The Washington Post, June 21, 1989; Susan G. Strother, "Anheuser-Busch Wraps Up Its Purchase Of HBJ Parks," Orlando Sentinel, December 1, 1989.
47. "Theme Park In Florida Is Nothing But a Memory," The New York Times, April 14, 2003; "Cypress Gardens sold for $16.8M," Orlando Business Journal, September 26, 2007.
48. Clave, *The Global Theme Park Industry*, 110.
49. Ben Rooney, "Sea World, Busch Gardens Sold for $2.7 Billion," CNNMoney.com, October 7, 2009, https://money.cnn.com/2009/10/07/news/companies/blackstone_anheuser_busch_inbev; Christopher Leonard, "Can InBev sell Anheuser-Busch theme parks?" FoxNews.com, July 15, 2008, www.foxnews.-com/wires/2008Jul15/0,4670,AnheuserBuschInBev,00.html.
50. Jason Garcia, "SeaWorld Parks & Entertainment Preparing to Go Public," Orlando Sentinel, December 17, 2012; David Benoit, "SeaWorld Files for an IPO," The Wall Street Journal, December 27, 2012.
51. "Blackstone to Sell 21 Percent Stake in SeaWorld for $429m to China's Zhonghong," Blooloop.com, March 24, 2017, https://blooloop.com/link/blackstone-sell-stake-seaworld-zhonghong; "Seaworld Terminates Zhonghong Theme Park Development Agreements," Blooloop.com, April 29, 2019, https://blooloop.com/news/seaworld-terminates-agreements-zhonghong-china-theme-park.
52. Dan Weil, "SeaWorld CEO Rivera Resigns After 5 Months, Continuing Turnover at Top," The Street, April 6, 2020, www.thestreet.com/investing/seaworld-ceo-resigns-after-five-months; Joel K. Manby, *Love Works* (Zondervan Books, 2020), Ch 10, 11, Kindle.

53. "Our Businesses," Herschend Family Entertainment, www.hfecorp.com/our-businesses.
54. Manby, *Love Works*; D. R. Jacobsen, *Herschend Family Values: A Collection of True, Inspiring Stories* (Herschend Enterprises, 2017).

12. REDEMPTION

1. "Waiting for Wizardry: Universal Orlando's The Wizarding World of Harry Potter Draws Thousands of Fans On Opening Day," The Tampa Tribune (Tampa, Florida), June 19, 2010.
2. Adam Chitwood, "'Harry Potter' Art Director Alan Gilmore on Helping Craft 'Hagrid's Magical Creatures Motorbike Adventure,'" Collider, June 19, 2019, https://collider.com/hagrids-magical-creatures-motorbike-adventure-harry-potter-interview-jk-rowling-involvement.
3. Themed Attraction, "#3: TA Podcast E3: Tom Morris Pt 2," ThemedAttraction.com (blog), October 25, 2018, www.themedattraction.com.
4. Tom Morris Interview.
5. Sarah Whitten, "14 Years, 4 Acquisitions, 1 Bob Iger: How Disney's Ceo Revitalized An Iconic American Brand," CNBC, August 6, 2019, https://www.cnbc.com/2019/08/06/bob-iger-forever-changed-disney-with-4-key-acquisitions.html.
6. Merissa Marr, "Disney's $1 Billion Adventure," The Wall Street Journal, October 17, 2007; Art Marroquin and Joseph Pimentel, "Disney Wants To Invest $1 Billion At Disneyland, California Adventure In Exchange For No New Gate Tax," The Orange County Register, June 26, 2015.
7. Ira West Interview.
8. Clave, *The Global Theme Park Industry*, 121.
9. Ken Elkins, "Latest Phase Of Carowinds Expansion Is All Wet," Charlotte Business Journal, October 28, 2016.
10. Tracy Kimball, "Carowinds Opens Saturday For 2017 Season With New 'County Fair' Attraction," The Herald (Rock Hill, SC), March 24, 2017.
11. Ken Elkins, "New Roller Coaster to Be Part of Carowinds' Largest Investment Yet," Charlotte Business Journal, August 30, 2018, www.bizjournals.com/charlotte/news/2018/08/30/new-roller-coaster-to-be-part-of-carowinds-largest.html.
12. James Koehl, "Let's Take A Walk Down Cedar Point's Frontier Trail," Theme Park Insider, June 2014, www.themeparkinsider.com/flume/201406/4097.
13. Cedar Point, "Steel Vengeance - Official Trailer," YouTube video, August 2017, www.youtube.com/watch?v=Y7Ww57UUrXw; "Steel Vengeance & Frontier Town Character Stories Confirmed—Cedar Point," Wild Gravity Travels, April 25, 2018, www.wildgravitytravels.com/steel-vengeance-frontiertown-character-stories-confirmed-cedar-point.
14. Merritt, *Knott's Preserved*, 168.
15. "Knott's Berry Farm Adding New Life To Old Log Ride," Los Angeles Times, April 24, 2013, https://www.latimes.com/travel/la-xpm-2013-apr-24-la-trb-timber-mountain-log-ride-knotts-berry-farm-04201324-story.html; "Knott's Berry Farm Breathes New Life Into Old Mine Train Ride," Los Angeles Times, April 16, 2014, https://www.latimes.com/travel/deals/la-trb-calico-mine-ride-knotts-berry-farm-20140413-story.html.

16. Brady MacDonald, "Review: Calico River Rapids Blends Storytelling With Thrills To Bring New Life To Aging Knott's Water Ride," The Orange County Register, May 16, 2019.
17. Merritt, *Knott's Preserved*, 119–122.
18. Merritt, *Knott's Preserved*, 167; E. Scott Reckard, "Knott's Independence Hall Reopens," Los Angeles Times, September 17, 1998; "Independence Hall," Yesterland.com, July 29, 2016, https://www.yesterland.com/independence.html.
19. Bradburn, "Historicist: 'The Dream..."
20. "2019 Canada's Wonderland Park Guide Reflects Big Changes, A New Themed Section And A Nod To History," Canada's Wonderland, April 10, 2019, www.-canadaswonderland.com/blog/2019/april/2019-canada's-wonderland-park-map-reflects-big-changes-a-new-themed-section-with-a-nod-to-history.
21. "South Bay Shores Waterpark," California's Great America, www.cagreatamerica.com/explore/south-bay-shores.
22. Six Flags St. Louis, Twitter post, March 2, 2020, https://twitter.com/SFStLouis/status/1234576734609125378/photo/1.
23. "Antarctica: Empire of the Penguin," SeaWorld, https://seaworld.com/orlando/animal-experiences/antarctica-empire-of-the-penguin; "Mako," SeaWorld, https://seaworld.com/orlando/roller-coasters/mako; "Sesame Street Land at SeaWorld Orlando," SeaWorld, https://seaworld.com/orlando/sesame-street; Sharon Kennedy Wynne, "First look: New 6-acre Sesame Street land opens at SeaWorld Orlando," Tampa Bay Times, March 28, 2019, https://www.tampabay.com/fun/first-look-new-6-acre-sesame-street-land-opens-at-seaworld-orlando-20190326.
24. Erin Glover, "'Legends of Frontierland: Gold Rush!' Begins Today at Disneyland Park," Disney Parks Blog, July 9, 2014, https://disneyparks.disney.go.com/blog/2014/07/legends-of-frontierland-gold-rush-begins-today-at-disneyland-park.
25. Doug Barnes, "#344: The Ken Parks Interview," The Season Pass: Your Ticket to Ride (blog), January 24, 2017, www.seasonpasspodcast.com; "Ghost Town Alive! Live New Adventures in the Old West," Knott's Berry Farm, Cedar Fair Entertainment Company, 2020, www.knotts.com/play/events/ghost-town-alive; "Ghost Town Alive! 2019 Review," Westcoaster, July 12, 2019, www.westcoaster.net/home/2019/7/12/ghost-town-alive-2019-review.
26. "Thea Awards 2018: Ghost Town Alive! - Knott's Berry Farm, Buena Park, CA, USA," Themed Entertainment Association, 2020, www.teaconnect.org/Thea-Awards/Past-Awards/index.cfm?id=7415&redirect=y.
27. Tony Clark, "Let's Explore Forbidden Frontier on Adventure Island," Cedar Point, February 15, 2019, www.cedarpoint.com/blog/lets-explore-forbidden-frontier-on-adventure-island; "Forbidden Frontier on Adventure Island," Cedar Point, 2020, www.cedarpoint.com/explore/forbidden-frontier-on-adventure-island; Scott Edmondson, "'Forbidden Frontier' Brings Role-Playing Interaction to Cedar Point," Theme Park Insider, May 31, 2019, www.themeparkinsider.com/flume/201905/6807; Tim Baldwin, "Cedar Point Goes Outside the Box With Forbidden Frontier on Adventure Island," Amusement Today, July 2019, http://amusementtoday.com/cedar-point-goes-outside-the-box-with-forbidden-frontier-on-adventure-island.
28. "Snake River Expedition," Cedar Point, www.cedarpoint.com/play/rides/snake-river-expedition; Tony Clark, "150th Anniversary Announcement," Cedar Point,

December 11, 2019, www.cedarpoint.com/blog/150th-anniversary-announcement.

29. "Justice League: Battle for Metropolis," Sally Dark Rides, 2019, www.sallydarkrides.com/dark-rides/justice-league; "Six Flags Introduces Justice League: Battle For Metropolis," PRNewsWire, August 28, 2014, www.prnewswire.com/news-releases/six-flags-introduces-justice-league-battle-for-metropolis-272996351.html.
30. Brittani Tuttle, "Six Flags Qiddiya Announced, Saudi Arabia's First Family-Oriented Theme Park," Attractions Magazine, August 26, 2019, https://attractionsmagazine.com/six-flags-qiddiya-saudi-arabia; "Six Flags Qiddiya to Bring Year-Round Thrills to Saudi Arabia," Blooloop, January 30, 2020, https://blooloop.com/features/six-flags-qiddiya; "Six Flags Qiddiya: About the Park," Six Flags, https://content.sixflags.com/qiddiya/about-the-park.

DUELL DESIGN 101

1. Onosko, *Fun Land USA*, 61.
2. Ira West Interview.
3. Ira West Interview.
4. Onosko, *Fun Land USA*, 65.
5. Onosko, *Fun Land USA*, 64.
6. Burt A. Folkart, "Randall Duell; Designed Magic Mountain, Other Parks," *Los Angeles Times*, December 3, 1992.
7. Folkart, "Randall Duell."
8. Ira West Interview; Onosko, *Fun Land USA*; Robert Coker, "1982 Interview With Randall Duell And Ira West Of R. Duell And Associates," ThrillRide.com, http://thrillride.com/RDuellinterview/RDuellInt1.html.

INDEX

ABOUT THE AUTHOR

Barry R. Hill is a professor of audio engineering, instructional designer, and writer. A member of the National Academy of Recording Arts and Sciences (Grammys), Audio Engineering Society, and the Themed Entertainment Association, he produces *The Themed Attraction Podcast* with colleagues who work in the themed design industry.

Other books include *Recording Audio: Engineering in the Studio*, *Podcast Audio: Make Your Show Sound As Good As Your Content*, *Mixing for God: A Volunteer's Guide to Church Sound*, and *Elizabeth City: Rediscover Home*. More information can be found at www.rivershorecreative.com.

Dr. Hill holds degrees in Instructional Design from The Pennsylvania State University, Music Technology & Interactive Media from New York University, and Music with Recording Arts from the University of North Carolina Asheville. He can be contacted at www.barryrhill.com.

Printed in the USA
CPSIA information can be obtained
at www.ICGtesting.com
LVHW020743031123
762649LV00042B/1174/J